This book is to be returned on or before
the last date stamped below.

The Ironic Harvest

English poetry in the twentieth century

For my Mother

The Ironic Harvest

English poetry in the twentieth century

Geoffrey Thurley

Edward Arnold

© Geoffrey Thurley 1974

First published 1974 by
Edward Arnold (Publishers) Ltd
25 Hill Street, London W1X 8LL

ISBN: 0 7131 5752 6

Printed in Great Britain by
William Clowes & Sons, Limited,
London, Beccles and Colchester

Contents

Acknowledgements

The author and publishers wish to express their thanks to the following for permission to reprint extracts from copyright works:

The author, George Allen & Unwin Ltd and Hill & Wang for extracts from *Little Johnny's Confessions* by Brian Patten; the author and Associated Book Publishers Ltd for extracts from *Map of Clay* by Jack Clemo; the author, Chatto and Windus Ltd and Harcourt Brace Jovanovich Inc. for extracts from *Collected Poems* by William Empson; the authors and Andre Deutsch for extracts from *Night Thoughts* by David Gascoyne, from *Brutus's Orchard* by Roy Fuller and from *King Log* by Geoffrey Hill; the author, J. M. Dent & Sons Ltd, New Directions Publishing Corporation and the Trustees for the copyrights of the late Dylan Thomas for extracts from *Collected Poems* and *Eighteen Poems* by Dylan Thomas; the author and New Directions Publishing Corporation for extracts from *Collected Poems* by Kenneth Patchen; the author, Faber & Faber Ltd and Oxford University Press for extracts from *Collected Poems 1921–1958* by Edwin Muir; the authors, Faber & Faber Ltd and Harper & Row, Publishers, Inc. for extracts from *The Whitsun Weddings* by Philip Larkin and for extracts from *The Hawk in the Rain, Lupercal* and *Wodwo* by Ted Hughes; the author and Rupert Hart-Davis for extracts from *Song at the Year's Turning* by R. S. Thomas; the author for extracts from *The White Room* by Lee Harwood; Donald Haworth for extracts from *Children of Albion* by Mark Hyatt; the author and Macmillan for extracts from *Collected Poems* by Dame Edith Sitwell; the author for extracts from *And it is a Song* (1959) by Anselm Hollo and Migrant Press, Worcester, England and Ventura,

California; the author for extracts from *The Less Deceived* by Philip Larkin; the author and Hope Leresche & Steele for extracts from *Penguin Modern Poets 10* by Roger McGough; the authors and Alfred A. Knopf, Inc. for extracts from *Collected Poems 1928–53* by Stephen Spender and for extracts from *Collected Shorter Poems 1930–44* by W. H. Auden; the author and Mrs I. Wise, the Macmillan Company of Canada and Macmillan, London and Basingstoke for extracts from *Collected Poems* by James Stephens; the author and Oxford University Press for extracts from *Collected Poems* by David Gascoyne; the author for extracts from *Once Bitten, Twice Bitten* by Peter Porter.

A WELL
FILLING WITH THEIR EYES
THEIR EYES WITH WATER AND THE WATER
WITH
THIS LIGHT BLAZING ITS TRUTHS
THE WORLD oh everything

impossible now to say—a whole gang of cowardly ironies beating up the few words I might have used, myself just watching idly by.

(Harry Fainlight, 'The Spider)

Total, constant sincerity as a constant effort to adhere to oneself is by nature a constant effort to dissociate oneself from oneself. A person frees himself from himself by the very act by which he makes himself an object for himself. To draw up a perpetual inventory of what one is means constantly to redeny oneself and to take refuge in a sphere where one is no longer anything but a pure, free regard. The goal of bad faith, as we said, is to put oneself out of reach; it is an escape. Now we see that we must use the same terms to define sincerity.

(Sartre, *Being and Nothingness*, p. 65)

In irony a man nihilates what he posits within one and the same act; he leads us to believe in order not to be believed; he affirms to deny and denies to affirm; he creates a positive object but it has no being other than its nothingness.

(*Being and Nothingness*, p. 47)

1 The Intellectualist Position

It has become customary over the past five years or so to distinguish at least two kinds of modern poetry. The word 'modern*ist*' is now in fairly general use to designate the heroic revolutionary art that emerged just before and just after the First World War. There is then a clear fracture between the formally experimental verse of that period, and the technical conservatism of W. H. Auden's generation and most poetry written since. In point of fact, 'modernism' reflects the influence upon English and American writing of French symbolism; for modernism, in English and American verse at any rate, is identifiable with imagism, and imagism is simply a characteristically Anglo-Saxon refinement of symbolism. There was a certain diminution of scale involved, a diminution reflected in the change in usage: an image today can mean more or less any metaphorical or symbolic device, and this fact denotes a reduced expectation. Since imagism, we have not expected from the poet's figures the deep resonances of the symbolist *symbole*. In becoming image, symbol lost the philosophico-religious orientation that had given it power in the poetry of Mallarmé and Valèry: the religion of art dwindled to an aesthetic programme.

But this is not the whole point. The fact is that English poetry of the second quarter of this century has been largely uninfluenced by imagism and symbolism: 'modernism', far from causing a disruption of the literary establishment, was allowed to pass away even before the death of James Joyce, leaving only its scattered ruinous monuments. In 1954, Donald Davie's *Articulate Energy* argued the case against imagism (and symbolism) with the forceful animus of a man with his back to the wall. But I cannot have been alone in my bewilderment: surely English poetry had been propped up by just the sort of discursive syntax and argumentative structuring that Davie regarded as indispensable to major poetry ever since the dust had settled on *The Waste Land*. It has only been in the past ten years that English poetry has shown signs of curing itself of an over-tidy sensibleness, a reliance upon rationality. Apart from isolated individuals like Dylan Thomas and David Gascoyne, who chose to subject themselves to the alien discipline of Surrealism, English poetry has remained firmly in the grip of an academic critical establishment which, though in some respects symptomatic of modern culture, was fundamentally out of sympathy with modern poetic consciousness.

This critical establishment—which, following William Empson, I propose to call the intellectualist[1]—emerged in the decade after the First World War, and its precepts, or at least its spirit, still prevail in university English schools and respectable literary journalism. When it first appeared, intellectualist criticism had a revolutionary force: it was certainly intended to shake up English reading-habits. But in point of fact it owed little to the modernist poetry and poetics introduced into England by Flint, Hulme and Pound. The Cambridge critics followed Eliot and Pound in being anti-Romantic, but in a strict sense theirs was a reactionary doctrine. Their poetic ideal was based upon the practice of Shakespeare and the Metaphysicals. Now this was in several respects a mistake. For although the Metaphysicals in general, and Donne in particular, served a useful purpose in purging off from poetry the vague, cloudy idealization that had made it so unrewarding a proposition for the adult reader in England, the attempt to recreate a quasi-Metaphysical idiom—which is what we have in effect in the poetry of William Empson and the American Fugitives—went hard against the grain of modern feeling. Briefly, we can say that poetry after the seventeenth century changes gradually in the direction of a greater and greater reliance upon the presentation of images, with a corresponding

---

[1] The phrase comes from Empson's review of Cleanth Brooks's *Modern Poetry and the Tradition*. 'A Masterly Synthesis', *Poetry* (Chicago, 1939), Vol. LV, No. III: 'Mr Brooks offers this as the consolidation of a critical position that many writers in recent years have been building up, what I suppose would be called the interlectualist position,' p. 154.

decrease in metaphorical involvement. The Romantic poets make images in montage take the expressive burden, and the expressive ideal becomes the orchestrated landscape that John Stuart Mill praised in Tennyson.[2] This is a matter of historical fact, and the criticism of the 'twenties, in its emphasis on conceit and metaphoric complexity, showed itself insensitive to its implications.

Proof of this general account, can be found in the poetry (as opposed to the criticism) of T. S. Eliot. As a poet, Eliot went closer than any of his contemporaries in writing a poetry from which non-image content had been eliminated. Eliot took his place naturally in a tradition beginning with Wordsworth and developing through Baudelaire and Mallarmé, so that his dissension from Romanticism was strictly strategic: his sensibility, like his poetics, was inherited from the Romantic and symbolist poets. We are all, as Dr Davie observed in a more enlightened moment,[3] post-Romantic. As critic, however, Eliot gave his support to the essentially reactionary criticism of Cambridge. Although he by no means inaugurated the new interest in Donne and the Metaphysicals, he did formulate their quality in an irresistibly eloquent way. In the process, moreover, he provided a persuasive framework for conceiving the history of English poetry since Shakespeare. Professor Kermode showed a long time ago[4] that the 'dissociation of sensibility' thesis is a difficult one to sustain, and it is not fashionable to use the phrase at all nowadays. Nevertheless, its implications are still tacitly assumed, by poets, by critics, by journalists, by university lecturers. For it was not so much the historical theory itself that mattered, as what it asked us to accept of the nature of poetry.

We recall, first, that Eliot argued that there was in the Elizabethan dramatists and poets 'something permanently valuable which subsequently disappeared but which ought not to have disappeared'. There was in these poets 'a direct apprehension of thought, or a recreation of thought into feeling'. The Elizabethans, Eliot argued further, were possessed of a 'mechanism of sensibility that could devour any kind of experience'.

---

[2] John Stuart Mill, *Early Essays*, p. 242.
[3] 'On Sincerity', *Encounter*, October, 1968.
[4] Frank Kermode, *Romantic Image* (London, 1957), Chapter VIII.

Eliot was quick to point out the similarity between this omni-
vorousness of the Elizabethans (the capacity for the 'direct
sensuous apprehension of thought') and the interestingly
dissonant complexity of the French symbolists,[5] citing Mallarmé,
and, with more point, the confused mêlée of Laforgue's
'Blocus sentimentale . . . .' Moreover, the verse of the symbolists and of the Elizabethans also comprised a calculated
discontinuity of tones and intractably 'unpoetic' imagery such
as would hardly have been allowed by Wordsworth or Shelley.
The successors of these poets, under the guidance of their high
priest Matthew Arnold, were felt to have traded in this omni-
vorousness of mind for a variant of Milton's Grand Manner—a
certain inflexibility of tone which, Eliot hinted, was against the
full use of the poetic sensibility. Eliot described the Romantic
poets as 'serious poets afraid of acquiring wit lest they lost intensity'. And this was the most grave consequence of the dissociation,
for the best poetry, Eliot hinted, is not frightened in this way
of losing intensity; on the contrary, only by subjecting emotion
to every sort of light is the true poetic intensity to be attained.

Undoubtedly, Eliot meant these arguments to have a wide
generality of application. Poetry *had*, he felt, lost something. Yet
it should not be forgotten that he elaborated the notion of wit
in trying to define the characteristic excellence of Marvell, which
was a seductive 'alliance of levity and seriousness'. Marvell's wit
bespoke an 'equipoise, a balance and proportion of tones', and
'an educated mind rich in generations of experience'. Behind
him was the moral sagacity of Ben Jonson, and the 'terrifying
clairvoyance' of Shakespeare. With the dissociation, 'poets
lost their hold on human values that firm grasp on human
experience.' Yet I wonder if Eliot felt entirely comfortable at the
suggestion that this quality of Marvell's—the poised yet sardonic
wit—could be set up as a criterion for poetic excellence in general?
To ally levity and seriousness might seem desirable for certain
orders of verse, but could it be seen as indispensable to *all* poetry?

I. A. Richards suggested something very like this in *Principles
of Literary Criticism* (1924). Richards distinguished between
'poetry which leaves out the opposite and discordant qualities of
the experience and second, poetry in which the imagination

---

[5] Edmund Wilson made the same point somewhat belatedly in *Axel's Castle*
(London, 1931), p. 19.

includes them, resolving the apparent discords and thus gaining a larger unity.' Poetry of the second sort corresponds, plainly, to Eliot's poetry proceeding from 'a mechanism of sensibility that could devour any kind of experience'. The poetry of the first sort 'will not bear ironical contemplation', just as Eliot's Romantics feared 'to use wit lest they lost intensity'. Eliot's seems the more precise formulation (I am not aware that he uses the word irony at all in those seminal essays). But his 'wit' and the 'alliance of levity and seriousness' surely correspond to Richards's 'ironical contemplation' and justify us in seeing here the basis of the intellectualist school.

The general trend of these new ideas was reinforced by Richards' pupil, William Empson. There is no evaluative programme in *Seven Types of Ambiguity* of the sort proposed by Eliot and Richards, but the concentration on the poetry of Shakespeare and the Metaphysicals and the several times expressed puzzlement with Romantic verse[6] confirm the direction of critical thought. For Empson, degree of complexity and/or ambiguity is practically equivalent to degree of excellence. It is plain that Empson too assumes a distinction between poetry which over-simplifies experience and which betrays its inadequacy to the facts in its simpler and less involved surface textures, and poetry which proves by its metaphoric involvement and verbal ambiguities that it takes a 'mature' view of experience. Richards had accused the poets of his first type (the over-simplifiers) of producing poems which were 'unstable', built out of 'sets of impulses which run parallel' and out of 'special and limited experiences': such cannot be, Richards argues, 'the greatest kind of poetry'. This latter, Richards assumes along with Empson, to be compact of balancing and self-righting complexities, which preserve it from sentimentality and partial vision.

Thus, Eliot's 'wit', Richards's 'irony' and Empson's 'ambiguity', though not exactly equivalent concepts, all spring from the same source and express a similar view of poetry, and of the history of poetry. For in each case, Wordsworth and his followers are condemned, implicitly or explicitly, for simplifying experience, or for being afraid to subject emotion to 'ironical contemplation'. What Eliot saw as the Romantic

[6] See especially, *Seven Types of Ambiguity* (London, 1930), pp. 20–21.

fear of 'using wit lest they lost intensity', Richards diagnosed as
'instability', and, by implication, incompleteness. The intellectualist school, in fact, aimed to restore to English poetry a
certain completeness, which it felt had been lost. Richards
spoke of a 'poetry of synthesis': this was to be achieved by
'using the mind'—the intellect,—in a way, so the argument
ran, alien to Romanticism. Romanticism aspired to the
'sublime', and specifically repudiated the 'mere' cleverness of
Dryden and Pope. But the greatest kind of poetry requires, so
Richards and Eliot argued, all the mind's alertness, and cannot
afford to let the intellect go to sleep, as Arnold with his expul-
sion of wit had in effect encouraged it to. By these means, the
notion of 'intelligence' was born, and the intellectualist school
acquired its true identity.

The creed received its plainest, if also its least subtle, statement in Cleanth Brooks's *Modern Poetry and the Tradition* (1937).
Here, Wordsworth is singled out for distinguishing between
'the wisdom of the heart' and the 'subtlety of the mind', and
found guilty of advocating a poetry devoid of mind. Coleridge,
similarly, contrasts 'work of the will which implies leisure to
reflect' with genuine creativity, 'the steady fervour of a mind
possessed with the grandeur of its subject'. Both poets, Brooks
argues,[7] are guilty of exalting 'inspiration'—an eye-shutting,
mindless sort of working up of enthusiasm—at the expense of
the intelligence. It is difficult now to see how anyone can have
thought that by 'steady fervour possessed of the grandeur of its
subject' Coleridge meant anything but the most powerful and
total concentration of the mind's faculties upon the most fundamental themes that can confront it. But it is enough for Mr
Brooks that Coleridge should have derided the 'ingenious and
the exact', Wordsworth the 'ingenuity of the fancy': clearly, he
argues, the architects of Romanticism reveal in these remarks
their distaste for the use of the 'mind' in poetry. And the poetry,
he further argues, bears this out: Romantic poetry is dissociated,
exactly as Eliot had demonstrated it must be, in its deficiency in
'secondary consideration' (Brooks' equivalent of Richards's
'ironical contemplation'). It is not, like the poetry of the Metaphysicals and the American Fugitives, 'inclusive poetry'

[7] In 'Metaphor and the Tradition', *Modern Poetry and the Tradition* (London,
1948).

('poetry of synthesis'). *Modern Poetry and the Tradition* is, it is clear from even so brief a survey, merely a doctrinaire elaboration of the basic notions of the intellectualist criticism of Cambridge. But it does have the value of making clear some important implications of this criticism.

For it becomes obvious on reading Brooks's book that the intellectualist notion of 'intelligence' really has a very particular sense. It has this sense in Richards, as well. But Richards had pinned his ultimate faith on tragedy,[8] and tragedy can validly be described in terms of its capacity for 'resolving the apparent discords, and gaining a larger unity'. With *Lear* in mind, we can assent to Richards's propositions about an 'inclusive poetry', and might even be prepared to accept some notion of ironical contemplation as a guarantor of a Shakespearean universality. But we would be wrong so to assent, and Brooks's book spells out the reasons why. For in point of fact the intellectualist emphasis upon Shakespeare and the various quasi-technical theories of wit are mere smokescreen for the attack upon Romanticism. That there was a need for a vigorous rejection of the enfeebled Romanticism that still choked English poetry at the time Pound crossed the Atlantic is beyond doubt. Nor is it to be questioned that irony—as it had already shown itself to be in France—was an excellent instrument for the purpose. But, as I have already argued, there could be no real 'rejection 'of Romanticism: post-Romantic, in Dr Davie's words, is what we are.

The rejection of Milton and the Romantics was facilitated by Eliot's dissociation theory, certainly not dictated by it. There is something reductive in this rejection, which had a profoundly narrowing effect on English and American poetry for more than forty years. And it is *Modern Poetry and the Tradition* which makes this most clear. 'Very many', Brooks asserts, 'indeed nearly all mature attitudes represent some sort of mingling of the approbative and the satirical.' Moreover,'The more complex attitudes are expressed . . . in varying degrees of irony: bitter, playful, whimsical, tragic, self-inclusive, etc.' The very crudity of this formulation elicits fairly enough, I think, some of the knowing stoicism that underlies Richards's own thinking. But what is more telling still is the range of examples Brooks calls upon to substantiate this position. Yeats's 'All Souls' Night'

[8] See *Principles of Literary Criticism*, Chapter XXXII.

is supposed to demonstrate the compatibility of a simple domestic image (a goldfish bowl) with a 'serious' statement. Yet this poem is surely banal and condescending in its deflation. Shakespeare is included in the ironical school on the strength of a rather bad pun from *Romeo and Juliet*, Keats largely in virtue of the repetition of *forlorn* in the Nightingale Ode, and such plays upon sound as 'Attic shape, fair attitude'. Wordsworth's great Calais Sands Sonnet, on the other hand, is found over-simplificatory because its imagery is 'poetic', ie, not recalcitrant, merely nice.[9] This last is one of many instances in *Modern Poetry and the Tradition* that alert one to the presence of something sheerly negative in the conception of poetry (the intellec-tualist conception in its most uncompromising form) upon which it rests. If the poet is not ready with pun, word-play and/or ironical reflection, Mr Brooks's analyses consistently seem to imply, then he is guilty of suppressing evidence, of tossing his awareness a drugged cake of 'inspiration': he has not subjected his emotion to all the possible critiques, and his poetry is there-fore partial, unstable and sentimental—*not* 'the greatest kind of poetry'. Thus, there is no sense in *Modern Poetry and the Tradition* of an underlying structure of values, of a *raison d'être*. Although seriousness is continually invoked and painstakingly discovered in every verbal irony or ironic sally, there is no real notion of the structural nature of seriousness: indeed the question of purpose in poetry is shelved altogether, in the interests of an all-purpose account of poetry in terms of irony and intelligence.

This account can seem plausible, as I have hinted already, especially if we think of the tragedies of Shakespeare as pro-viding a kind of poetic paradigm. Here we have a grand synthesis of all emotions: all tones, all shades, all discords, are fused and resolved in the great synthesis of Tragedy. But in point of fact there is no such ideal poetic idiom. Richards's account of tragedy is really circular: it invites us to join him in admiring the tragic synthesis, and then appears to deduce from its universality a theory of poetry based upon irony. But actu-ally every poetic idiom, even Shakespeare's, is severely limited in what (and to what) it can express. No poetry is really 'inclusive' in the sense intended by Brooks and Richards. Any

[9] All these instances are taken from Chapters 1 and 2 of *Modern Poetry and the Tradition*.

successful poem, on the other hand, does appear to be a 'synthesis'. Such terms as 'synthesis' and 'inclusive' are really not descriptive, but evaluative. Donne's ironies help him to articulate some things about sexual relationships, but they limit his expressive content, excluding some emotional shades in affirming others. They could form no part of Vaughan's poetry, for instance, with its intense and exalted natural mysticism. Does this make Vaughan's poetry more 'partial' than Donne's? Hardly: there is nothing in Donne of half the religious purity or exaltation of 'The Night'. And of course this line of argument is generally applicable. Marvell's sardonic yet equable wittiness incapacitates him for the extended spiritual flights of Milton as much as Milton's solemnity disqualifies him from wittily persuading a woman to come to bed with him. Idioms predicate content, and minds and purposes govern idioms. To posit an ideal poetic idiom capable of saying anything and everything is simply pipe-dreaming. Is it, then, the case that irony is 'consistently a characteristic of poetry (of the highest order)?' Unless we define irony out of usefulness, by identifying it with complexity or completeness, we cannot, I suggest, accept Richard's postulation: irony *is* after all ironical, and a poet who is judged ironical ought to be so judged in virtue of his essential attitude towards experience.

What kind of poetry, therefore, is the poetry we can honestly call ironical, the poetry of Donne, Marvell, Wallace Stevens, Apollinaire, Louis MacNeice? Is it, as I. A. Richards suggests, merely synonymous with good poetry? What are the real purposes of wit and irony?

Irony and wit are, in the first place, extreme ways of getting familiar words to yield new meanings. By setting the word or concept in a new dimension, the poet recreates it or, at least, gets further use from it. Often, this is done by transposing modalities, by using, for example, a concrete word with an abstract meaning, or an abstract word in a concrete sense. An example of the latter is the use of the verb 'upbraid' in Marvell's 'The Garden':

> And their incessant labours see
> Crowned from some single herb or tree,
> Whose short and narrow-verged, shade
> Does prudently their toils upbraid.

Emily Dickinson provides us with dozens of similar examples:

> At half-past three a single bird
> Unto a silent sky
> Propounded but a single term
> Of cautious melody.

What wit of this kind does to language, irony does to attitude, or stance. Most ironical verse needs awareness of the poetry immediately preceding it for its effect to be understood. Take, for example, the relation of Donne's poetry to the Petrarchan love tradition; or Laforgue's to the heroism of his immediate predecessors—Rimbaud and the Romantic conventions lying behind him,—the Hamlet-worship and the self-conscious bardicry of Victor Hugo. Laforgue still uses the poet-*voyant* myth of Rimbaud, but by his time it has become necessary to subject it to 'ironical contemplation' to restore to it some of its tension. Hence, his satiric obsession with the Hamlet stance, more familiar to English readers perhaps in Prufrock's 'No! I am not Prince Hamlet.' Laforgue stands Romantic ideology on its head: he ridicules the Romantics' moon-goddess, for example, and the traditional agonies—*Sanglots, Complaintes*, etc. Yet he is no less obsessed than they with these things. In Laforgue, there is a perpetually rebelling inner principle which keeps his work in a state of duality: irony has usurped its position, and become itself a source of obsession. The oblique cleverness, the even conversational tone, the tart, alert line, the saving sense of absurdity,—these things appealed to the young T. S. Eliot, though they did not influence his own most powerful creation.

Irony, therefore, enables Laforgue to retain his Hamletism: '*banale rancœur de notre farce humaine*'. It is the addition of the notion of banality, of course, that lends the declaration its irritating tone, the tone of the Diaghilev ballets with their *vieux jeu* skittishness, 'Jean, étonne moi', pastiche, *déjà vu*—French poetry indeed escapes this tone only at the cost of an embarrassing solemnity in the twentieth century. The Symbolist night-walking of Pierre Reverdy, for example, is a hollow imitation of symbolist gesture that makes the *Ballets Russes* skittishness welcome.

Outside France, the ironical bias of poetry emphasizes the general point that irony as a principle robs poetry of the full commitment essential to major poetry. Wallace Stevens is in many ways the perfect ironical poet—cool, detached, never committed either to statement or emotion. His poetry is put together. The fact that he did not publish until he was over forty goes to verify this.[10] He has not a feeling for words so much as an acute sense of situation and a total absence of sentimentalism. His poems are essentially cinematic: that is why one does not notice the lack of significant phrase-power. He works by variegated symbols, which he circles round and sketches with deft graphicity. He is the reverse of a poet like Lawrence, who is obsessive. Obsessive in fact is just what Stevens is not. At the centre of his work is the Bergsonian pre-occupation with flux and metaphor, the falsification of phenomenal flux and 'the human tragedy' in poetry.

Being a poet, as in 'Add this to Rhetoric,' he always betrays his doubts (by saying 'Look here is the moon' (world man death); and in the betrayal overcomes them:

> In the way you speak
> You arrange, the thing is posed
> What in nature merely grows.

The impersonalism of Stevens should not be confused with anything T. S. Eliot might be thought to stand for. Eliot's poetry is never less then intensely committed, his withdrawal of the personal pronoun a way of securing clarity. Stevens is completely withdrawn, and his poetry is impersonal in the limiting sense of having nothing powerful to communicate about his experience. There is little evidence in the Collected Stevens that he suffered much intense pleasure or real pain. His coolness therefore is a basic detachment cutting him off from any strong emotional or spiritual content. The perfect Stevens vehicle is 'The Snow Man', in which the entire poem is cast in the form of a speculation committing the poet-speaker to nothing—'One must have a mind of winter . . . .' The poem is syntactically and actually a hypothesis, an idea entertained and dropped. When Stevens attempts 'serious' commitment (an actual statement), the result is oratorical hollowness, the

---

[10] Only odd poems had appeared before *Harmonium* came out in 1923, when the poet was forty-four.

mauvaise foi of 'DryLoaf'—in which Stevens weakly attempts to universalize his accurately annotated experience of watching rooks:

> It was the battering of drums I heard
> It was hunger, it was the hungry that cried. . . .

But it was not, and Stevens is not telling the truth here. Stevens has remained a Sunday poet, and it is natural that he has found favour among the professors.

The bad faith of 'Dry Loaf' is signalized at once in its portentous platform manner: 'It is'—ahem—'equal to living in a tragic land To'—ahem—'live in a tragic time.' This declaration is of course the apology Stevens wants to make for never having engaged himself in what, in spite of himself, he clearly regards as being the 'great issues of our time'. (We need turn again only to T. S. Eliot or Hart Crane to understand exactly what, by way of engagement in these issues, Stevens so signally lacks.) It is with relief that we turn from this kind of throat-clearing—a prolegomenon to a statement the poet had the tact at least to refrain from embarking on—to the slight asides of 'Country Words', the poem which, in the edition to hand, follows 'Dry Loaf'. Here the characteristically clever improvisations ('I sang a canto in a canton'—cf. 'Le Monocle de mon Oncle') acquire more resonance than the heavy asseverations of 'Dry Loaf'. If we see Stevens's poetry as a series of such improvisations—'Asides on an Oboe'—we shall not take too seriously his ruminations about the 'Imagination' and the 'Blessed Rage for Order', and therefore perhaps refrain from condemning him too heavily for not being the kind of poet he was never equipped to be. His longer more ambitious poems address themselves to themes which may fruitfully exercise the wits of a professor or an amateur philosopher but which cannot engage—or, at least, the poet's tone and rhythm tell us have not here engaged—the deeper sources of the mind. Stevens is not *really* worried about the mind's habit of imposing a spurious order upon flux and chaos, nor is he *really* concerned about the necessity of imposing such an order. These themes are bookish. Imagination in Stevens is merely a logical property of vision; it does not, like Hart Crane's, outpace 'Bargain, vocable, and prayer'.

Emily Dickinson's reputation in this century gives a convenient graph of the growth of the ironist school, and its enthronement of wit. When *The Single Hound* appeared in 1914, everyone was too much concerned with *vers libre* to take in her metaphysics. It was only with the 1929 publication of *Further Poems* that the new critical establishment recognized a kindred spirit ('places her permanently among the enduring poets of the English language').[11] No one is likely now to want to question her place and quality: yet it is perhaps true to say that she never overcame a tendency to oscillate between wit and whimsy. Returning to her now, one is as likely as not to be aware of her limitations.

The worst of these is suggested by the facts of her biography. Her range of experience was restricted to such an extent that the realities which Baudelaire, Whitman and Rimbaud discovered through actual contact, came to her only as abstractions. Thus, her early poetry is vitiated in the main by the faults of the small-town naif—sentimentality, whimsicality, and generalization. There is such jingoism as 'If the foolish call them flowers', which justifies our dread of knowing superiority; and similar sentimentality, of bad Negro verse—'If I could stop one heart from breaking'. At the back of all these poems lie the same faults: abstraction and generalization. Generalization in poetry must succeed to an intense experience and be realized in more or less concrete terms. If she had not had greatness in her, she could not possibly have elevated herself above the position of prim verse-maker. Her most cogent pieces are the result of much suffering and the sinking of concrete and vivid imagery into the great common-places. In poems such as 'This merit hath the worst', the great commonplace (Edgar's speech in *Lear* is the source) lacks the element of suffering necessary for the production of great poetry. The result is a facile and uninformative juggling with dualistic opposites. In other poems of the same period one senses an experience appropriate to the theme: 'Softened by time's consummate plush', for instance, one feels compelled itself to be written: the theme is commonplace, the experience unique. Where she does not arrive at the great commonplaces by the shortcomings of bad poetry, her verse is live and swift.

[11] *Atlantic Monthly*, Vol. 143, January–June, 1929.

She is of course an 'intellectual' poet: that is, she is concerned more or less exclusively with the antithetical nature of poetry and experience, but the antitheses are both observed and ordered. What distinguishes her from Stevens, say, or Laforgue, is her gift for seeing both the disjunction and the conjunction of her experiences at once. Her language is vibrant with mental contact. She is gifted with natural synaesthesia,—'Tufts of tune', 'green chill', 'Like trains of cars on tracks of plush, I hear the level bee'—which affords her verse its concreteness. Above all she is gifted with the instantaneous vision of paradox and antithesis that underlies religion, poetry and the higher physics. Her obsession with antithesis—the dualism between expectancy and fulfilment, between attainment and failure, between anything and its converse—may be identified with her expression in metaphor, the innate grasp of opposites. It is her imagery which pulls the reader up, even when the rhythm remains sing-song:

> Shot the lithe sleds like shod vibrations
> Emphasised and gone—
> It is the past's supreme italic
> Makes the present mean.

The logic in such poems is ordered so that the emotional force is held back to a finely judged conclusion. The logic has a purely emotional value: the virtues of her mind are subservient to the dominant visionary power. She is able to realise a vision of heaven:

> Invisible as music
> Positive as sound.

This vision is expressed through wit, which is to say, through seeing the concrete in the abstract, the abstract in the concrete:

> These are the days when skies put on
> The old, old sophistries of June—

> . . . zero at the bone,

> Calvaries of love!

> Until the designated light
>   Repudiates the forge.

Or the reverse: 'Banks of noon', 'Siroccos crawl', 'Castles of sunshine', 'Inebriate of air am I, And debauchee of dew'.

Yet the wit is always close to whimsy,—as it is in Marvell. Marvell's

> And you should if you please, refuse
> Until the conversion of the Jews,

is parallelled by Donne's sagas of tear-floods, and Dickinson's

> What if the poles should freak about
> And stand upon their heads!

T. S. Eliot told us once to permit such playfulness in serious contexts. We are more likely now to overlook it as one of the occupational hazards of reading the poetry of wit. Certainly, in Dickinson's case, it seems part of a general lightness, indexed by the bad technique. Compared with Emily Brontë, she does not seem major. Guillaume Apollinaire, finally, is the poet of wit *par excellence*:

> *Bergère o tour Eiffel le troupeau des ponts bêle ce matin. . . .*

Yet beneath his worldliness, the Daighilev worldliness, how much of the anthologies there is:

> *Sous le pont Mirabeau coule la Seine*
> *Et nos amours*
> *Faut-il qu'il m'en souvienne*
> *La joie venait toujours après la peine*

—the ghost of Verlaine. And it is indeed very lovely. Yet the tart wit that protects the loveliness with worldliness also blunts the cutting edge of the mind. Apollinaire reflects with grace and humour the Paris and London of his age, rather in the manner of Derain or Marquet, sometimes even of Bonnard. Ultimately, then, the irony and wit seem self-important, superior, and simply lightweight, the graceful play of mind upon urban phenomena. T. S. Eliot outpaced Apollinaire by as much as Schönberg outpaced Stravinsky. Yet Apollinaire remains modish, for he is the perfect example of the poet of wit —aloof, yet comfortable, worldly, satiric, informed.

Clearly, this catalogue could be extended indefinitely. The

case I have attempted to present through these examples could be expressed like this: the poetry which we can properly call ironical—that for instance of Wallace Stevens, Louis MacNeice, Emily Dickinson, Marvell, Catullus, Rochester, Apollinaire, Tristan Corbière—is not, I submit, capable of the ultimate commitment of the self that forms an integral part of the greatest poetry. It is either divided against itself, like that of Laforgue, or coquettish in its attitude towards experience, like that of MacNeice, or simply cynical like that of Rochester.

Contrary to what Richards asserts, in fact, we can even say that irony must *not* form part of the *ultimate* statements of poetry. We are driven back upon some kind of distinction between reason and the creative activity, between the poetic and the prose consciousness. In one sense, all artistic work is a structure of thought which the artist to a greater or lesser degree attempts to define by attaining to the sense of existence necessarily accompanying it. In different artists, the thought-structure is more or less flexible, more or less sinuous. But however it is, there is a thought-structure which is at once the vehicle of thought and the thing itself. Now poetry attempts to define the structure of thought by *inhabiting* it. Prose describes the perception of which the structure is compact. Prose is therefore in a strict sense descriptive: the prose-artist is concerned with the act of perception, not with the 'ultimate reality' poets are supposed to be concerned with. Thus, prose is dualistic, existing in a tension between the act of perception and human behaviour-in-society. Poetry on the other hand is unifying: it is either the ultimate commitment of man to himself, or it is nothing. (The fallacious view of poetry so prevalent in modern criticism stems, I think, from Matthew Arnold's dictum that poetry should be a criticism of life, which had the effect of reducing poetry to the condition of prose.) As a means, irony can be valuable in poetry; taken as an end, it is destructive of the ultimate self-commitment we look for in poetry. The ruling poetic mode and end should always be given its consummation.

We are forced to conclude that the positing of irony as an end (which in effect is what we have in Richards) has some other explanation, an explanation not of a theory of poetry but of a particular mood.

The nature of this mood emerges most clearly in the criticism of F. R. Leavis, the most widely influential, perhaps, of all the intellectualist critics. In Leavis's criticism—which has remained remarkably consistent in attitude and tone for more than forty years—we find the same concern as we have already seen in Richards and Empson for ironical intelligence. Intelligence, it now appears, of a very particular sort. This is perhaps most apparent in *New Bearings in English Poetry* (1932). The whole book is really an argument for 'inclusiveness', compact of irony and ambiguity. The older established poets of the day—de la Mare, Hardy, Yeats—are dismissed for lacking the capacity for ironical contemplation, for preserving an inflexibly 'poetic' tone, and generally being incapable of handling mature experience. Ezra Pound and T. S. Eliot are then presented as characteristic of a new modern sensibility, principally in having this sort of 'intelligence'. It is Leavis's treatment of the early Eliot that is so revealing: 'Gerontion', for instance, is singled out for its 'intelligence', while 'Rhapsody on a Windy Night' and 'Preludes' (more powerful and significant poems in my view) are dismissed with a reference to their 'imagery of urban disillusion', and a passing warning about their possibly dangerous effects upon 'adolescent pessimists'. 'The Love Song of J. Alfred Prufrock', above all, is praised for its 'self-mocking, self-distrustful attitudes'. Now this seems to me a crucially significant phrase in the development of modern criticism: the unmistakable implication of Leavis's remark is that the self-distrust and the self-mockery are the source of the poem's strength. Why? Is it really praiseworthy in a poet to distrust himself, to mock himself? I am not aware that anyone before me has raised the question. Yet it begs to be asked; for the assumption behind this observation of Leavis's about 'Prufrock' is in fact pervasively operative throughout intellectualist criticism. Richards may dress it up in quasi-scientific mumbo-jumbo; Empson stick to the textual facts; Brooks merely jeer at the Romantic afflatus. But behind all these critical procedures there is the kind of belief manifested in Leavis's remark. We begin to understand the rejection of Milton and the Romantics afresh: Milton's *language* after all, as Empson early showed,[12] is rich in ambiguities

[12] See, for instance, *Seven Types of Ambiguity*, pp. 104–5.

and ironies: it is the whole stance of the man, his—yes, inflex-
ible assumption of authority and importance that lacks
irony. Milton's poetry simply does not ally 'levity and seriousness'.

No one expressed the intellectualist distrust of Milton more
powerfully than Leavis, though Pound and Eliot had already
established an attitude towards the poet that was to persist
until the 'sixties. Leavis accused Milton of lacking self-awareness: 'Milton has so little self-knowledge, is so unqualified
intellectually that his intention . . . and what he contrives as a
poet to do, conflict with disastrous consequences.'[13] Milton was
crippled, Leavis asserts, by a fatal combination of qualities: 'On
the one hand there was his heroic self-confidence, his massive
egotism . . . . On the other hand, only a great capacity for unawareness—unawareness in the face of impossibilities, his own
limitations . . . could have permitted him, after pondering such
an undertaking, to persist in it.' I am not concerned with the
Milton controversy itself here. Recent trends indicate that
Leavis's treatment of Milton is little more than a historical
oddity;—but it is a very revealing one, for our purposes. For it
shows two importantly related things in the clearest possible
light: the deep distrust by the intellectualist school of the
'egotistical sublime' (the 'vatic stance'), and the real function
of irony as a guarantor of 'self-knowledge'.

Milton's 'humourlessness' had been a standard joke long
before the first cracks appeared in the poet's 'classical standing'.
But this had usually been accepted as a price worth paying for
Milton's particular sort of seriousness: after all neither Dante nor
the prophet Isaiah seems overburdened with wit and humour.
But the intellectualist school in its emphasis upon irony and wit
had provided an instrument for turning this solemnity of Milton's
against him. Eliot's dissociation theory turned crucially upon
Milton, especially as he appeared in relation to Marvell and
Dryden (poets who preserved the flexible fantasy and sardonic
wit so glaringly absent from Milton). It was not the humourlessness itself that seemed to matter so much, *as the appearance of
scorning a proper sense of the ego's limits*: Milton's absence of 'wit'
and irony seemed to bespeak a certain blindness in him, a kind
of moral stupidity. He did not, like the Eliot of 'Prufrock',

[13] 'Mr. Eliot and Milton', *The Common Pursuit* (London, 1952).

'mock' or 'distrust' himself. Dr Leavis expressed this by saying that he did not know himself.

It seems to me that this characteristic emphasis on self-awareness of Leavis's, taken together with his no less constant stress upon irony and 'intelligence', gives us the clue to the real foundation of the intellectualist school. Richards's 'irony', Eliot's 'wit', Empson's 'ambiguity' and Leavis's 'intelligence' meet up along the line of self-knowledge. The real purpose of irony is to guarantee self-awareness, and the synthesis or inclusiveness of 'the greatest kind of poetry' derives from the poet's willingness to subject his impulses and emotions to every sort of reflective light—as Milton, in his bigoted self-righteousness, so the argument runs, did not. But if the irony is really a guarantor of self-knowledge, self-knowledge itself, as this school of critics conceives it, has also a special and restricted meaning. After all, there *is* a sense in which self-knowledge can be said to be the end and goal of the greatest art: Rembrandt's self-portraits, *King Lear*, Beethoven's last string quartets,— these works, supreme works in the western tradition, do seem to present the findings of a life-long investigation of the self, to be the profoundest documents of man's search for himself. With these works, moreover, we are conscious of an absolute and ultimate *confidence*, confidence born of the certainty that all illusions have been shattered: this, we are sure, is the *truth*, and it is a truth that does seem to have a lot to do with self-knowledge.

But the fact is that the self-knowledge the intellectualist school has in mind is of a different sort: by self-knowledge critics like F. R. Leavis really have in mind an acknowledgement of personal limitation. The poet is to get credit for his intimations of his own unworthinesses, his pettinesses, his minor absurdities and betrayals, his duplicities, his self-doubts. This is the real reason why Richards posits irony as an element of 'the greatest kind of poetry'. He obscures the fact by elaborating a theory of an inclusive imaginative idiom in terms of a purely technical irony. Irony *in fact* (as opposed to theoretic smoke-screening) is conceived as a constant check upon being deceived, taken in, deluded. In other words, the irony of the intellectualist school, far from guaranteeing a poetry of all shades and tones, really dictates a very limited order of poetry. The ironical

poet keeps a vigilant check on his own dishonesties, and pre-
serves his own integrity. Hence, Leavis's praise of 'Prufrock'
for its 'self-mocking, self-distrustful attitudes'. Hence, also, his
praise of the later Yeats for its admission of bitterness and
defeat: 'He does not deceive himself about what he has lost,
but the regret itself becomes in the poetry something positive.'[14]
Leavis speaks also of Yeats's 'difficult and delicate sincerity',
and 'extraordinarily subtle poise'. The latter study of Yeats
defines the excellence in terms of 'tormenting complexity of
experience', 'sardonic irony' and 'bitterness'.

What has happened to poetry over the past thirty years is,
roughly, that a sense of inadequacy and defeat—expressed in
the ironist ideology, though not, of course, created by it—has
infiltrated into the poetic consciousness. This process is clearly
conditioned by important historical and political factors. The
ironist school itself typifies the intellectual state of England at
the time at which its empire, its traditional sense of greatness,
and its class-system were beginning to crumble. To this extent,
the part played by the Great War cannot be over-estimated:
what we see in the poetry, philosophy and criticism of the
inter-war years is the self-analysis or self-castigation of a nation
which felt itself teetering into anonymity. Thus, the literary
criticism of Cambridge in the 'twenties—the Cambridge of
Russell, Keynes and Forster—is only a symptom among many
others of a general malaise. Of this malaise perhaps no symptom is more significantly general than the impasse reached in
dialectical thought in Europe.

For at this stage, it seems important to generalize the
judgement to include not only English but also French and
German culture. The Hegelian dialectic in German and
French thought had become a weapon of evasion, an instrument by which each and any position reached could be sub-
verted by its possible dialectical opposite. In the music of
Mahler at the beginning of the century we find 'mit parodie'
as a score direction, not just now and then, but endlessly, as a
mode of feeling: the conductor is encouraged by the composer
to join him in ridiculing his own inspirations. In *Doktor Faustus*
(1947), Thomas Mann's satanic artist, Adrian Leverkühn,

<hr>

[14] F. R. Leavis, 'Yeats: the problem and the challenge', *Lectures in America*
(London, 1969).

writes an opera based upon *Love's Labours Lost*, in which everything is mocked 'in strict chamber-music style, a delicate airy
filigree, a clever parody in notes, ingenious and humoristic,
rich in subtle high-spirited ideas'. The piece, the composer's
disciple Zeitblom reports, 'in every way mocked and parodistically exaggerated itself . . .'. We know that Mann himself at the
time of writing *Doctor Faustus* had faith only in parody, in this
seeing his alignment with James Joyce.

What is interesting is the way Mann turns the twelve-note
theory of Schönberg (a composer largely free from the parodistic
mania that dogged Mahler) into a means of evading what were
felt to be the impossibilities of the artist's situation in the twentieth century: the 'kingdom of the banal' was threatening 'to
swallow up art itself'. It is not difficult to find one's way through
Mann's layered ironies to catch in these words of Serenus
Zeitblom an expression of Mann's own fears: 'With deep
concern I asked myself what strain and effort, intellectual tricks,
by-ways, and ironies would be necessary to save it, to reconquer
it, and to arrive at a work which as a travesty of innocence
confessed to the state of knowledge from which it was to be won!'
We can see in this tortuous logic, of course, the characteristic
German weakness for the plausible yet far-fetched rationalization, the inability to out-think semantic systems, as Lawrence
and Joyce in their different ways both did. But underlying
Mann's dilemma is the more general predicament of European
thought and art in his time. The ironic bias of English criticism
and poetry in the second quarter of the twentieth century
sprang from the same general conditions: Leavis, Richards and
Empson rationalized a general European conviction that the
qualification, negation or ironic inversion of the old values
would serve to create new ones. The music of *Les Six*, the
neo-classicism of Stravinsky (itself a precursor of many quasi-
parodic regressions), the antics of Dada, the classicist pastiche of
Picasso and Braque, all these phenomena of *entre deux guerres* art
testify to the profound uncertainty vitiating Western European
civilization after the Great War. It may at first sight seem
perverse to yoke the Cambridge critics to a band-waggon that
would to them have seemed irresponsible and time-servingly
flashy. Yet the preoccupation—the obsession—with irony which

creeps into European art from the time of Laforgue and Corbière to that of Thomas Mann cannot be unrelated to the intellectualist criticism in England in the 'twenties.

What is peculiarly English about the Cambridge ironist tradition is what we have observed to be so dominant in Dr Leavis: the consistent under-valuing of the individual by himself. The role of irony in modern poetry has been to cut the ego down to size; so that irony itself grew naturally out of the 'twenties atmosphere. What Lytton Strachey did to the great Victorians, Pound and others were ready to do to Milton.

A sense of importance would seem a natural part of the poetic enterprise. Yet the ironist tradition, with its insistence upon self-qualification, has thrown this in doubt: the ironist tradition has laid all its emphasis on the importance of one part of the poetic venture—the sometimes salutary self-awareness with which the poet at times needs to revitalize a language over-burdened with sleeping grandeur. Moreover, the poet easily slips into an unthinking acceptance of the gesture and tone of his own immediate forebearers. The case being argued here is that this reliance upon irony is only justified at certain times: the Symbolists exploited the properties of irony to redefine the terms of an overblown romanticism, just as certain seventeenth-century poets practised upon the rich language of the Jacobeans ironic variations which sharpened their awareness. But in the twentieth century this strategy has become over-dominant: irony itself has lost its tension. Hence, the ironist critic has come to regard a saving sense of irony as part and parcel of the poetic enterprise. Yet many men engaged upon the most important work possible to man neither suspect, nor need to suspect, themselves of duplicity, dishonesty, or absurdity, and ultimately the intellectualist exaction is that the poet should do this.

2 F. R. Leavis and the English Existential Tradition

So far I have alluded only to one aspect of Dr Leavis's criticism —his insistence both upon self-knowledge as a goal and a criterion for serious poetry and upon a deflationary irony. Yet Leavis is associated most often with so-called 'positive values'— with Lawrence and Life. One might argue on the strength of what we have seen to be true of the ironist school in general, that this positive emphasis has always been partly negative—an instrument for detecting and expelling self-importance, rhetoric and the Grand Manner. Sometimes this seems to me to be undoubtedly the case: there is an element of sheer negativity, it seems to me, in the almost emotional need to debunk Milton. On the other hand, much of Leavis's finest criticism has been devoted to the praise of those virtues (moral and technical) which are the obverse of the Miltonic pride and the Swiftian bitterness—the modesty of Keats and Hopkins, the solid simplicity of Bunyan, the blazing common-sense of Blake. This aspect of Leavis's criticism is in fact wholly consistent with the first, in the same way as the cult of irony grew out of an embarrassment in the presence of the 'sublime'.

Dr Leavis's treatment of Wordsworth is interesting from this point of view: Wordsworth is praised for his 'distinctively human naturalness, with sanity and spiritual health'.[1] It is easy to feel that, subtle and sensitive as it is at its best, there is something missing from Dr Leavis's account of Wordsworth— something importantly associated with the Egotistical Sublime Leavis finds so abhorrent,—with that high sense of authority T. S. Eliot noted in the poet.[2] This pattern exists throughout

---

[1] F. R. Leavis, *Revaluation* (London, 1962), p. 170.
[2] T. S. Eliot, 'Wordsworth is really the first, in the unsettled state of affairs of

Leavis's criticism: constantly, we find an insistence upon 'sanity' and 'spiritual health', going along with the distaste for 'egotism' (a word frequently met with in Leavis) and a corresponding appreciation of modesty and other related human virtues. Gerard Manley Hopkins, for instance, has 'the rarest integrity ... rarest humility'. At the same time, Hopkins is praised for exploiting the 'naked thew and sinew of the English language'.[3] In the same way, Keats, accepted one feels in a spirit which emphasizes what are felt to be Shelley's weaknesses, makes a 'realizing use of the body and the action of the English language', and a 'full-bodied concreteness ... pervasive strength in the use of words'.[4]

The nexus between the moral and the textual aspects of Leavis's criticism is clear: he requires of poetry a naturalness of movement, a non-rhetorical manner, and a certain 'solidity' of texture to body forth a certain modest, outward integrity of feeling.

Now at one level this complex of requirements constitutes a typical English refusal of the abstract, of metaphysics, and also of conceit, exhibitionism, 'showing off': the English detest personal flamboyance as much as they distrust metaphysics. The poets Dr Leavis rejects by silence as often as by specific reference—Marlowe, Milton, Shelley, Yeats, Joyce, Baudelaire, Rimbaud, it's a long and impressive list—tend to be addicted to the transcendental in theme, and characterized often both by a glamorous abstraction of language and a heroic arrogance of personality. They are all outstanding poet-heroes, upholders of the 'vatic stance'. In this dual insistence upon irony and evidence of 'self-knowledge', and the rejection both of any kind of transcendentalism and of the 'vatic stance', Leavis's criticism is absolutely central to modern thinking and writing. And nothing is more significantly symptomatic of this thinking than the implicit assumption that 'self-knowledge' is incompatible with what Milton was doing, for instance, or Shelley, or W. B. Yeats. The absence of irony, or a sardonic self-doubt,

---

his time, to annex new authority for the poet, to meddle with social affairs, and to offer a new kind of religious sentiment which it seemed the peculiar prerogative of the poet to interpret.' J. Hayward (ed.), *Selected Prose* (Harmondsworth, 1953), p. 163.

[3] F. R. Leavis, *The Common Pursuit* (London, 1952).

[4] *The Comman Pursuit*, p. 16.

in Shelley and Milton, for instance, indicates self-deception. Since Shelley and Milton plainly lack the pervasive irony thought essential to the creation of 'inclusive poetry', or 'poetry of synthesis', it must be that they bought their scale, their sense of having some supremely important function in life, at the expense of their intelligence. Their solemnity, their high drive, like Wordsworth's distrust of wit, must indicate lack of self-awareness—signs of dissociated sensibility, indeed, wit having got itself divorced from 'high seriousness'. To put it bluntly, Dr Leavis has shown an increasing tendency to identify any evidence in a writer of a sense of the importance of his role with self-delusion.[5] Nothing less than the highest seriousness will satisfy Leavis, but this seriousness is severely limited in what it may attach importance to. I shall put my case in the clearest possible light by stating that Leavis's emphases upon self-knowledge, humility, modesty and integrity *in fact* have had the effect of limiting the scope of the poetic imagination. Self-deception is certainly incompatible with the writing of poetry, but we need not necessarily conclude that the object of poetry is therefore self-knowledge. The idea of self-knowledge may be quite irrelevant to the aims and purposes of a great poet. He may quite simply, have something *more important* to communicate, something which needs to be able to take its own honesty and integrity for granted. To posit self-knowledge (as irony) as an end may ultimately be corrupting and stultifying.

Dr Leavis established his reputation with a work which argued the virtues both of the ironical poetry that modernism had inherited from post-symbolist France and of a native English tradition that undercut the 'Romantic' poetry of de la Mare and the Georgians. It is in playing this role that he occupies the central position in modern English criticism. Underlying the surface differences between Laforgue and Apollinaire and the finest English poetry of the later nineteenth and early twentieth century—that of Hopkins, Hardy and Edward Thomas—there is a common concern for self-awareness. French poets like Apollinaire proved their integrity (as well as their sophistication) by the ironical view they took of their suspect impulses and of the pretensions implicit in their values. There is

[5] In his later criticism, words like 'uninhibited' and 'confident' are often used with a subtle reliance on a pejorative force.

little of the Parisian sophistication in Hopkins and Edward
Thomas, but there is by compensation a ferocious determination *not to be fooled* which manifests itself in an awesome sobriety
of tone and at times an almost appalling directness of approach.
The tone of their finest verse is, I think, unique to English
poetry of this period.

Historically, it is a tone which only slowly emerges out of the
intense subjective rhetoric of the Romantic poets. For all its
introspection and self-involvement, the nineteenth century
rarely seems concerned with being 'honest' with and about
itself. Its very strength, in fact, is that its subjectivity—its
intense interest in its own sensations and reactions—is put at
the service of an unconsciously inherited and adopted scheme of
attitudes and values. The lyrics of Shelley and Keats—the
greatest, perhaps, in the language—are sustained by a rhetoric of gesture and stance that transcends the self and *ipso
facto* sets that self—wholly given in its unconsciousness—in a
perspective greater than itself. Wordsworth's emphasis upon a
natural style is a historically important one. But his own poetry
exploits as much rhetoric as it requires to sustain its own great
scale: we need only compare the blank verse of *The Prelude* with
that of Robert's Frost's narrative poems to see how far poetry
had to go before something like Wordsworth's professed ideal of
a natural style could be achieved. Corresponding to the increase in naturalness goes a decrease in scale. The Romantic
poets as a school in fact use rhetoric in the quite valid way of
getting personal images in a perspective that transcends without falsifying the origin of the emotion.

One of the poets of the Romantic period, however, John
Clare, approaches at moments a stark directness which under-
cuts the subjective rhetoric natural to Romanticism:

> I am, but what I am who cares or knows?
>   My friends forsake me, like a memory lost
> I am the self-consumer of my woes.
>   They rise and vanish in oblivious host
> Like shadows in love's frenzied, stifled throes. . . .
>
>   (John Clare, 'I am')

With Clare's existential statement in Northampton lunatic
asylum a new tone comes into English poetry. Philosophy has no

monopoly of the word existential, of course, and I deliberately avoid the form of the adjective associated with the writings of Kierkegaard and his descendants. Nevertheless, in important respects, the parallels suggested by the label can and must be sustained. Clare's great poem is existential in that it affirms existence and nothing but existence: he has penetrated to a bedrock condition at which nothing of the social man or his acquired character remains: he knows only that he exists. He *is* —and he is abandoned, as Kierkegaard felt himself to be. His statement is not a cry for help, such as we hear in Cowper's 'The Castaway'; its value indeed lies less in its courage than in its directness of gaze. Clare has slipped the halter of mask, personality, character, custom. Hence, the eschewal of rhetoric and gesture. When Keats says 'My heart aches and a drowsy numbness pains/My sense', or Shelley that he could 'lie down like a tired child and weep away this life of care', they speak with unique personal voices which are nevertheless the voices of conscious or unconscious artistic personae: they are speaking an 'art-language': and they speak with style, eloquence and the authority of transcendence. The greatness of Romantic poetry indeed lies precisely in preserving so beautifully a subtle balance of the subjective accent and the objective persona.

At the time Clare was writing *The Shepherd's Calendar*, the strength of English poetry was going into the verse of the spiritual and ideological descendants of Blake and Wordsworth —Keats, Shelley and Byron. The spiritual ideals and the philosophical concepts of Romanticism began to lose their vitality as the century wore on. If we contrast Clare with Keats, we cannot feel that Clare's greater 'realism' is a sign of any greater vitality or power. On the contrary, Clare seems to us now, with all his strengths allowed for, a poet of limited vision and circumscribed emotion. The absence in his work of the exalted visionary dimension of Shelley and Keats seems a positive hindrance to his attaining the deepest kind of poetic truth. But later in the century we do begin to feel that, in Swinburne's case, for instance, the Romantic stance has been maintained at the expense of what counts in the creation of major poetry. Swinburne is a poet of major endowment, and his failure to produce a body of work of the order of *Les Fleurs du Mal* must, I think, be explained in terms of his acceptance of the Romantic posture at a time when this posture had lost the spiritual tension that informed it at the time of Shelley and Keats. As Swinburne was writing the first *Songs and Ballads*, Baudelaire was beginning to outgrow the Poe-distorted Byronism that mars so much of his own earlier work and to explore a new spiritual realism. The pain and disillusionment in poems like 'L'Aube Spirituelle' and 'Le Cygne' owe a great deal of their vividness to the clear, straightforward contexts and situations in which they are set—a Paris street at dawn, a shabby room, a dreary suburb at dusk. The despair of Tennyson and Swinburne—no less real and understandable—fails to engage us to the same extent largely because of the by now conventionalized eloquence with which it is retailed. The Romantic gestures, the rural settings, too often seem to us to dilute the intensity of the initial responses to life they are meant to embody. Much the same goes for the nature-writing. To turn from even so good a poem as Swinburne's 'The Sundew' to the Notebooks of Hopkins or to a poem like 'Inversnaid' is to make the transition from 'literature' to reality. How much greater is the effect of this contrast when the subject is the spiritual state of the poet. Swinburne failed to produce a body of work commensurate with his endowment, and the failure is ideological. He failed, broadly speaking, to see the implications of his position; which is as much as to say, that he misapprehended his position itself. By the time Swinburne was an old man poetry had experienced the full impact of social alienation. Romantic despair is, of course, itself an expression of the cultural and spiritual isolation we nowadays call alienation. But between Wordsworth and Swinburne came Marx and Dickens and Baudelaire. There was no excuse for maintaining the Romantic eloquence, which had itself been an intelligent adaptation to new circumstances of the neo-classic rhetoric.

In the last decades of the Victorian age the real strength of English poetry was going into a compressed dour verse which, rural as its settings often were, acknowledged the fact of alienation, as the 'Romantic' melancholy of Swinburne and, say, Bridges, did not. This poetry I call existential. Poets like Hardy, Thomas and Housman abstracted a quality from certain poets. Taking, as it were, the path of most resistance, they tried to find something upon which to establish a life, an authentic mode of being. That something was no less than—or should we say, no more than—existence itself, existence without attributes or qualities, mere existence.

This is outstandingly true of Hopkins. England produced numerous bohemian wavelets in the later nineteenth century, but no true *avant garde*. It produced, that is to say, movements which rationalized their sense of isolation with a half-heartedness which betrayed an inward cleaving to the social monolith which at once spurned and sustained them. This is the sense in which we can say that the failure of English poetry in the later Victorian period is ideological. Instead of an authentic *avant garde*, England threw up, alongside its official poets and semiofficial bohemians, a small number of poets who fit into no style, movement or programme, but who successfully solved the dilemma in which every nineteenth-century poet found himself. Of these poets, Hopkins is by far the most important. Poets like James Thomson, Francis Thompson and Coventry Patmore expressed themselves in more or less individual variants of the accepted post-Romantic manner. Hopkins alone succeeded in forging for himself an idiom which both eluded the content of the various late Romantic idioms (those of Keats, Shelley and Wordsworth—Byron is a notable and interesting absentee), and honestly declared its author's relation with society and God. He was, in fact, a one-man *avant garde*. No one has improved on Dr Leavis's statement of the case 'for' Hopkins,[6] and the case of course no longer needs arguing, strengthened as it has been by the ineptitude of the New Critical attacks on him. What I want to emphasise is the direction insisted by Hopkins's very success.

Hopkins was a nature poet in the romantic sense of the word;[7] he was, that is to say, spiritually anchored in the countryside where Verlaine, Baudelaire and Rimbaud were so significantly anchored in the city (if anchored is the word). But although in this following the general trend of English poetry, Hopkins manifests significant hardening of texture and feeling: the sensitivity so abundantly evident in the early verse and the Journals is pressed into the service of an increasingly intense spiritual drive towards absolute 'honesty', and an acquaintance

[6] See *New Bearings in English Poetry* (London, 1932), and 'Gerard Manley Hopkins', *The Common Pursuit* (London, 1952).
[7] But see Dr Leavis's remarks on the subject in 'Gerard Manley Hopkins'.

with the spirit's bedrock. To some extent, his progress parallels the experience of John Clare. Like Clare, Hopkins investigated Nature with a minuteness that in a sense killed the overall grasp we witness in Wordsworth and his Romantic successors. There seems to me to be a significant relation between Hopkins's analytics—his investigations into inscape, instress, etc.—and his whole evolution towards a poetry of existential awareness. I do not wish to deny the range of Hopkins's poetry—its important exultance, its strength and vitality —but I should like to suggest that the work for which he is most likely to be remembered, and the contribution which seems the most valuable, is to be found in the later poems—especially in the so-called Terrible Sonnets. The vitality indeed, far from being negated by these poems, was indispensable to their creation. We know from 'The fine delight that fathers thought', if not from the Notebooks and earlier poems, how intense was Hopkins's exhilaration in the presence of Nature—of God. But if we may assume for a moment the position of Hopkin's religious *Weltanschauung*, can't we say that suffering is what Hopkins's God meant him for? Isn't his suffering—suffering of abandonment, loneliness, absolute despair—what Hopkins had most richly to offer?

> Self-yeast of spirit a dull dough sours. I see
> The lost are like this, and their scourge to be
> As I am mine, their sweating selves; but worse.

Hopkins's Christ begins as a bird of prey, a dauphin, Orion, a Herculean hero; he ends as an ambiguous Blakean torturer who inscrutably scrutinizes the poet:

> But ah, but O thou terrible, why wouldst thou rude on me
> Thy wring-world right foot rock? lay a lion limb against me
> Scan with darksome devouring eyes my bruised bones?

The poet feels exposed to hammer-blows on an anvil, suspended over 'cliffs of fall'; his pleas are like 'dead letters' sent to a God he knows has moved away (an astounding instance of Hopkins's originality of metaphor). Nothing remains to him, apparently, but his self, and that not as a personality, but as the 'sheer'

capacity to experience: *J'existe donc je suis*. This absolute abandonment is nowhere more powerfully evident than in the poet's
refusal to 'despair':

> I can;
> Can something; hope, wish day come, not choose to be.

'I am that which chooses not not to be': somehow this is so much
more terrible than actually choosing not to be.

The *I can* of Hopkins and the *I am* of Clare are the corner-
stones of what we could call the English existential tradition,
peculiarly modern statements which help man to define himself
in his new existential situation. Turning from such poems to the
best poems of Thomas Hardy we can hardly help being aware,
if not of the same spiritual intensity, at least of a similar concern
with an almost stultifying fidelity to the appearance of Nature
and with a kind of undeceivable sobriety. Hardy wrote poetry
for nearly sixty years, yet it is in a sense from the first hyper-
mature poetry—a poetry of emotion recollected not so much in
tranquillity as in disillusionment. It is a poetry of patterns
discerned too late and at too great a distance. His is a poetry
destroyed in a sense by its own modesty, self-effaced to the point
of annihilation:

> I am the one whom ringdoves see
>   Through chinks in boughs
>   When they do not rouse
>   In sudden dread,
>   But stay on cooing, as if they said,
>   O, it's only he.

Hardy's nothingness, as it were, gives him his role. This poem
appears in the *Winter Words* collection of 1928. Yet such a
preoccupation with the nullity of human emotion can be seen
in much earlier verse:

> The smile on your mouth was the deadest thing
> Alive enough to have strength to die;
> And a grin of bitterness swept thereby
> Like an ominous bird a-wing. . . .

No other poet has caught man and Nature at quite such a low ebb as this: there is an almost exquisite relish for the degree of the neutrality. Consistently, Hardy annihilates display, exhibitionism, play, effusion, and the associated philosophical and psychological activities—metaphysics, mythology, transcendance, rhetoric. Like Hopkins's, Hardy's poetry takes place at a level where all traces of myth and role—unless of the peculiarly invisible sort we have seen in 'I am the one the ringdoves see'—have been obliterated.

Edward Thomas took over from Hardy the weird, grim penetration of vision that consistently 'saw through' human life, and in seeing through it, annulled it. In 'Under the woods', for instance, Thomas imagines, as Hardy does in 'At Nightfall', a time in a forest when the keeper will not be there; the poem returns to the present, after his death, with a characteristically subtle image:

> But now that he is gone
> Out of most memories
> Still lingers on
> A stoat of his,
>
> But one shrivelled and green,
> And with no scent at all,
> And barely seen
> On this shed wall.

The 'meaningless' physical object which, in surviving the human lives in which it has been involved, becomes symbolic of them, is an old device of poets; but never, surely, has it been used with more subtlety than here: we can hardly apprehend the resonance, as we could hardly see the stoat-skin. Thomas's great strength lies in a refinement of feeling, which, associated as it is with a morbid awareness of mortality, enables him to figure forth moods and intuitions all but ungraspable to human apprehension. What most men of fine feeling might at times be able to sense with instinct—the presence of death, the nothingness of experience, the strangeness of the ordinary—Edward Thomas felt as articulately as a trained philosopher feels a concept. What is presented in poems like 'Adlestrop', 'The Gallows', 'Cliff-top', 'Ambition', is perfectly available to us in

Thomas's imagery and rhythm, but we have absolutely no other means to paraphrase or suggest what it is. Thomas learnt his craft, we are told, from Robert Frost; the pay-out of the lines and certain tricks of feeling (evident for instance in poems like 'Tall Nettles') tell us of Thomas's debt to the American. But Thomas never acquired Frost's suave ease of movement (note the occasional awkwardness of rhyme in even so good a poem as 'Lights Out'). Yet nor did he acquire the glibness that so often short-circuits Frost's explorations: Thomas's verse makes all but the very best of Frost seem simply meretricious. And the way of feeling behind this verse derives not from Frost, but from Hardy:

> There was a crow who was no sleeper,
> But a thief and a murderer
> Till a very late hour; and this keeper
> Made him one of the things that were
> To hang and flap in rain and wind,
> In the sun and in the snow.
> There are no more sins to be sinned
> On the dead oak tree bough.
>
> ('The Gallows')

The basis of Thomas's verse, as of Hardy's, is the English nature tradition, of course. English poetry had failed, we have seen, to foster a significant *avant garde*. In default, it had intensified its awareness of the natural world to the pitch we have seen it assume in Hardy and Edward Thomas. The run of English verse, in short, remains within the confines of Wordsworthian ruralism; but there is a significant difference between poets who, like Blunden and de la Mare and Brooke, assumed the stance of the Romantic rhetoricians, and poets belonging to what I have called the existential tradition. If all poetry is, as T. S. Eliot suggested,[8] meant to be overheard, this is surely the least meant to be overheard in existence:

> As for myself,
> Where first I met the bitter scent is lost.
> I, too, often shrivel the grey shreds,
> Sniff them and think and sniff again and try

[8] T. S. Eliot, *The Three Voices of Poetry* (London, 1953), p. 6.

Once more to think what it is I am remembering,
Always in vain. I cannot like the scent,
Yet I would rather give up others more sweet,
With no meaning, than this bitter one.

                                        ('Old Man or Lad's Love')

What lies behind the peculiarly straight gaze of this existential
poetry is surely suggested in the last phrase just quoted: better
to hold on to this bitter scent *with meaning*, than relinquish it for
another that is sweeter but meaningless. The need for meaning,
and the inability to compound for the vaguer *sense of meaningful-
ness* associated with poetic rhetoric,—these are the twin drives of
existential poetry. They merge together in the total eschewal of
rhetoric, effect and posture, and produce a mental stillness so
complete that no voice disturbs it. It is peculiar, in my view, to
the best English poetry of this period.

There is nothing in American poetry with anything like the
sheer straightforwardness of this poem of D. H. Lawrence, who
inherited the Hardy–Thomas tradition:

A yellow leaf from the darkness
Hops like a frog before me;
Why should I start and stand still?
I was watching the woman who bore me
Stretched in the brindled darkness
Of the sickroom, rigid with will
To die; and the quick leaf tore me
Back to this rainy swill
Of leaves and lamps and the city street
      mingled before me.

                                        ('Brooding Grief')

Turning from this to the contemporary elegies of American
poets like Jeffers, Masters and Robinson, it is impossible not to
feel that Lawrence's lines have 'what counts' in poetry, and the
Americans have not. If we trace a line from the 'I am' of
Clare to these lines of Lawrence, the skeleton of a distinct
existential tradition begins to emerge clearly enough. What
happens over the course of the nineteenth century is that an
almost morbid awareness of 'what counts' in poetry—absolute
honesty, total absence of deception—assumes greater and

greater importance in the work of the relatively few poets who resisted the disintegration of the Romantic ideal. The finest poems produced with this ideal can hardly be surpassed in their honest simplicity, their subtle tenderness, their softly blazing mystical vitality. The finest poems of Hardy, Hopkins, Edward Thomas, Lawrence and later R. S. Thomas and Jack Clemo make most poetry of their respective times seem foolish and non-serious.

Yet the truth is that it was not healthy, it was not long possible, for poetry to exist in these conditions, with these spiritual aims. Too much had to be sacrificed, for one thing, and the range of mood that could be expressed was restricted. This was a poetry *in extremis*—existential, denuded, disabused. It was marked by sobriety, and was founded upon the work of poets who had penetrated to the bedrock layers of the human condition. Without the extreme states of mind behind the later Hopkins, say, or Edward Thomas, the poet was left only with a disabling concern for his own integrity, with maintaining the naked absence of illusion forced upon the existential poets themselves by dire experience.

All of these tendencies and trends are summed up in the person and writings of F. R. Leavis. Dr Leavis has analysed the Englishness of English poetry, and provided modern English poetry with its rationale and its justification. Thus, English criticism, like the poetry it works upon, is opposed to metaphysics, transcendence and any display of personal arrogance or pride, and in particular, the 'act' of being a poet. Now, to a large extent the poet must be aware of 'being a poet'; and some of the natural by-products of such an awareness—a certain swagger, or exhibitionism—are not enough to disqualify the man who displays them from the serious exercise of his art. The sense of 'being an artist' so detestable to Dr Leavis[9] is, I should want to argue, an essential part of the poet's emergence into mature poetic consciousness. Paradoxically, 'maturity' in the sense that Dr Leavis and his followers are apt to intend when they use the word, may actually hinder a poet in the process of finding himself. The poet's subject-matter in the modern cultural world is crucially involved with the sense of

[9] See for instance the Yeats essays, and the essay on *Anna Karenina* in *Anna Karenina and other Essays* (London, 1968).

role and function, and it was not healthy for the perfectly
natural pride and even arrogance that so often attend this
consciousness of poetic talent to be as inhibited as the intellectualist insistence upon irony and 'self-awareness' (in the limited
sense I have already indicated) have made it. A sense of being
distinguished by Fate or God or Society, of being marked out
for some important mission, is an important part of the poetic
venture. It may be nicer or more acceptable to the rest of
society if this sense is worn invisibly and modestly—but that
may not have anything to do with the stature of the poetry that
results. Dr Leavis has done English poetry a disservice, I
think, in making poets too conscious of some of the sillier
follies of the bohemian stance. Sitwellian exhibitionism may be
foolish, but dandyism, bohemianism, beatnikery, hippiness—
these are simply variants of probably indispensable strategies by
which poets in this century have survived neglect and protected their talent by making a place for themselves and
arriving at a conception of themselves.

The obsession with irony in the nineteen-twenties clearly
assisted an inhibiting process that went back to the existential
consciousness of poets like Hardy and Edward Thomas. Irony
enforces an awareness of the limits of the self; it cuts the ego
down to size, and this can be all to the good. But it can also
disable the poet for the more adventurous projects open to him.
For myth, persona and metaphysical transcendence are all
important instruments in the development of the poetic personality, and the poetic personality must exist before poetry can
be written. Poetry is not looking-into-the-heart-and-writing,
though the concern for an absolute honesty in the English
existential poets suggests that it is. Denying himself the projective
power of myth, the poet is left with the situation-report, and the
situation-report is only possible intermittently.

It is time for me to put all my cards on the table. I believe
that a preoccupation with irony and self-knowledge has secured
a dislocation of sensibility exactly the reverse of the synthesis
Richards, Eliot and Leavis intended to guarantee. In striving
after a unity of vision, compact of serious experience and ironic
awareness, the intellectualist critics drove a wedge between the
mind and the free exercise of its highest and strongest faculties.
In fact, their greatest achievement was to rob poets of a sense

of the importance of their task—of living the life of a poet in the sense which has been integral to Western poetry since Dante, if not earlier. They succeeded in making poets sceptical of a wide or an exalted scale, in making them nervous of taking on the most important themes for fear of seeming portentous, above all in inhibiting the capacity for frank and full self-declaration which must in the last analysis form part of the poet's utterance. They destroyed the capacity for intense feeling by inculcating the fear of appearing naive: 'Am I being absurd? Am I deceiving myself? Do I really *feel* this?' These are the questions that intellectualist criticism taught poets to ask themselves; they are questions and doubts which are basically incompatible with the creation of 'the greatest kind of poetry'. This was the harvest of irony.

The argument of this book is that unless the poet can regain possession of the importance of his function that informs the work of the sense of the great Romantic and symbolist poets, poetry must remain in the inferior category it has allowed itself to be allotted. Moreover, it is essential, I believe, for English poetry to rid itself of the notion that poetry is fundamentally a 'criticism of life', and that its main object is self-analysis. Self-knowledge is valuable only if it accrues unsought-for: taken as an end in itself it is apt to be corrupting and disabling. A poetry adequate to our time, one which openly confronts the deepest issues, can only derive from a revolution in attitudes. Such a revolution has in fact taken place over the past fifteen years. Commenting on academic poetry and values in England today, Michael Horovitz writes: 'In the synthesizing mind, the wildest overflow of powerful emotions can co-exist with "high seriousness".'[10] A tilt at the intellectualist dem and for 'ironica contemplation' and its identification of power and possession with myopia and sleep. I should go still further: 'high seriousness' is only possible when all impediments to the mind's fullest functioning—conscious ambiguity, ironical contemplation, watchfulness, self-consciousness—have been removed, and the mind's ends are not fore-ordained.

[10] Michael Horovitz, 'Afterword', *Children of Albion* (London, 1968), p. 351–2.

3 'Partial fires':
Empson's poetry

There is no precedent in English writing for the influence of the intellectualist critics upon the creative practice of the poets who emerged in the decades following the publication of their seminal works. For various reasons, which it would require a social historian to evaluate properly, the poetry of the 'thirties, 'forties and 'fifties is characterized by a certain tone or range of tones for which the word academic is the only adequate descriptive label. It was nothing new for a group of poets to be associated with a particular university: but it was certainly new for the attitudes and techniques of poetry to be determined by the thinking of literary critics teaching at universities. 'Academic' is an adjective that I will use a lot in the following pages, often with no claim to have shorn it of the rather stale pejorative aura it has acquired. As we shall see, there were strong reasons why this influence had to be constrictive, and the pejorative associations are justifiable and inevitable. Unlike literary criticism, poetry depends on a way of life lived with a degree of force and freedom often impossible within the confines of the university.

For Dr Leavis, English writing more or less ceases to exist after Eliot's *Four Quartets*. As the very interesting *Afterword* he wrote to the 1950 edition of *New Bearings* makes clear, nothing could have persuaded him to accept Auden, or to alter his opinion of Auden as an essentially meretricious poet, incapacitated by background and environment from making the most of his (undenied) gifts. Yet in the final analysis, the gap between Oxford and Cambridge poetics was really no greater than the traditional differences between the intellectual climates of the two universities. Oxford poets and critics really worked upon the basic Cambridge concepts the kind of mutation worked by Ryle and Austin upon the philosophy of Russell, Moore and Wittgenstein. It is significant that the Oxford Movement of the 'fifties called itself Empsonian. The Augustanism of the Movement is substantially set out in Leavis's *Revaluation*, and Davie's *Articulate Energy* is largely a re-working of Ricardian and Empsonian principles. Moreover, Empson was only the Cambridge equivalent of Auden—shaggier, more wily, more intellectually dogged, yet square, and lacking in style.

The early verse of Empson is based conscientiously upon the practice of the Metaphysicals. This would be apparent from the movement alone:

> Drawn taut, this flickering of wit would freeze,
> And grave, knot-diamond, its filagrees.
>
> ('Sea-Voyage')

As strikingly pasticheur in spirit is the rifling of scientific lore and mathematical symbolism to provide imagery and structure. Whole poems, finally, are built upon the extended conceit in the manner of Marvell and Donne. The poem Empson wrote for his mother, 'To an Old Lady', for instance, is constructed upon the metaphor of space-travel, complete with space-landings, rockets and blast-offs:

> Ripeness is all; her in her cooling planet
> Revere; do not presume to think her wasted.
> Project her no projectile, plan nor man it;
> Gods cool in turn, but the sun long outlasted.
>
> Our earth alone given no name of god
> Gives, too, no hold for such a leap to aid her;
> Landing, you break some palace and seem odd;
> Bees sting their need, the keeper's queen invader.

The focus of the metaphor shifts, slightly, as the poem develops: once the telescope is trained upon the old lady-planet in the line following these stanzas, the imagery is more conventionally geared to domains and rulers. At the end of the poem, she reappears as a star:

> And but in darkness is she visible.

The poem is parallel in many ways to John Crowe Ransom's 'Here lies a Lady'. In each case the subject—fragile fine breeding, an out-of-date hauteur that seems half-heroic—is celebrated with a courtly gentility that stands curiously opposed to the Metaphysical toughness the whole ironist movement was supposed to have restored to poetry after the Romantic decline. Ransom, like Empson, deals courteously and delicately with his subject:

> What was she making? Why, nothing; she sat in a maze
> Of old scraps of laces, snipped into curious shreds.
>
> Or this would pass, and the light of her fire decline
> Till she lay discouraged and cold as a thin stalk
>   white and blown,
> And would not open her eyes to kisses, to wine.
>
> ('Here lies a lady')

It doesn't seem inappropriate that both Empson and Ransom, in some ways the respective key-figures in the English and American wings of the intellectualist movement, should excel in the presentation of refinement and gentility. For their is in essence a gentlemanly art and their common preoccupation with irony refers back to a common interest in the restoration of 'tone' to poetic traditions which were felt to have lapsed through weak-fibred romanticism into indulgence and self-absorption. It is no longer possible to be as excited by Ransom's ironies as Cleanth Brooks once was, or to be as impressed by Empson's intelligence as the author of *New Bearings in English Poetry*; the reason is not so much that these critics were wrong in their judgement, as that they overestimated the significance of what they praised. The gentlemanliness of both Ransom and Empson invites both praise and censure: praise for the undeniable sturdiness of gait, and for the disavowal of the merely clever and of the flashily self-assertive; censure for the very modesty and reserve which seem to keep each from a wholly daring commitment of himself to himself. It is not absence of vulgar declamation and hysterical self-pity one deplores in their verse, therefore, but rather the presence of an inhibiting self-consciousness imposing upon the imagination the necessity of irony and self-qualification. One might attempt to establish the point by going to T. S. Eliot for contrast. No-one is going to accuse the author of 'Marina' or 'Ash Wednesday' of lacking either poise or control, and yet these are achieved not in spite of but because of a total self-projection. For Eliot each poem was an adventure, an act of self-commitment which left him hung out over a void:

> let me
> Resign my life for this life, my speech for that unspoken,
> The awakened, lips parted, the hope, the new ships.
> ('Marina')

If we think of verse like this, we shall find it hard to remain satisfied with the ironies of Ransom and Empson, which far from guaranteeing synthesis or inclusiveness (whatever might be intended in those expressions), succeed rather in damping down the spirit.

Empson's 'The Ants', for instance, subtly and thoughtfully exploits facts of entomology to present with an almost Augustan calm a commentary, rather than a comment, on our own values:

> How small a chink lets in how dire a foe.
> What though the garden in one glance appears?
>
> Winter will come and all her leaves will go.
> We do not know what skeleton endures.
> Carry at least her parasites below.

The poem is 'academic' not so much in its learning—it is proper for a poet to tap all his roots—but in the manner in which its lesson is offered, and in the extent of the lesson's relevance. As often in Empson, the implications of the poem's logic are narrow and confined:

> Carry at least her parasites below.

The parasites—Empson's note apprises us—are green flies protected by the ants for their own needs. It is hard to carry away any but a slight shudder of acknowledgement from the poem. We see the point, but little else happens. We do not, after

all, feel deeply altered or affected by the reflection that nature's
obscure rituals and humble scavengers often conceal a rationale
we might be pleased, one day, to have applied to our own
behaviour patterns. Furthermore, the tone of what does affect
us is unashamedly classical:

> Winter will come and all her leaves will go.

This is a graceful literary gesture, the sort of thing one might
find in de la Mare. It is significant that expression is not always
assisted by complexity in Empson; that, on the contrary, the
concern for an intellectually justified complexity frequently
hampers expression. The possibility arises whether this is not,
in some obscure way, intended: complexity, it appears, may
have an obscurantic function in Empson.

Certainly, there are occasions when Empson establishes an
ironic relation between the slightness of an experience and the
load of philosophico-scientific speculation it is made to bear:
the heavyweight intellect is placed at the service of the banal
experience, with a pleasant irony. 'Rolling the Lawn' maintains throughout its bulky disquisitions the fine tone of humour
with which it starts:

> You can't beat English lawns.

—You can't beat them, both because they'll always get the
better of you, and because they are the best. The final parody-
religious invocation hits just the right near-Restoration tone:

> World, roll yourself; and bear your roller, soul,
> As martyrs gridirons, when God calls the roll.

The poem keeps in touch with its objective starting-point, and
also keeps a tight rein on the relations between the slightness
of the experience and the necessarily ironic direction of the
engendered 'thoughts'. The heave of the thoughts, indeed,
mimics the laboured physical ritual that originated them. The
whole poem is a good specimen of the genuinely ironical
poem.

Empson uses this objective, physical origin as a platform for
intellectual rumination. In the case of 'Rolling the Lawn', he
doesn't let us forget the fact, and the irony depends very mater-

ially on his being sensible about what level of seriousness he is entitled to. To some extent, all poetry must use initial experiences in this sort of way: the experience, however important, is always occasional, like Yorick's skull. But there are fairly strict rules governing the relations between the experience and the poetic implications derived from it. Hamlet's 'thinking-about' death, for instance, is marvellously natural, both within the gravedigger scene itself, and within the continuum of his own morbidity: it is, moreover, beautifully poised, its gravity being nicely disproportionate to the accidental occurrence of the skull itself. The grave-digger's coarse irreverence and Hamlet's willingness to humour him in it further prepare us for the shock Hamlet experiences at being confronted by the real fact of death (about which he has been so wittily deep) in the revelation of the skull's belonging to someone he has known, and the world of recollection this occasions. Hamlet's own knowingness about death is shown up for the unthinking thing it had been, and in the process he learns something really worth knowing about it.

Empson's use of his learning to elaborate his experiences rarely has this kind of tact. Too often overweight, awkward yet casual, it fails the experience by moving from the known and felt to the merely thought-about. This is outstandingly true of 'High Dive', perhaps the trickiest of all Empson's poems. Working hard at his Notes, and cross-referring diligently enough to the text of the poem itself, one can attain at most to a mild cerebral satisfaction that something so trivial as diving into a pool can be transcribed into such pretentious terms. (The Notes encourage us to follow the poet into speculations about mathematical equations for the movement of water, the god-like pretensions of the diver, Norse and Egyptian myth, and Cornford's theory about primitive cosmology.) We don't think Empson is showing off here: the tone is too matter-of-fact for that. It is rather that the speculations do not carry us far enough into interpretation of the experience—into meaning, in fact: they do not amount to anything more important to us (or to him) than the experience itself.

If we compare the poem with Mallarmé's 'Petit Air' ('Quelconque une solitude'), for instance, with which it is oddly analogous, we cannot but feel that Empson's piece is cumbrously learned. With a suaveté that seems at all times aware of its own 'pretentiousness', Mallarmé describes (or does he?) a girl diving into a river. He avoids all but the most evanescent detail, as though to intimate the vulgarity of approaching the goddess too closely. The final celebration of her 'jubilation nue' both successfully consummates the poem and creates the splashing of the water as she goes in. It is a delicate triumph of good sense, always gently ironical about what is being said, yet genuinely ceremonial and even exalted. Delicate sophistication of this kind ought not, given his critical preconceptions, to figure among Empson's virtues, and I do not intend to insist upon any close parallel between the two poems. Yet the reader familiar with Mallarmé's poem cannot fail to be aware of the breaches in tact in Empson's; breaches which refer back to the intellectualist prejudice in favour of a poetry which flaunts intelligent self-possession as a credential. There is little of the overt preoccupation with self-awareness in Empson. But there is, by compensation, an equivalent common-sense, a matter-of-fact steadiness, which informs us of the poet's freedom from the Romantic possession: Empson's concern with 'not being carried away' seems singularly well-evidenced in the structure and development of his poems. It was suggested above (p. 2) that there might be dangers to the Metaphysical influence on twentieth-century English poetry. Here is one of the most marked: Empson's poetry constitutionally shifts into and out of focus, now clearly visualised, now obscured in intellection, now brightly relevant, now woodily entangled in its own ramifications. 'Sleeping out in a College Cloister' is the exception (or one of the few exceptions) to a generally obtaining rule; a more or less totally successful piece of witty notation, which at the same time bulks larger than its aperçus at first suggest it will. It is the reverse, in other words, of those of Empson's poems which hang too much conceit and speculation upon too little genuinely grasped experience. The basis of the poem's success is undoubtedly its eschewal of the Metaphysical penchant for metaphoric involution, in favour of the nineteenth-century strategy of holding steadily in focus the perceived realities of ordinary experience. Where 'High Dive' for instance, starts out from actual events and soon loses itself in internal speculation, 'Sleeping out in a College Cloister' remains straightforwardly documentary, its odd angle on things at once literal and metaphorical:

> It must be later you look round and notice
> The ground plan has been narrowed and moved up;
> How much more foliage appears by star-light;
> That Hall shelters at night under the trees.

The poem reminds us forcibly what a very strange mind Empson has: how curious is his way of seeing things, how humorous, both consciously and unconsciously, are his responses. This accounts for a good deal of sheer eccentricity in both verse and criticism; for the fact that, for instance, the Seven Types of Ambiguity have never become part of the critical background of Empson's readers, although the book itself is a mine of insights. In the present poem, this oddity of vision affords Empson an insight of great depth: just as in trying to pay homage to the remote strange beauty of an old lady, Empson had recourse to science-fiction imagery, so, here, he leaves his body to take a look at the earth:

> Earth at a decent distance is the Globe
> (One has seen them smaller); within a hundred miles
> She's *terra firma*, you look down to her.
> There is a nightmare period between
> (As if it were a thing you had to swallow)
> When it engulfs the sky, and remains alien,
> When the full size of the thing coming upon you
> Rapes the mind, and will not be unimagined.

This writing has been heightened rather than undercut by the space-photographs the last decade has surfeited us with. The next observation, linked to this analogically, is perhaps less nightmarishly relevant; but the perception that 'The creepiness of Cambridge scenery... consists in having trees, And never ... looking "wooded" ...' yields Empson a natural bridge to the final generalization, that

> What was planned as airy and wide open space
> Grown cramped, seem stifled here under traditions,
> (Traditor), their chosen proportions lost;

This isn't the most rivetting thought, and one might argue that the poem's ambience has infected it to excess: it is precisely this kind of reflection, derived at once too easily and with too much strain from the preceding *aperçus*, that later formed the basic strategy of the poetry we usually call academic, with justified reliance upon the pejorative force of the word. A poem is academic when the relations between motivation and subject become estranged. Robert Lowell's poem 'Mr. Edwards and the Spider', for instance, is academic, though the poem of Edward Taylor upon which it is based certainly is not. The academic poet lies in wait for the 'subject' of the poem, where it should properly lie in wait for him. The conclusion of Empson's poem is academic: the inference is fair enough, but its real inner relevance is slight. Nevertheless, 'Sleeping out in a College Cloister' shows what Empson could do when the world of real experience was allowed to generate its own significances.

Pedantry was always a risk Empson was prepared to run, and there are times when his weighty learning structures poetry of equal heft. But intellectualist critical criteria should not be allowed to blind us to the fact that much of his verse is not intellectual but *merely* pedantic. And the formula for this pedantry is the imbalance between the slightness of the 'experience' or the motivation and the bulk of the learning expended upon its articulation. Or rather, the fact that the 'experience' is not really articulated at all, but merely serves as a springboard for philosophizing. The philosophizing itself can be either interesting or merely academic, of course. The thought about Cambridge civilization in 'Sleeping out in a College Cloister', for instance, seems to me to be based upon bookish and conventional ideas about Order (poetry turning upon Order is invariably tedious and almost as invariably spurious).[1] The flight of fantasy in the second section of the poem on the other hand seems a real poetic inspiration, a projection of the poet's own psyche which eludes the rather heavy strictures he normally places upon it. One loses, for once, the obtrusive matter-of-factness of Empson's voice, the common-sensical reassurance that all this is not to be got out of proportion, or

---

[1] Ulysses's speech in *Troilus and Cressida* confirms my point: its theme is political order, not the quasi-mystical abstraction of Empson's poem.

taken too seriously. He has gone on a 'trip', and risked himself out in the void where all really good poetry originates.

The question now arises, why does Empson want to place these ironical restrictions on himself? Why does he want to play it down, to diffuse intensity, insist on the qualifications and speculations that weigh so heavily in his poetry? Part of the answer to these questions must relate to the facts of Empson's own personality and remain unstated here. That his is a powerful, shrewd yet diffident character is apparent from the hints divulged in the poems. And it is perhaps the fact that the hints are hints, not explicit statements, that should give us pause: Empson is afraid, it is clear, to make a strongly revealing statement about himself, and he uses the intellectualist critical rationale as a means of evading issues that count. So far we have considered his tendency to swamp an experience in strictly extraneous rationalization. We come now to a more crucial feature of Empson's poetry: his use of irony as a smokescreen for emotion. This is most evident in those poems when Empson might—or another poet might—have written a love-poem. It takes a good deal of conviction to launch oneself into a declaration of love, in poetry or in real life.

In 'Camping Out', Empson shyly and tentatively attempts a love-statement under the protection of his own irony. Mocking the love-poem, the poet puts out a hand towards the woman who

> half-awake
> Milks between rocks a straddled sky of stars.

The milk is the toothpaste she ejects into the lake-water, and she is restoring to the lake 'its glass of the divine' because the mist keeps out the stars and she compensates by giving it her toothpaste galaxies (the Milky Way, of course). A little strained, perhaps, but the brackets and self-qualifications intimate the poet's sense of this and anyway the poem is in the tradition of the sixteenth-century tribute, in which hyperbole is of the essence. The second stanza, however, loses all contact with this delicate tenderness—tenderness the more delicate for being only half-revealed—and at the same time with the actual experiential basis of the statement. The first stanza is 'about' camping out; the second takes off from 'Soap tension' and the woman's reflection in the water ('Madonna through-assumes the skies') but almost immediately loses itself in internal rumination about gravity and relativity. Empson's later Note on the poem not only throws no light on it, it positively confirms our impression of poeticized 'thought' which has no reference to the poem's meaning.

> Who moves so among stars their frame unties

is glossed thus: 'if any particle of matter got a speed greater than that of light it would have infinite mass and might be supposed to crumple up round itself the whole of space-time.' This may be so. But the relativity-notion has nothing to so with Empson's poem, the Madonna has been forgotten, and they might never have been out camping. This seems a classic instance of the evil influence of the Metaphysicals: it was perfectly natural to the seventeenth century poets to draw their sexual and amorous experiences into the orbit of their intellection. But in the twentieth century the direction has been reversed: we demand now a consistent relation of the poem to the experience, or rather we insist that the experience itself should dominate the intellection, not merely serve as an occasion for it.

Empson himself later deplored the influence he exercised over the young academics of the 'fifties. Commenting on the Empsonian school, G. S. Fraser observed: 'Yet what attracted the best of these young poets to Mr. Empson was not, obviously, merely the "noble, frank, and manly" style which he shares with Dryden but the fashion in which, in his best poems, a mind of the first order can be seen exercising an ironic control over an inner core of passion. The problem about the disciples is whether they have merely the irony, without the core.' [2] The truth seems to me rather that Empson himself rarely if ever gives expression to any core of passion. I do not know which poems Mr Fraser was referring to. Certainly it is difficult to find any evidence of passion in the *Collected Poems*. Irony is, as we have seen, used in various ways, to deflect emotion, to smokescreen real feeling, to deflate the poet's own heaviness. But the main impression we take away from these poems is of a man too

[2] G. S. Fraser, *Poetry Now* (London, 1953), Preface, p. 23.

shy and stifled to get at the 'core of passion' that *might* lie within him. For there is every reason for believing that a man capable of real passion sees to it that it receives expression. Certainly, there seems little brief for saying that Empson controls passion, or exercises control over it: that would suppose far more integrated poetic power than is on display in Empson's work.

Yet there is nevertheless a muscle to Empson's strongest pieces—'Doctrinal point', 'Aubade', 'Missing Dates', 'Courage', 'Success'—that betrays powerful feeling, and bespeaks a good deal of genuine transmutation of material. The idea of tunnelling, of cavernousness, of being inside Time, of being, for example, one's own determination,—often enough Empson succeeds in giving such ideas body and follow-through. Perhaps it is this Mr Fraser intended when he spoke of a 'core of passion'; that still seems too strong: we are dealing, I think, with something less burningly important to the poet. But it is true that Empson at least gives the impression of being a man *capable of* strength of feeling, where his Movement disciples simply seemed pleased with themselves. Consider for instance 'Value is in Activity'. *Appleness* is strongly rendered at the outset, 'an acid green canvas hollow', and the central stanza of the poem is a small *tour de force*:

> Nor heeds if the core be brown with maggots' raven,
> Dwarf seeds unnavelled a last frost has scolded,
> Mites that their high narrow echoing cavern
> Invites forward, or with close brown pips, green folded.

An odd angle of things, surely, but this is Empson's gift. Much more seriously, Empson succeeds, in 'Doctrinal Point', in bodying forth the Free-Will-and-Determinism conflict as perhaps no-one else quite has:

> Magnolias, for instance, when in bud,
> Are right in doing anything they can think of;
> Free by predestination in the blood,
> Saved by their own sap, shed for themselves,
> Their texture can impose their architecture;
> Their sapient matter is always already informed.

> Whether they burgeon, massed wax flames, or flare
> Plump spaced-out saints, in their gross prime, at prayer,
> Or leave the sooted branches bare
> To sag at tip from a sole blossom there
> They know no act that will not make them fair.
>
> ('Doctrinal Point')

—And hence are free, free 'by predestination in the blood'. It is more than the sense that Empson has spent a lot of time looking at magnolias (the one in the courtyard of the University library at Cambridge in particular, perhaps) that is so impressive; the inextricably close union of mind and body, union of the empathy has enabled the poet to body forth the tree, and the intellect has enabled him to find in it a natural law and an example. Significantly, the poem almost at once deteriorates into chattily discursive speculation. The instance is merely generalized to take in Professor Eddington on physics and the Heaviside layer.

Paradoxically, Empson's verse is strongly physical: paradoxically, because it ought, one feels, to be disembodied by its own intellectuality. Poems like 'Doctrinal Point' prove that there is not only no conflict between the thinking behind Empson's verse and the strongly physical way it is often presented, but on the contrary that the physical embodiment is essential—even to the thinking. For the fault in Empson's verse is not its cerebralism, but the way this cerebralism is allowed to take the poet away from his point. He shares Donne's weakness for the irrelevant and obtrusive elaboration,[3] and his hold upon 'reality' (as opposed to the more or less indefinite world of the private psyche) is intermittent. The best of his poems, needless to say, are free of these vices. 'Missing Dates'—possibly his best single piece—is clean and straightforward in movement. The same is true of 'Aubade' and 'Success', though a certain furtiveness has replaced the earlier shyness. Yet it is in these poems that we can trace the fundamental limitations of Empson's poetry most clearly.

The later poems in the Collected Empson were written in the shadow of Munich, and the rise of German–Japanese militarism. This is evident not only in that poem which refers, rather

---

[3] The bullet conceit in Donne's 'The Exequy' is quite as absurd as anything in Empson.

bravely, I feel, and intelligently—to 'the wise patience' of England,[4] but from the general preoccupation with flight, cowardice, courage, a kind of terminal debate on the dissolution of the old heroic values. 'Courage means Running' discusses the 'thirties situation in a way that contrasts interestingly with Auden's best verse of the same period. Where Auden expresses a kind of thrilled horror, Empson talks about the traditional values and virtues with calm and precision:

> As to be hurt is petty, and to be hard
> Stupidity; as the economists raise
> Bafflement to a boast we all take as guard;
>
> As the wise patience of England is a gaze
> Over the drop, and 'high' policy means clinging;
> There is not much else that we dare to praise.

The thread of rumination in this poem is continued in 'Ignorance of Death', 'Success', 'Missing Dates' and 'Aubade'.' Just a Smack at Auden' rightly (up to a point) satirises the element of irresponsibility chiliastic toughness in the Pylon school; yet Empson himself is really in the same boat. He, too, felt that there was not much to praise, that the world he had grown up in was coming to an end, that the time of the assassins really was at hand. The inward defeat of the 'thirties poets was expressed not only in the Marxism of Auden and Spender (such as it was), but in the self-consciousness of Empson and Bottrall.

This self-consciousness in Empson is, I think, what really kept him from ever being the major poet Dr Leavis once took him for. His poetry constitutionally avoids and evades the strong personal statement, his irony and his intellectuality equally serving him as escape-routes. And again, if it should be thought that D. H. Lawrence, for instance, is being set up as a kind of all-exclusive standard, I should make it clear again that I believe that the so-called impersonalism of T. S. Eliot shows up the absence of strong personal commitment in Empson at least as dramatically as Lawrence's more direct intensity.

For, in consonance with both the intellectualist tradition and

---

[4] Later, Empson felt it necessary to apologize for this. See the corrigenda in the *Collected Poems* of 1955.

the older native line from Wordsworth and Clare to Hardy and
Lawrence, Empson eschews myth and the poetic projection of
myth; this explains, I think, the anecdotal, chatty basis of his
poems, and the constant care taken to make sure that we, his
readers, do not think he is trying anything on. Empson's
poetry is studiously casual about 'being a poet': it tries as hard
not to sound 'poetic' as the Georgians tried to sound poetic.
Again, this fits in perfectly well with his own criticism, and that
of the other intellectualist critics. It is for all these reasons that
the best Empson celebrates failure. For in the context of
intellectualist thinking, failure, or the admission of failure,
becomes a kind of intellectual Nirvana. In 'Missing Dates',
Empson finally makes his confession:

> Slowly the poison the whole blood stream fills.
> It is not the effort nor the failure tires.
> The waste remains, the waste remains and kills.

In case these lines should be misunderstood, let it be stressed
that the 'failure' of which Empson speaks here (the failure not
in his view to be deplored) is the failure of a man like Yeats,
who has striven whole-heartedly. What 'Missing Dates'
celebrates and deplores, by contrast, is the much more fundamental failure, the failure to launch oneself into action at all.
This failure produces 'partial fires':

> from partial fires
> The waste remains, the waste remains and kills.

What personal incidents or non-incidents are referred to here;
and whether the poem expresses the perennial intellectual's
atrophy, are irrelevant considerations. Some of the poems
adjacent to 'Missing Dates' in the *Collected Poems*—'Success',
'Reflection from Anita Loos'—seem to turn, somewhat
evasively, upon sexual impotence, either feared or disappoint-
edly overcome. But the poem's relevance is far more fundamentally important than this. The fires are partial, in a word,
because Empson's entire intellectual and social code requires
them to be This is not to posit any simple causal relation

between Empson's intellectual convictions and his poetry and life; it is not a matter of causation. What we are confronted by in Empson's poetry and criticism is a whole phase of English life: Empson writes what he is, and what he is both reflects and is reflected in the decisions about life and art his work embodies. The partiality Empson sees as smothering the life of the 'fires' is precisely equivalent to the ambiguity-consciousness expressed in his criticism, and indeed to the ironist bias to the entire intellectualist tradition. To this tradition, 'Missing Dates' could serve as an epitaph. If we take Empson's notion of partiality as roughly equivalent to Richard's concept of inclusiveness, we shall not be far from an appropriately ironical verdict on the whole movement. Irony, in a word, was needed as an acid to purge off the vestigial pastoralia of the Georgians; it then, unfortunately, proceeded to eat away the life of the body.

It seems to me justifiable to attempt the following extra-polation. The 'partial fires' of Empson's poem are partial because the philosophical strategy behind all Empson's thought, as behind the whole intellectualist tradition, insisted upon a kind of constitutional ambivalence, a reverence for the ambiguous, the undecided, the ironically qualified. Ambiguity suggests that things are not as they seem, and probably the reverse of what we think; to be on the safe side we had better hedge our bets, qualify our utterance so that we cannot be caught out (caught out actually saying something, presumably). This whole process is abetted by the concern for self-awareness. It can never be wrong (to say it again) to urge self-knowledge; but as a method, self-awareness may be irrelevant to our needs, and destructive to any concerted effort of the will. Self-deception is a form of stupidity inimical to the writing of poetry; but self-awareness as an end, as a policy, may reflect a decline in mental vigour and a loss of interest in the world around us. Such a decline seems to have taken place in English writing under the influence of the intellectualist school.

4 W. H. Auden: the image as instance

It was suggested above that no very great gulf separated the poetics of Oxford and Cambridge in the years between the Wars. When undergraduate Auden told undergraduate Spender 'who was good' in the late 'twenties, the list of names he offered confirms the whole trend of my argument: 'Wilfred Owen, Gerard Manley Hopkins, Edward Thomas, A. E. Housman, and, of course, T. S. Eliot'.[1] The 'of course' has the unintended effect of underscoring Eliot's foreignness to the context. For Auden's list shows that the native existential tradition still dominated English thinking about poetry.[2] Auden's list of 'who was good' in fact confirms Leavis's own selection in *New Bearings* (published shortly after this exchange between the two Oxford poets took place). The glaring exception—A. E. Housman—strongly supports this assertion: for Housman wrote a consciously 'basic' poetry, denuded of illusion and comfort, that reads often like a parody of Thomas Hardy or Edward Thomas. Leavis was right, in my opinion to exclude the pseudo-classic economies of Housman, but that is not the point: Auden's choice of the *Shropshire Lad* poet proves that Auden's bearings and Leavis's were much the same. Spender provides further corroboration: 'Self-knowledge, complete lack of inhibition and sense of guilt, and knowledge of others, were essential to the fulfilment of his aims. Unless one knew oneself, one could not know what one wanted, and plan to obtain it.'[3] For Auden, as for Leavis, self-knowledge is the chief end of poetry.

[1] Stephen Spender, *World Within World* (London, 1953), p. 43.
[2] Since this was written, Dr Davie's book *Thomas Hardy and British Poetry* has appeared. See p. 142 (n.) below.
[3] Spender, *World Within World*, p. 46.

Self-awareness, I have argued, can be a frustrating and even corrupting object for a writer. It may appear only negatively, in a refusal of transcendence and adventurousness, in the sturdy integrity of William Empson. But it may more positively back-fire: in Auden's case, the result of the hunt for self-knowledge was the exact opposite of the release and abandon he had anticipated. In point of fact, a refined sense of personal guilt is an inevitable consequence of an excessive concentration on 'knowing oneself'. What we witness in the poetry of Hopkins and the later confessional writings of Tolstoy is an equivalent consciousness of sin: there is perhaps an indissoluble nexus be-tween the desire to know oneself, and a sense of original sin, the consciousness of the latter leading directly—in an honest man—to the pursuit of the former, and the attainment of the former intensifying the latter. Auden's expressed admiration for a cer-tain order of basic, 'honest' poet (Edward Thomas, Gerard Manley Hopkins), as well as his overt interest in 'complete self-knowledge', suggests what I think is true, that his early Marxism was motivated less by political and social than by personal and moral factors. Auden was Marxist (in so far as he was Marxist), less because he felt Marx was right about econo-mic history than because he was sure he and his own class were in the wrong. Thus we find, in Auden's 'social' poetry, a variant of the ironical theme: class-guilt is bodied forth by means of irony and a consistent self-qualification, working on the principle that to find oneself in the wrong guarantees a certain degree of moral probity and mental alertness, and redeems the class guilt. In point of fact, it does nothing of the sort: a concern for personal integrity is irrelevant to the needs of the proletariat and the theoretical foundations of Marxism, and it is rightly condemned by genuine Marxists as bad faith.[4] This applies not only to English fellow-travellers like Orwell, Auden and the young Spender, but to French intellectuals like Sartre and Aragon. These people, in so far as they had any influence at all on contemporary affairs, merely delayed serious social action by simulating a political consciousness conducive to change, when in fact they were simply throwing up a smoke-screen of well-meaning bad conscience. It is clear, at a second

[4] One could invoke here Sartre's hero Mathieu Delarue (of *Les Chemins de la Liberté*). The phenomenon is general.

glance, that the writers concerned *knew* that they had no
intention of engaging themselves in serious revolutionary action;
this class-guilt was simply symptomatic of the Western intellectual's confusion in the inter-war years, and further proof that
the whole intellectualist movement in criticism and poetry
allows of, and ultimately perhaps requires, an interpretation in
ideological terms.

As much is suggested in Empson's spoof-poem, 'Just a smack
at Auden':

> What was said, by Marx, boys, what did he perpend?
> No good being sparks, boys, waiting for the end.
> Treason of the clerks, boys, curtains that descend,
> Lights becoming darks, boys, waiting for the end.

Empson's poem is a significant indication of the Cambridge
attitude towards Auden. It was not simply the affected slickness
('Hell is hard to bear', 'At Dirty Dicks and Sloppy Joes') that
offended Leavis and Empson: after all it is fairly apparent to
even a hostile reader that it did not fool Auden as it fooled some
of his admirers (one thinks of Christopher Logue). It was rather
the easy assumption of knowledge, which, if acquired at all,
ought to be acquired with horror or at least with a sober sense
of responsibility. Auden's crowd played at waiting for the end in
only a slightly less exaggerated way than Empson's brilliant
parody suggests. Empson has put his finger on a serious source
of intellectual corruption—the facile familiarity with per-
sonalized class-guilt ('Treason of the clerks, boys') that annuls
the actuality of the guilt itself, and therefore becomes an evasion
of that actuality. But this is precisely the kind of mechanism I
have been suggesting within the ironist tradition of which
Empson himself is so outstanding an example. Empson's
matter-of-factness, his sturdiness, his shyness, his disabusement
—these qualities amount in sum to an abrogation of the
responsibility incurred in the possession of poetic talent at least
as grave as Auden's cheery cynicism. The inward defeat of the
'thirties poets is expressed equally in their Marxism and in their
conscious uncertainty. Life, as well as art, demands that we
make up our minds (to put it in the simplest possible terms) on
the most important issues confronting us, on pain of forfeiting

our character. The poet's mode of 'making up his mind' is the forging of a consistent poetic personality by an act of self-commitment sabotaged as much by Empson's methodological dither as by Auden's Marxist self-condemnation. The defeatism we witness in the 'thirties poets is condemnable not just because it is somehow nicer to be cheerful and optimistic, but because there is in it a fatal degree of distortion—a kind of biological mendacity—involved in the inability to commit oneself to action which is so characteristic of ironist poetry. The writer's right to a final disillusion, or to a fundamental pessimism, is not in question: T. S. Eliot is a far more frightening poet than either Auden or Empson. But he is not, like them, defeatist; he launches himself into the spiritual action of poetry as they do not.

Nevertheless, it seems to me important at this point in time to be just to Auden. He is, in the first place, not only a very brilliant but a very intelligent poet. Whatever reservations we ultimately have about Auden—I shall suggest some of them later—they are not to be couched in terms of 'intelligence'. Auden is as *intelligent* a poet as ever put pen to paper, and it is misleading to use the word, as Dr Leavis is inclined to use it, with a special meaning that makes it applicable to Hopkins, for instance, and not to Auden. Intelligence is intelligence, and Auden would appear on the face of it to be a more *intelligent* man than much greater poets like Hopkins or Keats. Their superiority over him is simply not to be expressed (or should not be expressed) in terms of intelligence. Auden's best poetry raises cleverness to a point where the word loses its usually pejorative force:

> Sir, no man's enemy, forgiving all
> But will his negative inversion, be prodigal:
> Send to us power and light, a sovereign touch
> Curing the intolerable neural itch,
> The exhaustion of weaning, the liar's quinsy,
> And the distortions of ingrown virginity.
>
> ('Petition')

This is a display of intellect, an enjoyment of mental power such as we ought to be grateful for. Mr Alvarez has called it

'Shakespearean',[5] thinking presumably of the Hamlet solilo-
quy. But it is surely closer to Pope or Dryden:

> Prohibit sharply the rehearsed response
> And gradually correct the coward's stance. . . .

Certainly, it is impossible to deny the poem the intellectual
poise to carry off the Augustan style or the sheer mental agility
to baffle us with 'illustrations',[6] so instantly apt and so
economically fitted into the verse as to appear arbitrary. Auden
was one of the poets who created the impression that modern
poetry was 'difficult' or 'obscure'. Yet he is in this exactly the
opposite of Dylan Thomas: Thomas's verse is obscure but not
difficult, Auden's difficult but not obscure.

'Petition', it is true, falls away fairly drastically after the
couplet cited above:

> Cover in time with beams those in retreat
> That, spotted, they turn though the reverse were great;
> Publish each healer that in city lives
> Or country houses at the end of drives;
> Harrow the houses of the dead; look shining at
> New styles of architecture, a change of heart.

The grand personage to whom this petition has been addressed
—King, God or moon—would certainly have lost the track of
the courtier's plea at this point, and the more factitiously
carpentered syntax is paralleled in a sharp loss of momentum:
the octet of the sonnet moves forward urgently and rhythmically, energetically directing the mind and eye of the hearer.
The sestet pants for breath, and tries to disguise the fact in
Shakespearean 'strong' verbs ('Publish', 'Harrow'). But these
lines contain a glimpse—the only one in the poem—of a
method which Auden used with more consistent brilliance
than any other: I mean the line 'Or country houses at the end
of drives'.

Now it was Auden—not Eliot—who created the staple idiom
for alert English poets in the nineteen-forties, 'fifties and
'sixties, and the essence of this idiom lay in the skilful *montage*

[5] A. Alvarez, *The New Poetry* (Harmondsworth, 1963), p. 23.
[6] S. Spender, *World Within World*, p. 47.

of just such social observations. We shall look more closely at
this method later, when dealing with the poetry of Roy Fuller
and Philip Larkin. Here I want to emphasize what is perhaps
the most significant element in Auden's poetic vocabulary, a
certain generality of reference, which was both his strength and
his weakness. The 'Petition' sonnet shows Auden exploiting
this generality at a high philosophical level: the poem is typical
of Auden's best manner in being an arrangement of general
observations—'the liar's quinsy, the distortions of ingrown
virginity'—atypical in that these observations lack (l. 10
excepted) the social 'descriptive' realism of so much of his best
poetry. 'The Quest', 'The Lesson', 'Law', 'Paysage Moralisé'
—these poems proceed neither by the juxtaposition of symbolic
image, nor by ratiocination. They have their own convincing
rationale—based upon uncanny aptness in the selection of
image to demonstrate thesis. And it is this instantaneous con-
version of thinking into relevant image that distinguishes
Auden from any other 'thirties poet: Empson, by comparison
seems laboriously rationalistic, weighted down by conceit and
simile. Auden's images are more than annotation: they contain
the right amount and kind of significance relevant to particular
propositions in particular contexts but they are not, like the
symbols of T. S. Eliot, irreplaceable elements in a 'formula for
an emotion'. They are more like items in a lawyer's brief: they
possess vital and experiential life, yet they are not chosen for
their faithfulness to given situations. They contribute to their
context their life, and that context returns to them a heightened
point in reward for their pertinence:

> Caesar's double-bed is warm
> As an unimportant clerk
> Writes I DO NOT LIKE MY WORK
> On a pink official form.
>
> ('Fall of Rome')

It is only when one looks at Auden's images singly and separately
that one realizes how plain and general is their treatment:

> The piers are pummelled by the waves:
> In a lonely field the rain
> Lashes an abandoned train;
> Outlaws fill the mountain caves.

Taken separately these images have practically nothing of the 'concreteness' which has usually been supposed essential to poetic imagery. Yet together they create the effect of marvellous taut accuracy that is the hall-mark of Auden's best poetry. More, the effect Auden wants would be destroyed by any more specific particularization. I seem to remember a famous critic dismissing Auden with the remark that he 'couldn't pass an optician's test'; yet in fact Auden's notorious short-sightedness made a positive contribution to his art: it made possible to him certain cinematic techniques of composition. I feel sure there must have been some influence of the Russian cinema upon the young Auden: Dovzhenko, Pudovkin and Eisenstein all excelled in the evocation of socio-political atmosphere by the assemblage of disparate yet relevantly selected shots—by montage, to use Eisenstein's own term.[7] Now Auden's technique was cinematic in a very interesting way: it did not matter what the precise content of a shot was, so long as it was 'people rioting', 'an abandoned train', men 'roaring like beasts on the floor of the Bourse'. For in a curious way, cinema, the great art of the actual, is in reality the great art of the abstract and the general. Auden understood this with the strategic cunning of a Lenin: the magnificent realism of his best poetry is achieved by the unerringly shrewd choice of general, typical images. This means that the formal relations in his poems are not really linguistic and semantic at all, but kinetic and atmospheric. His poems are structures not of metaphor or symbol, but of 'shots'. What we deplore in his verse—if we deplore—is just this absence of 'concrete realization' ('Has he *seen* it?'). What we admire on the other hand—if we admire—is the never-failing knack of coming up with the right, the only image to prove the point or complete the montage, i.e. to stand as a valid instance. In Auden, to put it in a nut-shell, image is instance.

Corresponding to Auden's deficiency in local actualization, in fact, is a certain freedom of reference, which enables him to evoke with three or four strokes any one of a wide variety of social ambiances. How well, for instance, he has caught the Embassy atmosphere here:

[7] Eisenstein's book *The Film Sense*, gives a clear exposition of montage method and rationale.

> As evening fell the day's oppression lifted;
> Far peaks came into focus; it had rained:
> Across wide lawns and cultured flowers drifted
> The conversation of the highly trained.
>
> ('Embassy')

There are two major uses for the montage: montage principles can exploit widely differing images to create a complex totality by violent juxtaposition; or create atmosphere by cutting strategically from angle to angle within a given scene. The Embassy scene in Auden's poem is constructed on strictly cinematic lines: the atmosphere of tension is created by superbly intelligent cutting: evening—(far hills)—rain (flowers, wet-gravel dark)—lawns—flower-beds—talk—the well-dressed men—the gardeners —the chauffeur reading. There is no blur, no touch too many; we are so familiar with this kind of montage nowadays that it is easy to forget how original this poetry was in the middle 'thirties.

Auden excelled even more brilliantly with the first type of montage-sequence, however. In the best poems he wrote in the early and middle 'thirties, he cuts and edits selected shots to give us the feel of this most troubled phase of Western political history. Expressions like *Angst*, *Real-politik* and *Lumpen-proletariat* belong to the 'thirties as much as Oedipus fixation and father-figure to the 'twenties. Marx takes over from Freud, and it is Auden who is our best source of information on the transition, at least as far as English intellectual life is concerned. Again and again he creates the atmosphere of a State overrun, of civil-war, panic, treachery, social disintegration. The early volumes—*The Orators*, *The Dog Beneath the Skin*, *Look, Stranger*—are rife with unease, menace, political disorder, as if the hell of the dreaming unconscious were let loose upon the waking world. It seems to me fair to observe that none of Auden's contemporaries, either European or American, succeeded in evoking the nature of civic disorder and political barbarism as well as he did:

> The first time that I dreamed, we were in flight,
> And fagged with running; there was civil war,
> A valley full of thieves and wounded bears.
>
> Farms blazed behind us; turning to the right,
> We came at once to a tall house, its door
> Wide open, waiting for its long-lost heirs.
>
> ('The Lesson')

Our sense of the 'thirties, with its dread of the future chaos, its gangster politics and internecine conflict, comes not from George Orwell or Edward Upward or Christopher Isherwood, but from W. H. Auden, and it is simply pretentious to deny him his status. His nose for climate or for *Zeitgeist*, to use another favourite 'thirties expression, had, it's true, its negative aspect, which I shall come to in due course; but it is important at this point to underline that it was very much more than a journalistic facility for atmosphere: it was a mature appreciation and diagnosis of the causes underlying the atmosphere and creating it. It is the peculiar advantage of literature, as opposed to cinema and photography, to be able to present diagnosis co-presently with documentation, analysis with apprehension, interpretation with reflection. It would be a huge error to describe Auden's marvellous montage sequences and scenes as 'mere' political notation. Their sequential precision and implied commentary testify at all times to the active intelligence not of the journalist but of the poet.

The prime fact underlying this civic disorder was, of course, the accumulation of social injustices under high capitalism. I have referred above to Auden's Marxism as a by-product of his class-guilt, this being in turn itself an objectification of an obscure personal guilt. I think this is so. Nevertheless, it would be foolish to deny that the predicament of Auden and his contemporaries was an extremely difficult one. To grow to maturity after the Great War and under the shadow of the Depression and of rising Fascism was sufficient to make acceptance of Marxism practically an intellectual necessity. Auden's response to the situation seems not only to have been intelligent but also mature (not always the same thing quite). One must, surely, respect Auden's wise appreciation of where his own 'low dishonest decade' stood in relation to its own secret dreads, to its ideals, and to the oppressed and exploited classes which both generated those ideals and threatened them, and which justified and stultified its radicalism at the same time. Auden analysed better than anyone else of his time the peculiar ambivalences in the bourgeois intellectual's idealism. (Sartre by comparison seems an excited seminarist who refuses to see the implications of views he is adopting to spite his elders.) Auden's best political poetry, though informed with a genuine sympathy

for the victims of capitalism, stems essentially from an astute
awareness of his own real position in the class-war, and of what
things he most cherished in life.

For if we look closely at Auden's brilliant evocations of his
age, we see in them a steady, unvarying esteem for the old ways,
the advantage and privilege he knows to be at once essential
to civilization as he understands it and doomed by history:

> But happy now, though no nearer each other,
> We see farms lighted all along the valley;
> Down at the mill-shed hammering stops
> And men go home.
>
> Noises at dawn will bring
> Freedom for some, but not this peace
> No bird can contradict: passing, but is sufficient now
> For something fulfilled this hour, loved or endured.
>
> ('Taller Today')

It is hardly too much to say that the poet needs the contented
industry of the workers at the mill—their 'noises off'—to
complete his own sense of peace: the *satori* beautifully articulated in Auden's poem depends very materially upon the high
valuation the poet places on the quality of the experience, the
magic of life itself, which is significantly ranked higher than the
'freedom for some' the committed political poet is supposed to
prefer. Like most poets in fact, Auden is a conservative beneath
the radical armour (the dog beneath the skin?). Too much of a
poet's feeling and his sense of what matters is invested in the
past and his recollection of the past for him to contemplate with
much relish the obliteration of a familiar world. Intellectual
acumen and radicalism tended to go together in the 'thirties,
and there is nothing bogus about Auden's professions of a quasi-
Marxist dissatisfaction with Western democracy. But he never
deceived himself—as I think Day Lewis did—as to where his
own real interests lay, as to where he would, regretfully, finally
throw in his lot. He knew that what he really valued was a certain kind of order, calm and gentility that would inevitably go
under if the revolution really happened. What gives Auden's
best verse its tension in fact is just this balance of nostalgia and
disgust: as intellectual, diagnosing the social evils of his time, he

looks forward to the revolutionary future, as bourgeois poet he looks back to the safe harbourage of middle-class security and good breeding. And it is this security and breeding that are threatened:

> Once we could have made the docks,
> Now it is too late to fly;
> Once too often you and I
> Did what we should not have done;
> Round the rampant rugged rocks
> Rude and ragged rascals run.

('Doomsday Song')

The panic and sense of imminent chaos so characteristic of Auden's earlier poetry express this bourgeois dread of working-class vengeance—so skilfully evoked in the 'Doomsday Song' with the deft adaptation of Nursery rhyme—as much as, or more than, they indict the malpractices of the ruling classes. There is in fact a central ambivalence in all the poetry Auden wrote in the 'thirties under pressure from the political situation: the professed enemy is the Fascist, and the intellectual poet stands shoulder to shoulder with the Communist who opposes him. But in reality the endless flights, nightmare panics, abandoned trains and wrecked social amenities of Auden's verse testify more to the poet's fear of the brutalizing disruption which must ensue if the revolution he is committed to uphold really occurs. It is the workers Auden really fears, not the Fascists.

The class-guilt then is of a peculiarly intense kind. It is easy often to mistake fear for guilt: the man mastered by guilt often dreads retribution for his sins more than he regrets the sins themselves. The sense of being historically condemned emerges later in the sonnet I have already quoted (the first of those that make up 'The Lesson', 'The first time that I dreamed . . .'). The flight of the speaker and his companion leads to a house where a Kafkaesque clerk (sitting 'on the bedroom stairs/Writing') refuses them asylum: 'Our lives were not in order; we must leave.' A similar sense of guilt-born-of-fear informs Dickens's historical novels, *Barnaby Rudge* and *A Tale of Two Cities*, the greatest of all fictional accounts of revolution, I think. Dickens fully acknowledges the culpability of the ruling class, but in the final analysis he is more shocked still by the overturning of the established order. A more acute ambivalence of this kind, because it is fully unconscious, is to be found in Eisenstein's films *Strike* and *Battleship Potemkin*. (Auden must have seen at least the latter by the middle 'thirties.) On the face of it, the ideological stance of these films is perfectly straightforward: the villains are the fat capitalists (usually Jewish), and the officers and Guards who carry out their will. But one of the things which stays most persistently in one's memory of Eisenstein's films is the massacre of the innocent bourgeois on the steps of Odessa in *Potemkin*. And one's sense of the scene is determined by the images of ladies with parasols waving languidly to the battleship (unseen out on the bay). When the shooting starts, one of these ladies acts as a protectress to the children caught in the fire. Another unforgettable image equally emblematic of upper-class life is the ornate perambulator which bumps its way down to the bottom of the steps. The ideological assailants of these *bon bourgeois* are of course henchmen of the aristocracy; but film is nothing if not an immediate idiom, and the actual attackers—those we see pulling the triggers—are uniformed proletarians, just as the actual victims are in the main well-clothed and well-bred people out promenading. It is the bourgeois who are massacred, not the proletarians. When the film ends, revolution unconsummated, with the rebel ship sailing back into the ranks of the Tsar's navy, there is almost a sense of relief.

Auden had of course already expressed this ideological uncertainty in 'Which side am I supposed to be on?' (1930). One cannot help admiring his honesty and candour, especially when one goes for comparison to the gaseous surrealist propaganda of much of Eluard and Neruda, for instance. It is more maturely expressed, though, in the poem Britten chose to set in his *Spring Symphony*, 'A Summer Night'. Nowhere else perhaps does Auden celebrate with franker warmth the pleasures of the society he loved:

> Lucky, this point in time and space
> Is chosen for my working-place,
>   Where the sexy airs of summer,
> The bathing-hours and the bare arms,
> The leisured drives through a land of farms
>   Are good to a newcomer.

'Lucky' is a word Auden uses strategically and well, here as elsewhere ('Warm are the still and lucky miles'). There is something curiously beautiful about good luck: I am lucky to be here, Auden says, 'Equal with colleagues in a ring'—not destined, or fated or doomed—just lucky. And the poem's curious magic hangs upon this awareness. For if one part of the magic of good luck derives from its inexplicability, part also derives from our ability to imagine how easily things might have been otherwise. This is the real theme of 'A Summer Night', as the rising of the moon makes clear:

> To gravity attentive, she
> Can notice nothing here, though we
>   Whom hunger does not move,
> From gardens where we feel secure
> Look up and with a sigh endure
>   The tyrannies of love:
>
> And gentle, do not ask to know,
> Where Poland draws her eastern bow,
>   What violence is done,
> Nor ask what doubtful act allows
> Our freedom in this English house,
>   Our picnics in the sun.

Britten incidentally ends his setting here: with a musician's ruthless nose for relevance, he lets his soprano sink down to uneasy rest on the 'picnics in the sun', thus throwing the whole complex emotion—pity, secret gladness, guilt, unrest, foreboding—into sharp and unforgettable relief. Auden sacrifices this sharpness of focus to a more portentous elaboration of some of the poem's implications. The stanzas just cited are followed by a further four which present, in verse never less though rarely more than highly competent, the prophecy of disaster implicit in this fragile sense of luck: 'Soon, soon, through the dykes of our content / The crumpling flood will force a rent,' etc. Admittedly Britten's marvellous musical imagery (subtle lurking woodwinds, shocked wordless chorale, pure soprano) makes this superfluous; admittedly, too, Britten's is a simpler organism. (He eliminates the second, third and fourth stanzas of the poem as well.) But all the same, his setting points up a

lesson. Auden's poem goes off the rails here, largely by substituting discussion for presentation. The situation earlier
evoked with such tenderness carried with it its own meaning:
the country-house weekend *was* the historical situation of the
privileged classes. In the last four stanzas of the poem, Auden
underlines it all in an allegory. The coming revolution is seen
as a flood, with a new spring, regeneration etc. Symbolism
should have made this impossible:

> But when the waters make retreat
> And through the black mud first the wheat
>   In shy green stalks appears,
> When stranded monsters gasping lie,
> And sounds of riveting terrify
>   Their whorled unsubtle ears. . . .

This is Dryden browsing through *The Golden Bough*. Again, as
with Empson, we find English poetry of this time going against
the grain of its own sensibility. Just as Empson often substitutes
an inner abstract debate for the real self-determining movement
of symbol and image, so Auden sacrifices the integrity of his
observation (observation that in its relations to other observations declares its own interpretation) to an allegorical fiction. In
the case of 'A Summer Night', we can identify in the poem's
deterioration an equivalent falsification of emotion. The
balance of feelings had been superbly maintained: consciousness
of privilege generated guilt, but was qualified by a deeper
responsibility to Life itself: it seemed more important to savour
and appreciate the quality of the experience itself than to let
'petty' political considerations destroy it. This feeling in turn
generated a more real pity for those hunger does move, and was
underscored by the certainty that the very beauty of the
weekend in this English house—the perfection of the picnics in
the sun—must in some obscure but undivertible fashion bring
about its own termination. And so on; it is a genuine complexity
of feeling, and the poem takes its place with the novels of
Virginia Woolf as a record of a way of life that was doomed to
pass, and has passed in our own time. The later allegory in the
poem not only crudifies this complexity: it substitutes for it an
emotion which interests us less, and even rings false. We are
aware at the poem's end, of a tone we had encountered at the

end of the 'Petition': there too a decline in poetic pungency heralded the accession of a utopianism which though quite sincere, and even strongly felt, remained recalcitrant to poetic treatment:

> Look shining at
> New styles of architecture, a change of heart.

The last line is a good one, but appears too obviously to have been stored up for maximum effectiveness.[8] In 'A Summer Night', the flood allegory—itself a dissipation of the previously generated tensions—assumes a scale that Auden simply has not earned. He imagines a new generation rising out of the tidal mud left by the receding waters of revolution, and expresses the hope that the 'wrongs' he and his friends are responsible for, or are enjoying the benefits of ('These delights we dread to lose') may interpenetrate their experience and joy as children's voices 'through the drowned parental voices rise / In unlamenting song'. This is a bold schema: its pattern of sacrificial death, regeneration and transfigured continuity by far surpasses in scale and ambition the complex but limited perspectives of the earlier part of the poem. Yet its effect is of plausible sincerity rather than real poetry. Auden has simply bitten off more than he can chew, and what began as genuinely registered complexity has been diluted into fluent optimism. Of this degeneration, the utopianism is the sign.

There is nothing of course wrong with utopianism in art. The Ninth Symphony, 'And did those feet . . .', the finest poems of Shelley—this is all utopian. And when Rimbaud speaks of celebrating 'le noël sur la terre', his hope is utopian. But these artists had given much more of themselves to the ideas within the utopian schema than Auden has. Rimbaud and Shelley, for instance, paid the price of their utopianism in disillusion and pain. Auden's utopianism is merely a softening, a relaxation of vigilance—a 'hope', in fact, sincere but not worked for or

[8] By 1966 Auden had repudiated this line: 'For example I once expressed a desire for "New styles of architecture" but I have never liked modern architecture. I prefer *old* styles, and one must be honest even about one's prejudices.' Quoted in 'A Testament to Self-Control', *Times Literary Supplement*, 12 January 1973. It was, of course, the possibility of a 'change of heart' that Auden no longer believed in. Being honest about one's prejudices is sometimes a way of being *dis*honest about one's spiritual development.

wholly believed in. Like the doctrine of Christian love that gradually permeates his later poetry, Auden's political utopianism is more of a convenient intellectual answer than an experienced reality. The utopianism is in a way a means of evading the despair which his intellectual investigations have really made mandatory.

We are concerned here with more than a passing phase, or a local weakness: we are concerned with the very basis of even Auden's best poetry. It is not necessary to be a committed Leavisite to feel that there is something missing from his verse. 'Tonight a scrambling decade ends', he wrote in the *New Year Letter* of 1939, and the tired phrase seems to breathe a relief, as though a role has at last been dropped. I have earlier paid homage to Auden's acute sense of *Zeitgeist*, while allowing that it has its negative aspect. It is time now to say what this is. For, although his nose for atmosphere is a function of a poetic intelligence, the sign of someone 'fully alive in his own time', it is impossible to read much of Auden without feeling that the socio-political content, the representativeness, has excluded too much of the personal voice. It is the curious limitation of Auden's poetry actively to discourage an interest in his own personal development: the development that takes place in Auden the man is not reflected in the technique of the poetry, nor in its content. Development in Auden is almost purely a matter of 'attitude': the attitudes become broader, more catholic, more relaxed. But this affects the verse only negatively in an increasing slackness of rhythm and a deceleration of the cerebral processes. Auden's poetry loses its figure, but there is little corresponding accumulation in weight. Late poems like 'Goodbye to the Mezzogiorno' display great acumen and wisdom, but poetically they represent no advance whatever on *Look, Stranger*.

This has nothing to do with the impersonality cult, though this has played its part, I think, in the formation of Auden's poetic personality. What we have here, surely, is a characteristic withdrawal in poetry in the intellectualist era—influenced by or sharing intellectualist or ironist ideals—such as we have already seen in the case of William Empson. Very much more is concerned of course than the actual critical school itself: intellectualist criticism, to say it again, is itself only symptomatic of an entire phase of English cultural life. Auden's limitations, moreover, derive in part from factors of his own personality. We are nevertheless justified, I think, in holding that his curiously public confessions offer further evidence of the annihilation of personality which affects English poetry between the wars. Identifying the expression of personality with post-Romantic expressionism and afraid of the vulgar display of egotism, Auden and his contemporaries gradually lost contact with themselves and became incapable of making a powerful statement of any sort.

In Auden, this emerges in an absence of body in the verse, a certain weakness in stress and rhythm that is clearly related to that tendency of his noted at the beginning of this chapter to compose his poems in montages of instances, rather than by metaphoric involvement. His rhythm—to take it first—is typically swift and cerebral: the best adjective to describe it is probably his own favourite 'neural'. The almost preternaturally rapid transitions of Auden's montage-sequences produce a kind of Alpha-rhythm that is responsible for the thrilling tension of so much of his early verse. His best poetry answers swiftness of movement with relevance of instance:

> Now the leaves are falling fast,
> Nurse's flowers will not last;
> Nurses to their graves are gone,
> And the prams go rolling on.
>
> Whispering neighbours, left and right,
> Pluck us from our real delight;
> And our active hands must freeze
> Lonely on our separate knees.
>
> ('Autumn Song')

Auden's exploitation of nursery-rhyme rhythm and metre is a subject in its own right. It is no accident that his critical writings are so liberally sprinkled with references to Lewis Carroll, the Brothers Grimm and his Nanny. Childhood retained a special place in Auden's intellectual world: it signified not only innocence (we shall come to this later), but the security of a world unthreatened by the 'rude and ragged rascals'. In the 'Autumn Song', the rhythms of Stevenson's *Child's Garden* are brilliantly adapted to the flicker of Auden's neural awareness.

Poems like this are sustained by the sheer rapidity and urgency of thinking. There are other poems, however, in which this swift pattern is forsaken for a consciously Elizabethan delicacy of movement. In the following selection of opening couplets, we find a genuine lyric subtlety that recalls the best Campion:

> Dear, though the night is gone
> Its dream still haunts today . . . .
>
> ('A Dream')

> Lay your sleeping head, my love,
> Human on my faithless arm . . . .
>
> ('Lullaby')

> Look, stranger, on this island now
> The leaping light for your delight discovers . . . .
> ('Seascape')

> Warm are the still and lucky miles,
> White shores of longing stretch away . . . .
>
> ('Song')

In each case, the gentle unsteady pulsation is really there, a poetic fact, that reflects a different emotional inscape from the clever wry awareness of poems like 'Autumn Song'. Toughness and slickness have been replaced by a perhaps over-conscious tenderness. These are love poems, and it is the rhythm that tells us so. But the love-poem requires a particular assertiveness, a powerful confidence in one's own voice. And this is precisely what Auden's intellectual apparatus, like Empson's, is directed against. In every one of the exquisite lyrics just cited, the rhythmic pulse is allowed to die down into matter-of-fact syllable-counting, either consciously prosy and sensible, or overly languorous. In the 'Seascape', for instance, the subtle *élan* of the *light-delight* beat quickly peters out into professional carpentry. In spite of its Shakespearean machinery—'Oppose the pluck / And knock of the tide'—the poem becomes resourcefully imitative of a floating-balancing water-rhythm, rather than genuinely responsive to the lyric impulse. Copious use of feminine endings ensures a certain success:

> May wander like a river
> The swaying sound of the sea . . . .

> And move in memory as now these clouds do
> That pass the harbour mirror
> And all the summer through the water saunter.

This is adroit, competent writing—too adroit and competent, with none of the pointed relevance of the quick-tongued opening lines, which create in themselves that sense of longing and nostalgia so moving in Auden's best writing. There is a sense of indulgence, a sensuous languor, the reverse of the poet's more customary taut vibrance. A poet's strengths must support each other, and there is evidence of a deep schism in Auden, an inability to bring both his intelligence and his 'emotion' to bear at once upon his true subject-matter. This is confirmed, *mutatis mutandis* in the other lyrics quoted. In the 'Dream', for instance, the exquisitely tender opening couplet ('Dear, though the night is gone / Its dream still haunts today') gives way to the prosily informative:

> That brought us to a room
> Cavernous, lofty as
> A railway terminus.

As modern prosodist, Auden presumably thought he could get away with a line like 'Cavernous, lofty as', but he could not, expecially as 'lofty as' had to rhyme with 'terminus'. The procedure anticipates the nervous para-rhyming of Auden's successors (one thinks of Roy Fuller and Geoffrey Hill): without the rhyme-structure, the poet feels naked, insecure, but he has little or nothing to say with it, so that the result is an inertness corresponding to the weakness of the governing emotion. And this of course is the point. We have seen that a deep shyness, a certain moral and imaginative timidity, kept William Empson from any powerful emotional commitment in his love poems. In Auden, too, the self-consciousness encouraged by the intellectualist ideals makes it impossible for the poet to *risk* passionate declaration. Auden like Empson feels too conscious of his absurdities to be able to reveal himself as openly and bravely as the love-statement demands. He is of course no more absurd than anybody else, but self-consciousness is a slippery ramp to get on: Auden is too much the expert on private shames and embarrassments for his own good. Once more—the dangers of misunderstanding being extreme—I should emphasise that I am not assuming a norm based upon the worst excesses of expressionist hysteria. I am thinking of poems like Lawrence's 'Dijon Roses', Eliot's 'La Figlia che Piange', Yeats' 'He remembers forgotten beauty', Goethe's 'Ich denk' an dich'. The fullness of commitment I have in mind requires a great deal more of the poet than self-indulgence or even strength of feeling. It exacts a creative risk, a willingness to wager that private sense of safety which forms like a thorn-hedge around the ego of the poet in the intellectualist era.

In Empson this emerges most unmistakeably in the poet's tendency to retreat behind an intellectual smokescreen or to sabotage his emotion with irony when some powerful statement seems required. In Auden it appears as an inability to sustain momentum, to force through the rhythmic implications of his verse. Auden's failure in these love-lyrics is primarily a failure of total engagement in the act of writing. As much was implied in speaking of his montage-techniques. His verse is rapid and limpid to a degree unmatched elsewhere in modern poetry. Yet precisely the facility in finding the right instance afforded him by a preternaturally alert brain appears to have relieved Auden from the necessity of engaging himself wholly in the struggle to make language yield its hidden meanings, which is the very life of poetry. And this means that Auden gives up the struggle with life itself. Rhythmically this reveals itself in his tendency to cosset himself with the lyric rhythms of poems like 'Dear, though the night is gone', or to substitute the play of the brain (in which he feels secure from revelation or involvement) for the exploration of emotional complexity. The man feels and suffers, we know; but the poet steers himself away from that naked exposure of self which is, *au fond* the real justification of poetry. Metaphorically, it reveals itself in an inability to transfigure his material by the pressure of sustained thought.

It was argued above (p. 60) that the internal relations in Auden's poetry are not semantic but atmospheric; it was also suggested that his methods of composition by montage had their own validity. Nevertheless, there are many places in Auden's verse when something more seems to be demanded, when the process of smelting and transmutation which is what takes most out of a poet is evaded by Auden. To put it bluntly, Auden has little capacity for the kind of simultaneous perception of end and means, similarity and dissimilarity, that emerges in metaphor: he never successfully converts percept into concept by the pressure of imagination. Instead, he works either by means of montage, as I have already said, or by transposing one of his montages from one mental plane to another. That is to say, by the use of allegory. Some of Auden's best and wittiest pieces are in the form of allegory: 'Atlantis', 'The Quest', 'The Climbers', such poems and sequences allegorize experience in terms of expeditions, journeys, military campaigns. The method is ideally suited to Auden's mind: for the essence of allegory is the matching of one structure of ideas (life or experience) point for point with another (the figurative journey or campaign). It is no longer quite so easy to dismiss allegory as the work of secondary talents: works like *Bleak House, The Castle* and *Waiting for Godot* are fundamentally allegorical, in that the surface story or situation emerges as also emblematic of a more general universal condition.

Still, there is something evasive about Auden's use of the allegorical mode. Dickens', Kafka's and Beckett's allegories are 'earthed' in their personal experiences too deeply for us to doubt the strain and significance of the enterprise. Auden's are too often cleverly tricked-out structures, which in remaining parallel to the poet's consciousness, absolve him from the need to relate himself too painfully to them. In 'Atlantis' and 'The Quest', for all the brilliance of the performance (something we should perhaps just be grateful for), the *Zeitgeist* absorbs too much of the poet's meaning for the allegory to make real contact with his own predicament. Much the same is true of another type of allegory or quasi-allegory we find in Auden's earlier poetry, a more interesting variety which owes something perhaps to the *trompe l'œuil* techniques of Salvador Dali. In these poems, one area of experience is related to another area of a different kind. In the elegy for W. B. Yeats, for instance, the poet's corpse is allegorized in the terms of Auden's own political poetry:

> The provinces of his body revolted,
> The squares of his mind were empty,
> Silence invaded the suburbs,
> The current of his feeling failed . . . .

The poem is successful because of the ease and subtlety with which Auden moves from one context to the other: the great poet is seen as a lost guardian of sanity in a mad world in which 'the brokers are roaring like beasts on the floor of the Bourse'. It is winter, not only in the year (1939) but in the life of Europe, and the natural mourning for a great man merges into the anticipatory mourning for the end of European civilization, over which the dead poet had kept such vigilant watch.

A still more brilliant example is the superb 'Barbed Wire'. Here Auden marshals his political *aperçus* with a skill that surpasses even his own previous best:

> Across the square,
> Between the burnt-out Law Courts and Police Headquarters,
> Past the Cathedral far too damaged to repair,
> Around the Grand Hotel patched up to hold reporters,
> Near huts of some Emergency Committee,
> The barbed wire runs through the abolished City.
>
> Across the plains,
> Between two hills, two villages, two trees, two friends,
> The barbed wire runs which neither argues nor explains
> But where it likes a place, a path, a railroad ends,
> The humour, the cuisine, the rites, the taste,
> The pattern of the City, are erased.

This is what we have come to expect of Auden: incomparable montage evoking the atmosphere of a troubled decade. But the wire has acquired a life of its own ('where it likes a place'): it has become animated, like something out of Grimm. The poem's most brilliant stroke continues the transformation of the political into the unconscious world:

> Across our sleep
> The barbed wire also runs . . . .

The poem works, there and then, before our eyes: it is quite irresistible, even when known and expected.

In both the Yeats elegy and 'Barbed Wire', the socio-political instances are consciously and deliberately translated onto a different plane, so that the montages in effect become allegoric. There is however a further order of effects to be considered. These are close to the true symbolism of Mallarmé and Valèry. In the 'Song' already quoted, the emotion of longing is symbolized in the white shores which have already been evoked:

> Warm are the still and lucky miles,
> White shores of longing stretch away . . . .

Now what Auden is doing here, in the phrase 'white shores of longing' is offending against the genius of modern poetic idiom in precisely the way I have suggested already that both he and Empson consistently do offend. It is something Ezra Pound long ago warned against:

> Don't use such an expression as 'dim lands of peace'. It dulls the image. It mixes an abstraction with the concrete. It comes from the writer's not realizing that *the natural object is always the adequate symbol.*[9]

I have italicized the last clause because it encapsulates the whole symbolist aesthetic, and crystalizes the spirit of modern poetry so violated by intellectualist criticism and the poets influenced by it. We need look no further than an immediately contemporary poem to feel the inadequacy of his method:

> From the wide window towards the granite shore
> The white sails still fly seaward, seaward flying
> Unbroken wings

Eliot does not say 'Unbroken wings' of childhood or longing or anything else: the emotion caught so precisely by the symbol is genuinely unstateable in any other way; it would be limited and hampered by the affixing of the over-determinative phrase. Yet if we turn from Auden's 'white shores of longing' to the concluding lines of the same poem, we are aware of a sharp difference:

> Restored! Returned! The lost are born
> On seas of shipwreck home at last . . . .

'seas of shipwreck', 'light of recognition'—such phrases slip all too easily off Auden's tongue, and tend to lack any real basis in experience. The 'white shores' on the other hand *do* analogize

---

[9] 'Imagisme', *Poetry*, Vol. 1, 1913. Quoted in J. P. Sullivan (ed.), *Penguin Critical Anthologies: Ezra Pound* (1970), p. 42. My italics

longing, and their meaning has already been indicated by the previous line, 'Warm are the still and lucky miles' (one of the most beautiful in the whole of Auden). Description here has become symbolization. In another poem already cited, 'Autumn Song', Auden again successfully symbolizes something ungraspably beautiful:

> Cold, impossible, ahead
> Lifts the mountain's lovely head
> Whose white waterfall could bless
> Travellers in their last distress.

Here Auden's interest in Freud (a master-collector of symbolic devices), in mythology and in allegory, all coalesce to produce the symbolic insight. The earlier stanzas of the poem have evoked a scudding, flying sort of day, with children trapped in perambulators, and nurses hurrying through humdrum routines, while men's hands 'freeze / Lonely on . . . separate knees'. The social perceptions (the nurses' routines and the public-park loucherie) have been force to yield an image which has been there, glimpsed beyond the trees, all the time.

In the *New Year Letter* of 1940—an uneven poem betraying the decline in tautness to be so characteristic of Auden's American period—a still more penetrating perception yields a still more inwardly reverberant symbol:

> O unicorn among the cedars
> To whom no magic charm can lead us,
> White childhood, moving like a sigh
> Through the green woods unharmed in thy
> Sophisticated innocence

Again, this is neither rhetorical trope nor instance, but genuine symbol: Auden has said something so deeply and widely true of childhood and the loss of innocence that we are conscious here, as perhaps nowhere else in Auden of the tremor of truly great poetry. Although the rhetorical structure remains the same for a further twenty lines, a change takes place; the feeling cools, the intensity slackens, and what had begun as a cry, turns into a device, a device moreover, of the kind rightly condemned by Pound: 'O dove of science and of light' etc. 'O dove of science' is an idea, a yoking together that limits rather

than expands its elements. But Auden had not said 'O unicorn
of childhood': the unicorn was really seen, glimpsed, like the
waterfall in the 'Autumn Song' through the trees of sad adult-
hood. 'O dove of science' is a tired apostrophe, of the sort
Dryden might have been expected to produce for the Royal
Society. 'O unicorn among the cedars' is a *cry*—the first and
only cry throughout Auden's work.

What we are confronted with in Auden's poetry, it seems to
me, is further evidence of the self-alienation of the intellectual
in the twentieth century. Poets like Auden and Empson
eliminated all but entirely an indispensable element—the felt
pressure and vibrance of the self in its need for articulation,
expansion and definition. Modern poetics and aesthetics had
encouraged poetry to regard itself as the self-consistent arrangement of internally related semantic particles. In Mrs Langer,[10]
for instance, the emphasis is all upon the process of 'symbolization' by which private self-expressive elements are converted
into valid artistic form. The argument she uses is circular (what
is artistically excellent being defined as successful symbolization,
and successful symbolization being defined in terms of artistic
excellence), but that is not the point. What happened over the
latter half of the nineteenth century was that poets became able
to project themselves into percepts, which became *con*cepts of
experience—or symbols, without the mediation of declarative
or discursive language. T. S. Eliot articulated this into the
impersonality business, allowing him to write some of the most
intensely 'personal' poetry in English. The intellectualist
critics—especially the New Critics in America—encouraged a
quasi-structuralist approach to the analysis of poetry by cross-
examining poems for their internal relations, with no reference
to 'expression'. The result was the divorce of intelligence and
emotion Richards and Eliot had been so anxious to remedy.
The deficiencies of New Critical methods make a subject of
their own: it remains to be shown that they are seriously inadequate for the detection and appreciation of factors like
in-tension, voice, vibrance etc., which are, often, what distinguish the merely good from the great. More seriously, the
poets of the intellectualist era evince a marked incapacity for
the powerful expression and articulation of emotion.

[10] S. K. Langer, *Feeling and Form* (London, 1953).

5 A Kind of Scapegoat:
a retrospect on Stephen Spender

If Spender is not the most unfashionable poet in the world at the present time, it is certainly difficult to think of a *more* unfashionable one. He is known universally as a Poet, and as a Social Poet. Yet there are reputable anthologies of middle twentieth-century verse which exclude him altogether, and in the universities he is likely to be scorned. Contempt rather than oblivion has been Spender's lot—contempt for the lapsed fellow-traveller, for the vegetated poet, for the confessor who never quite came clean. The *Encounter* association and divorce only reinforced the common image of the faded pink whose left hand was so ignorant of the right hand's doings that it could work for ten years against its own real interests.

Yet Spender was, I believe, Auden's superior as poet, and, with David Gascoyne, the most powerful English poet of his time: he became, not entirely through his own fault, the victim of the *maladie Anglaise*, a kind of scapegoat. His poetry assumes greater significance today: if we turn to Spender, to David Gascoyne, and Dylan Thomas, ignoring both the more facile Pylon verse and the more gaseous New Apocalypse writing, a different picture of English poetry emerges from the 'thirties, one that suggests a new future and avoids the poverty of New Lines and The Movement. Such a tradition harks back to D. H. Lawrence rather than to Hardy, to Eliot's poetry rather than to his criticism, and to Wilfred Owen rather than to Edward Thomas; it develops through Ted Hughes rather than Philip Larkin. If such a tradition is a conscious construction rather than an actuality, so is any tradition in so far as that tradition affects the way people aware of it think and write. What inscape in the past we see there depends very largely upon what someone has taught or told us to identify and pick out. In such a re-casting of a poetic and critical tradition, then, a just appraisal of Stephen Spender assumes considerable importance.

Spender himself has largely connived at his own dereliction. He suffered the savage fate of a too early and too complete acceptance, that was based upon a serious misunderstanding— or rather upon an even worse half-understanding. For Spender was accepted as a triumvir, the author of 'The Pylons', a sidekick of Auden's. Scorned at Cambridge as the 'new Shelley', Spender sank into a curiously public decline, which he seemed willing to accept as heartily as anyone else. Thus, in his brilliant long story, *Engaged in Writing*, he catches himself beautifully, mirrored in the distorting pebbles of Sartre's glasses (the French philosopher is thinly anagrammed as Sarret):

> They approached him as one attending the funeral of his career.
> He did not altogether regret their sympathy.
>
> (*Engaged in Writing*, p. 20)

—*Pauvre type!* Spender appears to have endorsed the verdict with dogged glee.

Yet he is much closer than Auden to what, for example, a Polish or a Spanish or a Russian poet or critic would regard as *a Poet*—and this fact seems to some extent to explain his fall from grace. The English do not like a Poet, unless he is Celtic: and Spender has always been 'being a Poet'. He has been both hampered and helped by this consciousness of role. Much of the self-conscious symbol-mongering of his later verse stems directly from it. He becomes, as one works through the *Collected Poems*, more and more 'literary' until he cannot open his mouth but to hold forth like a translation of Rilke or Seferis—

> Again, again, I see this form repeated . . . .

At the same time, the appearance he has of being at all times 'a Poet' is not entirely a matter of mistaking the career of the man of letters for the activity later dubbed poetic, nor of laboriously impersonating the style and rhetoric of the classics. Spender appears 'more a poet' than either Auden or Empson because

his verse strives more continuously than theirs for a unifying
context both transcending and undercutting the immediate
perception. Both in rhythm and body of verse, Spender's best
poetry is more powerful, and more deeply organized than
Auden's. And this reflects the kind of serious commitment of
himself that is inherent in the choice of the life of a poet. What
is most important here probably is the awareness that a choice
has been or has to be made.

It is the early verse, naturally enough, that demonstrates this
best. *Poems* of 1933 seems now an impressive achievement. Less
precocious than Auden's *Poems* of 1932, less dazzlingly sure of its
indefinable subject-matter than Dylan Thomas's *Eighteen
Poems* of 1936, it is still a declaration of promise which the later
work was never wholly to fulfil. It is startlingly naïve: *viz.* 'How
strangely this sun reminds me of my love', which is a good
poem, in fact. But the naïveté *is* Spender, or at least an important part of him: it goes along with a genuine innocence of
eye, and a capacity not only for being easily and deeply moved,
but for honouring that emotion in strong and direct expression.
But there is also a most impressive energy here, arching and
bracing the stanzas with a strongly emotional physicality,
which reminds one of Ted Hughes's *Hawk in the Rain* manner.
(Spender's *Collected Poems* came out in 1953—to be savaged in
the Leavisite *Delta*—while Hughes was an undergraduate at
Cambridge.) This is best seen in the poems which directly
address the important question shelved by Auden and Empson
in the interests of a vigilant self-awareness,—the obligations
inherent in the possession of poetic talent. Auden and Empson,
as it were, pretend not to know they are poets. But the young
artist is necessarily a hero-worshipper. Hence, Spender's quite
legitimate tendency to think 'continually of those who are
truly great'. The resignation and envy in the very title of this
poem (it makes it clear the poet knows he isn't one of them) are
significant in fact. But the awareness of the sort of spiritual quest
involved is equally important: it is a far more mature recognition
of the nature of the task confronting him than the sincere but
inadequate social conscience the volume also flaunts. A more
impressive instance of this *Kulturmythologie* is the frankly
adulatory poem on 'Beethoven's Death Mask'. Once again,
Spender puts a distance between himself and the 'truly great'

man, which is clearly going to incapacitate him for the sustained spiritual flight. But again, also, the acknowledgement of
the peculiar role of genius is intelligent and constructive. It is
also quite legitimate that Spender should explore the possibilities of the spiritual aspiration through the actual achievement of Beethoven—the transition from Scherzo to Finale of
the Fifth Symphony in this case:

> Then the drums move away, the Distance shows;
> Now cloud-hid peaks are bared; the mystic One
> Horizons haze, as the blue incense heaven.
> Peace, peace. . . . Then splitting skull and dream, there
>   comes
> Blotting our lights, the Trumpetter, the sun.

Spender's talent is far better exercised here, in the naive
imitation of a master (an Imitation of Christ, *mutatis mutandis*),
than in the would-be sophisticated knowingness of 'An "I" can
never be a great man', in which received twentieth-century
ideas are crossed with Negative Capability in an image-less
confusion.

   Much more impressive than the latter poem in a related vein
is 'What I expected' (poem XIV in the book), which makes an
interesting parallel or contrast with Auden's contemporary
allegories of the intellectual life,—'Atlantis', for instance, or
'The Quest'. Where Auden parabolizes in studious disenchantment, Spender eschews the extended allegorical schema, confident in the capacity of a loosely connected sheaf of activities—
climbing, struggling, fighting—to coalesce into a composite
image of the spiritual experience:

> What I expected was
> Thunder, fighting,
> Long struggles with men
> And climbing.
> After continual straining
> I should grow strong;
> Then the rocks would shake
> And I should rest long.

The next stanza introduces us to the disabusement anticipated in
the tense of the first, 'the gradual day/Weakening the will/

Leaking the brightness away'; the third, to the objective causes of this process, 'the watching of cripples pass/With limbs shaped like questions/In their odd twist,/And pulverous grief/Melting the bones with pity.' It is these facts that inhibit the exercise of that sense of a personal destiny in the Romantic manner, and Spender speaks here for all the poets and intellectuals of his generation. The last stanza of the poem maintains the pluperfect disillusionment, but presents through the tense the redeeming-image the whole poem is meant to embody—'The created poem, Or the dazzling crystal'.

Structurally and methodologically, it is a beautiful piece of work, the parts related simply and subtly to the whole which they modify as they create it, yet still holding the air of an honest and honestly outraged personal testament. Like all the best poems Spender produced at this time, it embodies the message it enunciates: in pursuing the structural argument, one experiences the poem. And this capacity in Spender has a lot to do with his conception of the poem as an act, rather than as a statement. It is this which most distinguishes him from W. H. Auden, with whom he was fatally associated for so long. The Auden association seems to me to have been a disaster. No poet could have been better chosen to expose Spender's deficiencies and undermine his self-confidence than W. H. Auden. Nor, at the same time, could any poet conceivably be further removed from Auden in mind and ability than Spender. They are in fact polar opposites: as so often happens in the history of thought, two temperaments more or less exclusively contrasted become fixed in a polarization at first stimulating, then destructive. As with Wordsworth and Coleridge, the weaker character went under and suffered in the process more or less crippling damage to his self-esteem and identity. In the present case, the extra-verted abreactive brain of Auden, scientific and sharply exact in its annotative habits, decisively demoralized the vacillating religiose vagueness of Spender. The decline of Spender's reputation set in when those who had bracketed him with Auden first realized how far he was from fulfilling the Auden norm, a norm he was hopelessly ill-equipped to attempt.

Like Day Lewis, Spender laboured hard to compete with Auden without ever understanding that Auden's 'precision' was based, as I have suggested above, upon an always semi-ideational mode, a conceptual 'case' argued with brilliant selection of instance. Thus, they did not see that the effect in Auden's verse of sharply focussed observation derived at least in part from the mental manipulation of 'idea', and that Auden, in short, rarely had to bother to 'get' the precise visual phenomenon in its particular inscape: it was enough for him to introduce the typical instance—the pier pummelled by waves, the cave full of outlaws, the rioters in the square.

Spender never really understood this fact about Auden. His weakest lines are those which attempt to fix the politico-social facts with what he seems to have felt was an Audenesque precision. Now precision is exactly what Spender characteristically lacks—precision and swiftness: the movement of his verse is laboured, heavily stressed, bound up with its own rhyme echoes. If we compare a poem like the much-anthologized 'Fall of a City' with any of Auden's political poems, Spender will appear naïve and amateurish:

> All the posters on the walls,
> All the leaflets in the streets
> Are mutilated, destroyed, or run in rain.
>
> ('Fall of a City')

Auden would, in the first place, hardly have bothered noting the observations down—he would not have *seen* them as 'images' at all. They are too much the earnest sixth former's great-eyed search for 'material'. At most, he might have noted the single detail of leaflets or torn posters in the rain. Now, Spender does little to really fix the impression: there is no distinguished touch to the lines. And yet the heavy-handed emphasis on the three verbs—'multilated', 'destroyed' and 'run-in-rain'— does something beyond and beneath the actual visual content of the words. In fact, what at first appears its embarrassing ineptitude (the fact that the three verbs together tell us little more than any one of them might have alone) emerges as its real strength: the compassionate pathos that rubs off or through onto the inhabitants of the city. More, the suggestion in these lines of tears is something Auden would either not have caught, or would have been embarrassed at: it is the limitation of very clever people that they can often only see suffering as a reason for pity, without being able to feel pity itself.

Auden's apperceptive rapidity—we remember that 'neural' is a favourite adjective of his—marshals the instances much more brilliantly and effectively than Spender's slow-moving introspection, but at the same time succeeds often in merely registering or demonstrating the 'truth' without the pity being generated. Spender's clumsiness, in the instance under discussion as in many others, derives probably from the fact that he had to make a conscious effort of will to focus the external facts (the posters and leaflets) from which Auden, bad eyes or no, would have extracted the essence in a trice.

Yet the difference between Auden's mind and Spender, lies deeper than this. I have already noted certain similarities in their use of allegory to express the struggle of the intellectual life. Another type of allegoric poem both poets liked to exploit concerns sexual and emotional situations. Here the allegoric narrative is replaced by a single symbol, as in Rilke's great poem 'Exposed on the mountains of the heart', from which both English poets, I fancy, learned something. Spender's 'Your body is stars whose million glitter here' recaptures much of the ecstasy of Rimbaud's *Illuminations* in its frank hyperbolic celebration of the act:

> Our movements range through miles, and when we kiss
> The moment widens to enclose the years.

The explorers invoked in the second half of the poem are not Auden's jaded delinquents—swillers of rare liqueurs in Graham Greene bars—but acolytes, 'explorers of immense and simple lines'. It is in fact, an immense and simple poem, despite its post-coital deflation, which seems less an intimation of disenchantment than a pain of exclusion welcomed as part of a ritual:

> The promise hangs, this swarm of stars and flowers,
> And then there comes the shutting of a door.

Again, as in 'What I expected', Spender combines several loosely associated images—beholders, explorers, the sky, branches, mountains, flowers,—trusting to the validity of the emotion to fuse them all into a coherent whole.

We note, by contrast, the purely 'literary' origination of the mountain symbol in Auden's Sonnet, 'The Climbers': the poem becomes a mere exercise, presenting the labours of love in terms of a climb. Imagery of kitting-out, setting off on a gruelling expedition which is not literal but figurative is, I have noted, a common property of Auden's universe. The sonnet sequence 'The Quest' explores the possibilities better than anything else of his perhaps; in a more overtly allegorical form, 'Atlantis' provides another example of the genre, an at times exciting mélange of school-boy adventure story (Hadath and Henty), literary myth and Freudian double-think. 'The Climbers' seeks to combine narrative and lyric. Yet it *is* allegory, and the comparative facility of the medium contrasts badly with Spender's more compact symbolism. Thus, Auden writes,

> with excuse concocted
> Soon on a lower alp I fall and pant,
> Cooling my face there in the faults that flaunt
> The life which they have stolen and perfected.
>
> ('The Climbers')

In spite of the apparent complexity of meaning (he cools his face not in snow but in 'faults' that have 'stolen' the poet's life, and 'perfected' it), the result of Auden's manipulation of the mountain-climb symbol is to rob it of its immediacy and to return it to allegory. Spender, forsaking the clever ramifications of the symbol, achieves a far greater intensity and reality of experience:

> Here is our goal, men cried, but it was lost
> Amongst the mountain mists and mountain pines.
>
> ('Your body is stars whose million glitter here')

Something of Spender's greater relevance in the contemporary scene can be gleaned from a glance at Dom Moraes's beautiful 'Snow on a Mountain', which sustains the symbol with a narcissistic sensualism and an overall strategy not really present in Spender's more ambitious poem:

> One moment past my hands had run
> The chanting streams of her thighs;
> Then I was lost, breathless among the pines.
>
> ('Snow on a Mountain')

Auden's Sonnet could not have helped to midwife so fine and
fresh a piece. One turns with a mixture of weariness and disgust, on the other hand, from the inevitable self-accusations of
'The Climbers': phases like 'Excuse concocted' and 'Cooling
my face in the faults' amount almost to self-parody. Why, we
ask ourselves, can Auden only prove his integrity by demonstrating his awareness of his own mendacity and failure? In
spite of its confessional nature, Spender's poetry is free of this
characteristic vice of ironist verse, and it is the consequent
openness and fullness, coupled with the greater volume and
rhythmic power of his poetry, that establishes his superiority
over Auden. These particular quotations suggest, it is true, a
disparity between their gifts that does not always obtain.
Spender is not always that good, nor Auden often that bad.
'The Climbers' has been anthologized (in a collection con-
taining not a line of Spender)[1] and appears at first glance a
plausible enough offering. Only closer scrutiny shows Auden at
an unusually weak moment: 'excuse concocted/Soon on a lower
alp I fall and pant' is deplorably feeble *just as verse*: the words
are slack, the lines lack all inner cohesion. By contrast, the
Spender has an Olympian ease and strength: 'lost/Among the
mountain mists and the mountain pines'. The placing of 'lost'
really *does* something in and for the poem, and the following
line expands with an impressive relaxation.

In general Auden's actual versification *does* less, and it is
probably this transparency of texture, through which the
instances are meant to be seen, that has kept him in bad odour
in circles where he ought to be admired, and which does in fact
justify ultimate reservations as to his stature. By the same token,
Spender's higher rate of prosodic 'work' earns him the higher
Parnassian niche, and justifies an increased interest in his
poetry today. The strenuousness of Spender's language and
rhythm is easily demonstrated. It derives from the poet's slow
involvement in his emotionally possessed and surrounded
objects and observations. The strength and inner life of his
metre explain—as they are explained by—that very naïveté
and sluggishness which seemed initially to make him such a
hopeless straggler in the 'thirties field:

[1] Maynard Mack *et al.* (eds.), *Modern Poetry* (New York, 1952).

> Only the world changes, and time its tense
> Against the creeping inches of whose moons
> He launches his rigid continual present.
>
> ('No Man's Land')

In these lines, Spender compels a slow, tensed-up reading—it is not possible to hurry the verse along in the way that Auden encourages us to hurry his, to glance at things in passing, without being really aware of the words being used. The strategic placing of 'tense', with its grammatical ambiguity, enforces a stiff concentration, much as the shadow creeps across the 'rigid continual present' ('continual' is possibly just an oversight, but certainly its implication of something nagging, wearying, suits the mood of the lines better than the correct 'continuous'). The slow strenuous movement of the time is maintained in the following triplets by means of the cinematic concentration on the growth of grass, which is finally seen piercing the skin of a dead soldier 'as through a drum'. Much of the tension of the piece stems from the contrast between what is normally felt to be a gentle sensationless process (the moon shining, the grass growing) and the immense physical restraint Spender exercises on his verse. I submit that there is nothing in Auden of comparable weight.

The Spanish Civil War poems are probably on balance the most satisfying in the Collected Spender. Significantly, the fighting and death afforded Spender a profounder vision into reality than they afforded Auden. Where Auden communicates an exciting sense of disaster and anarchy, Spender sees both sides engaged in a conflict which ultimately transcends their partisan differences; he achieves the classic serenity that marks off the merely good from the momentarily great:

> Clean silence drops at night, when a little walk
> Divides the sleeping armies, each
> Huddled in linen woven by remote hands.
> When the machines are stilled, a common suffering
> Whitens the air with breath and makes both one
> As though these enemies slept in each other's arms.
>
> ('Two Armies')

The last line suggests that Spender can achieve maximum engagement in a poem only in the presence of a near-erotic

element. Certainly, some of his finest pieces stem directly from
personal relationship. 'The Room above the Square', for
instance, presents its 'shatteredness' with an impressive
straight-forwardness:

> Now I climb alone to the high room
> Above the darkened square
> Where among stones and roots, the other
> Unshattered lovers are.

The powerful slowing vowel-structures, 'alone—room—
darkened—square—stones—roots—lovers—are' strengthen the
stanza-structure (note the excellence of the 'square–are' half-
rhyme) in a manner quite unknown to the reader of Auden.
Essentially, though, it is that same capacity for the open gaze as
we observed in 'Fall of a City', sensitized by Spender's almost
professional capacity for being wounded, which lends his
relationship poetry its force. 'A Separation', hardly less successful than 'The Room above the Square', treats its eminently
representative situation with equally admirable directness (it is
the naïveté, of course, that makes this possible):

> Yes. The will decided. But how can the heart decide,
> Lying deep under the surface
> Of the level reasons the eye sees.

The heart cannot, of course, and the body must endure along
with it the consequences of the will's decision:

> Under sleep, under day,
> Under the earth, in the tunnel of the marrow,
> Unchanging love swears all's unchanged, and knows
> That what it has not, still stays all it has.

The heart-reason distinction the poem is based on is hardly
promising; yet Spender has made it his own, and given it verbal
embodiment, precisely because he uses it to make sense of an
actual situation: the distinction serves the moment, the poem
does not embroider the distinction.

Spender's successes come when he has forgotten the wrangle
with symbol and image that bogs down so much of his verse;

conversely, his poetry loses its point when the symbol takes over. This almost wrecks the central stanza of 'The Room above the Square'; in 'Meeting', the strikingly original opening section is suffered to give way to the studied preciosity of this kind of Metaphysical riddling:

> Distances between us are of crystal
> Traversed with diagonals of rays
> In which our eyes meet when, near or far, they
>   gaze. . . .

Yet despite the strength of the poetry of relationships, some of Spender's most powerful writing has been dictated by his peculiarly emotional apprehension of political situations. At moments in the Second World War poems, he attains to the hard transcendentalism of the best Spanish Civil War poems. 'June 1940' fumbles its way through a good deal of inconclusive dialogue to reach a cold visionary statement that might have come out of the underground limbo of Owen's 'Strange Meeting':

> I am cold as a cold world alone
> Voyaging through space without faith or aim
> And no Star whose rays point a Cross to believe in,
> And an endless, empty need to atone.

The 'need to atone' of course derives very much from the Spenderian psyche: confession, atonement, abasement—these are emotions he understands and even relishes. Yet here he has struck through to an impersonal layer of generality, as indeed he does in the amazing 'Rejoice in the Abyss', surely one of the finest examples of Blitz poetry. The tone of Christopher Smart penetrates Spender's sleep in a weirdly prophetic ecstasy:

> I saw whole streets aflame with London prophets,
> Saints of Covent Garden, Parliament Hill Fields,
> Hampstead, Hyde Park Corner, Saint John's Wood,
> Who cried in cockney fanatic voices:
> 'In the midst of Life is Death!'

The poem opens powerfully—'The great pulsation passed'
—and throughout a somewhat haphazard, quasi-rhapsodic
development, manages to sustain a queer dream-like momentum:

> Then in the sky, indifferent to our
> Sulphurous nether hell, I saw
> The dead of all pasts float on one calm tide
> Among the foam of stars
> Above the town, whose walls of brick and flesh
> Are transitory dwellings
> Of spirits journeying from life to death.

Like 'Beethoven's Death Mask', 'Rejoice in the Abyss' breaks
through to a visionary world in which a voice speaks that is not
the poet's own, one possessed of a felicitousness unknown to the
waking man:

> For hollow is the skull, the vacuum
> In the gold ball under Saint Paul's gold cross.
> Unless you will accept the emptiness
> Under the bells of fox-gloves and cathedrals,
> Each life must feed upon the death of others

The felicitousness of 'Under the bells of fox-gloves and cathedrals' goes along with the authoritativeness of the moral man-
date—'All human aims are stupefied denial'. To penetrate so
far beyond his habitual diffidence represented a considerable
victory for the demonic principle within Spender, unless that
diffidence is itself less than ingenuous.

The strenuousness (body, rhythmic strength), which I have
tried to illustrate in Spender, ties in with his genius for
metaphor, or his weakness for it, as it often appears. Metaphor
is not only Spender's most natural mode of expression; it is
part of his conceptual apparatus—everything is seen in terms of
something else. Each image breeds an analogical double.
Spender has often been described as 'introspective', usually in a
loose way, referring to his awkward self-consciousness. It is not
merely his penchant for thinking 'continually of those who were
truly great', however, that justifies the label. Spender's mind is

introverted in a more precise sense, that relates to his actual
manner of perceiving reality. Certainly it is no accident that so
many of his successful poems take the form of a commentary on
his prolonged rumination (it is this, rather than meditation).
'I think continually' is a much more Spenderian poem than
many of the political pieces contained in the same volume.
'Beethoven's Death Mask' and 'Dark and Light', also exem-
plify the ruminative envelope within which so much of his
poetic thinking takes place, and which it tries so hard to break
out of. Another, slightly different, example is the sympathetic
piece he wrote on the 'thirties unemployed, 'Moving through
the silent crowd'. This poem is carried off largely in the social
imagery of the kind more brilliantly handled by Auden:

> Moving through the silent crowd
> Who stand behind dull cigarettes. . . .
>
> They lounge at corners of the street
> And greet friends with a shrug of shoulder. . . .

The technical immaturity (the articles omitted for reasons of
scansion) in this case suits well with the awesome naïveté of
feeling—'Now they've no work, like better men/ Who sit at
desks and take much pay'—which suggests the direct influence
of Wilfred Owen. But what makes the poem specifically
Spenderian is the final move, when, the objective scenes behind
him, Spender returns to his interior silence:

> I'm jealous of the weeping hours
> They stare through with such hungry eyes
> I'm haunted by these images,
> I'm haunted by their emptiness.

The first couplet skilfully places Spender's own position—the
well-heeled young poet, over-emotional, and envious of the
Romantic despair of the unemployed. In the last couplet, when
the withdrawal into the inner world is complete, we accept
fully and in good faith his assertion that he is 'haunted'. In
one way, the superiority of the poem over so many of Auden's
much more impressively adroit social poems could be expressed

quite simply by stating that it transmits a far greater 'pity' than is ever present in Auden. Yet what is really interesting about Spender's poem is that emotionally it is *more* sophisticated than Auden's poetry on comparable themes: Spender pursues his compassion with an almost erotic avidity. The poem woos the workers with a woman's softness. The flow of the verse, too, testifies to the technical skill that underlies so much of Spender's almost willed gaucherie.

Spender's genuine introversion of temperament is much better suited to interiorisation of this kind than to the kind of reportage attempted in the popular 'Landscape near an Aerodrome'. This poem, like the equally often anthologized 'Elementary School Classroom', though not offensive in its class-attitudes, remains heavily 'descriptive', its emotion really squirted on to its somewhat turgidly 'precise' observation: fundamentally, Spender remains unengaged. The opening stanza of the 'Landscape' is certainly well achieved with its characteristically tender animism (the 'moth' image, with its 'furry antenae' could only come from Spender), and he has 'done' the aircraft descent for us. But beyond its general accuracy, it fails to justify an interest in the moral indignation that follows. In this case, the indulged sensualism of the animistic metaphor clashes with the social compassion: we get an exercise in social criticism instead of the strongly motivated emotionalism of 'Moving through the silent crowd', in which the poet's near-erotic engagement in the subject fuses into or identifies with the social sympathy. In the present case, the Dickensian social protest—'Figures frightening and mad' and 'squat buildings/With their strange air behind trees'—is artificially yoked to the beautiful descent imagery of the first stanza, so that the final Blakean warning—'Religion stands, the Church blocking the sun'—falls with a platitudinous thud.

The successful interiorization of 'Moving through the silent crowd' and the animistic moth image at the beginning of the 'Landscape' represent two aspects of Spender's introversion of temperament. For the animism could be predicted of his mind. Metaphor itself represents an attempt to activate or vitalize phenomena. It is often implied in critical writing that such an act of animism informs all metaphor in poetry, but as I have tried to show with Auden, this is not really so. In a poet like Spender, we see at work something like the primitive animism, almost fetichistic in its intensity, that galvanizes the descriptive writing of Dickens. The moth image at the beginning of the 'Landscape' assumes an alarming furry reality: the 'plane becomes a moth, just as the harbour walls of Port Bou, in the poem of that name, become a child's hands holding a pet. The pet is the sea, trapped in the harbour that

> looks through the gap
> To outer freedom animal air.

('Port Bou')

The pent-up energy in the clutched animal is transferred to the sea, thus lending the 'description' animated vitality it could not otherwise have had.

This kind of energy-transference, the province often of the witch-doctor or the psychoanalyst, is radical to Spender's metaphor. At its best it is charged alternately with a tremulous tenderness, or a circumscribed virility. At its worst, it merely seeks some objective justification in the given image for the metaphoric transformation the poet automatically needs to effect upon it. 'Seascape', for example strives for the symbolic immanence of Valéry's 'Cimetière Marin' (though the feeling is closer to Shelley), and succeeds only in laboriously establishing average-to-good analogies: the ocean, for instance, is like 'an unfingered harp'. Such *Correspondences*, of course, have been the goal of the poet ever since Baudelaire, although the source for an English poet is directly available in Wordsworth. In 'Cimetière Marin' Valéry lifts the entire plan of his dazzlingly Platonist poem to an exalted spiritual revelation by means of a *Correspondence* between the sails of the ships at sea and the sight of doves pecking upon a roof.

The latent academicism of Spender's symbolist programme in 'Seascape' is mitigated and in part redeemed by the image of the 'motionlessness of the hot sky' that 'tires' to produce the 'sigh, as a woman's' from inland. There is also the characteristically tender image of the two butterflies 'like errant dog-roses' that get themselves drowned (a narrative awkwardness Valéry would have shuddered at, yet somehow carried off by Spender). It is the true naïveté of such images here that keeps Spender

from stiffening into an academic symbolist laboriously culling
the analogies that have long since lost their Symbolist resonance.
The lines following the drowning of the butterflies shockingly
betray this naïveté—

>   Fishermen understand
>   Such wings sunk in such ritual sacrifice.
>
> ('Seascape').

The modish interest in 'ritual' (there is nothing ritualistic
about the episode as narrated by Spender) effectively mars the
naïveté, and in doing so, underlines it. The final stanza of the
poem gives everything up for a mélange of literary echoes
involving visions of Atlantis, the sea-change, *The Tempest*.

It was Rilke, however, and not Valèry, who set for Spender
the most dangerous precedent, for it was Rilke rather than
Valèry who made the most absolute claim for the symbolist
Correspondences. The *Duino Elegies* are the Koran of symbolism
and their success or failure must be held to refute or confirm
the acknowledgement of bankrupty declared in *Une Saison en
Enfer*. As we move through the *Collected Poems*, the hand of
Rilke exercises a more and more inhibiting restraint upon
Spender's native metaphorical sense. He displays a greater and
greater concern for finding analogical correlates for phenomena
which do not especially seem to have struck him, and his own
natural metaphorical animism gives way to an increasingly
literary symbolism.

Ultimately the effort to compete with Rilke (this is how it
registers) broke Spender. The single image in which he most
seriously strives after a Rilkean universality—'The Vase of
Tears'—unequivocally announces the failure of Spender's
adoption of Rilkean profundity:

>   And one by one these bitter drops collect
>   Into my heart, a glass vase which reflects
>   The world's grief weeping in its daughter.

A co-translator of the *Duino Elegies* ought to have been more
aware of the care with which Rilke ensures a feasible analogical
form for his symbols. The cause of Spender's failure in these

lines is the absence of any visual or other actual support for
the symbol. To call his heart 'a glass vase' was bad enough—
the metaphor lacks any real analogical basis. But to go on to
picture the vase *reflecting* was disastrous: we are forced to conclude that Spender was leaning entirely upon the reader's
stock response to the loaded words—heart and tears.

'The Vase of Tears' was published in the 1937–9 collection,
Love and Separation. Thereafter the imagery and metaphor show
an increasing self-consciousness that borders often on the
mechanical. The metaphors and similes succeed more and more
in fixing only a limited visual effect. An air raid at Plymouth
for example, provokes Spender only to a series of more and less
successful parallelisms—the searchlight-beams 'fuse in a cone',
or smash the aircraft's image like a cup; they are like fencing
swords, or they makes geometrical patterns, trying to mark the
spot with a cross of doom. The cross they make is of course at
once a geometrical intersection, an omen of doom, and then the
cross that marks the pilot's grave. This kind of ingenuity
betrays the gravity of the events observed. The concern for
analogical accuracy destroys or precludes any serious feeling
Spender might have entertained. He might be describing a
firework display or a circus instead of a struggle in which some-
body—the aircrew or the inhabitants of Plymouth—is likely to
get killed. The last stanza's Christian sermonizings do not ease
matters: on the contrary, the laboured accuracy now connives
at a knowing wit—'the waves/Chuckle between the rocks'!
No-one who has read Edith Sitwell's 'Still falls the rain' is going
to be impressed, either, by Spender's final crucifix reference:

> Man hammers nails in Man
> High on his crucifix.

This kind of image-hunting is still more shocking when
the subject is Belsen or Buchenwald. The pilot was out of sight,
and after all he was a Nazi. Confronted by the living skeletons
of Belsen, Spender—who has shown himself so enormously
compassionate, so profoundly moved by suffering in poem after
poem; who is dangerously vulnerable to emotion, and half-
Jewish at the same time—retreats into a hunt for the appropriate image that genuinely appalls: their skin 'tars the bones'

with a 'thin varnish'; their faces are like 'clenched despair' 'Knocking at the birdsong-fretted air'.

Failure in the face of Belsen and Hiroshima cannot be held against any artist: they are beyond sympathy. The attempt to treat them in artistic form is at best misguidedly immature, at worst presumptuously self-important. It was inevitable that someone of Spender's endowment—tremulously emotional and accessible to suffering—should be forced into a total withdrawal of himself in the face of the Nazi camps. Hence, his poem on the subject (self-mockingly called 'Memento') not only reveals no evidence whatever of genuine emotional response, it is positively offensive in its unscrupulous seeking after effects: 'birdsong-fretted' in particular, with its Shakespearean overtones, hits an unpleasantly literary note. We resent this display of technique in the context of such suffering, just as we reject the elegance of Sydney Nolan's Auschwitz drawings, and the pious pomp of Britten's War Requiem. All of these performances seem insulting in the circumstances, their 'sincerity' an impertinence, their articulations heartless. Only silence will do, and silence is a failure.

6 David Gascoyne:
phenomena of zero

Everyone knows that the 'thirties amounted to more than the Pylon School on holiday in Spain. From time to time someone protests. But to all intents and purposes, the 'thirties still mean the social poetry of Auden's school, with Empson and Bottrall trying to live up to Dr Leavis's great expectations over at Cambridge. Yet the 'low, dishonest decade' also produced Lorca and Eluard, and Surrealism, the first real international style since Symbolism. The closer we look at the continental scene between the wars, the more vehemently we are led to regret the insularity of the English cultural tradition. In this case, English isolation meant not the magnificent eccentricity of a Blake or a Hopkins, but the conservatism of Auden, and the reticent cleverness of Empson. Cut off by its class timidity and self-consciousness from the life-source of D. H. Lawrence, and unable to carry on the momentum of T. S. Eliot's breakthrough, English poetry in the 'thirties atrophied into a wanness of disbelief.

The point is emphasized by exceptional poets, like Dylan Thomas and David Gascoyne, who, subjecting themselves to the discipline of Surrealism, plugged in to a broader tradition. In one way, David Gascoyne's adoption of Surrealism is odd; for at first glance no poet could seem less apt for the mode. Surrealism is built upon swiftness of association, the abnegation of the self, its necessary consequence, the immolation of the personal voice. Such at least is its programme: for the personal voice represents the will, the ego, the Freudian slave-master the whole movement was meant to overthrow.

Gascoyne—as his later development shows—is essentially a master, an ego, and he never succeeded in eradicating the

traces of his own voice. The photographs of the poet reveal a
sombre, brooding face, heavy with will, the very anti-type to,
say, D. H. Lawrence.[1] Seen from the Lawrentian viewpoint, in
fact, there is little to admire in Gascoyne with his insistent ego
and harshly sober intellectuality, ungainly in movement, never-
resting, ceaselessly imposing itself upon the flow of experience,
preoccupied with itself even in the act of love (for example,
Gascoyne's obsession with mirrors in poems like 'Camera
Obscura' and 'The Fabulous Glass'). A moralist in fact, even
in his immoralism; a moralist who has sinned, and whose
sinning fuels his moralising. If Lawrence is the Noble Savage,
Gascoyne is the Original Sinner, and unlike Stephen Spender,
who was quite ready to accept the need for atonement provided
he could be evasive on the deeds for which it might be necessary,
Gascoyne insists at times on morbid confessionalism.

But Surrealism is more than a technique: Surrealism takes its
place in a complex metaphysical tradition more exciting
intellectually even where it seems less sheerly *serious* than the
English tradition. Moreover, this continental tradition is
merely the continuance into the age of scepticism of the great
Catholic tradition of the Cathedrals and of Dante: the world of
Surrealism is geared to axes of damnation and bliss, of *Spleen et
Idéal*. And it is evident that Gascoyne felt naturally in these
terms. If he is, as I have suggested, essentially a moralist,
Surrealism, despite its whimsical by-products, was essentially a
moralistic idiom, a product of a world-situation of plethora
and horror. Gascoyne was a Marxist in the 'thirties, and the
body of his indignation is carried not in social comment, but in
the Surrealist attempt to create purity in form out of ordure.
The Surrealist believes that conscious intervention in his work
must be false since its structure is governed by necessity and
entailment without freedom. This deep distrust of the conscious
mind stems from disgust with what the conscious mind has
achieved in society—the world of war, depression and hunger.
Hence, Gascoyne's Nazis are the persecutors of Christ—

> See, the centurions wear riding-boots,
> Black shirts and badges with peaked caps,

[1] I have seen only one photograph in fact, in Derek Stanford's *Freedom and
Poetry* (London, 1946).

Greet one another with raised-arm salutes;
They have cold eyes, unsmiling lips;
Yet these His brothers know not what they do.

('Ecce Homo')

Thus, Gascoyne's Surrealism reflects a disturbed moral sense. So that, basically, the best of the Surrealist poems do not differ from the finest of the poetry that follows, except for the stage of development they indicate. In them Gascoyne creates symbols of horror and obsession with the dream-apparatus made available by Surrealist association techniques:

Garments of the sensory
Worn by the nocturnal expedition
By all the chimaeras
Climbing in at the window
With lice in their hair
Noughts in their crosses
Ice in their eyes

Hysteria upon the staircase
Hair torn out by the roots.

('Charity Week')

'These are the phenomena of zero', Gascoyne observes at the end of this poem ('Charity Week'—dedicated to Max Ernst). And thereby betrays how 'conscious' is his manipulation of the Surrealist props. Sometimes it appears debatable whether Gascoyne was ever strictly speaking a Surrealist poet at all, as for example Kenneth Patchen, the young Dylan Thomas and Paul Eluard all were. For Gascoyne nearly always provides a conscious frame 'placing' the irrational phenomena, and this act of legitimization in a sense contravenes Surrealist principle. The question is academic (good poetry is good poetry is good poetry), but interestingly so:

The worlds are breaking in my head
Blown by the brainless wind
That comes from afar
Swollen with dusk and dust
And hysterical rain

('Yves Tanguy')

What matters is that even though the imagery here is legitimately internalized (by the phrase 'in my head'), Gascoyne has struck through to the essence of the psychic phenomena afforded by the twin researches of Surrealism and psycho-analysis.

Surrealism does not of course have any magic formulae or any privileged access to the unconscious. The man who believes he has the unconscious on tap understands neither psychoanalysis nor his own mental processes. But to choose Surrealism as a mode is to reject certain patterns of thought and the imagery collateral to them, and to reject also certain strict entailments of mental activity regarding suitability, order and logic. It is at the same time and by the same token to make available to oneself certain types of experience and certain orders of meta-phor inaccessible to the Gestalt-bound rationalist. A poet like Auden exploits the contents of Freudian handbooks: his treat-ment of the 'unconscious' is purely conceptual and external. He uses the Freudian projection to chart a landscape in which unconscious anxieties and inhibitions are symbolized (by civil war, for example, or barbed wire). But this is mere psycho-analytical lore, and Auden has no real traffic with the pheno-mena concerned. If we move from Auden's 'Barbed Wire' to Gascoyne's 'Rites of Hysteria', we cannot remain unaware of the contrast between the Freudian tourist armed with a guide-book, and the natural denizen. This difference is explained by the concept of availability: the poet determines or limits his range of imagery by his pre-taken decisions about life and art. Images like Gascoyne's 'chimaeras . . . with lice in their hair . . . ice in their eyes' simply could not have occurred to Auden.

The myths of Surrealism are articulated by means of wit. The wit of Surrealism is present in Lautréamont's formulation —'the chance meeting of an umbrella and a sowing-machine on an operating table'. It is there also in the visual puns of Ernst and Duchamp. For Surrealist writing there were broadly speaking two main avenues of wit: the creation of static dream-objects (more or less on the model of what the painters had achieved), and linear metaphoric transformation, or meta-morphosis. Since even the static juxtaposition of two alien objects amounts to a metamorphosis of both, we might put forward the suggestion that the metamorphosis is the basis of Surrealist mythology. David Gascoyne's Surrealist poems divide fairly easily between the two modes. His more successful pieces fall in the category of the painterly dream-symbols, static and unmoving:

> An image of my grandmother
> her head appearing upside-down upon a cloud
> the cloud transfixed on the steeple
> of a deserted railway-station
> far away
>
> ('The Very Image')

Here, the 'effect', in so far as we can isolate the source of its magic, derives from the witty displacement of context by context: Gascoyne makes us hunt out the background for the old lady—we think of chintz, crowded Victoriana, birdcages—and then confounds us first by placing her head on a cloud (all right, because she might be in heaven, all wrong because upside down); then, by forcing us to see in the same spatial plane her close-up (a miniature or faded portrait photograph) and the necessarily reduced scale of the station 'far away'. The poem thus imitates the form of visual art by presenting a static symbol, yet demands a kind of dynamic of understanding: to 'see' the image, that is, defined not in space which can be apprehended at one glance, but in time, it is necessary for us to make a sequence of adjustments. In grasping one image and context, we make it possible for the poet to work upon us; he forces us to make the transition to its next aspect. Moreover, we are forced to realize that what we first 'saw'—the image of an old lady's head, for example, was not the whole truth, nor even the truth itself. The action of these poems is the action of this perpetual adjustment and readjustment.

Many of Gascoyne's best Surrealist poems are cast in this form for the obvious reason that his is basically a deliberate, even slow-moving mind. Certainly, his least successful Surrealist poems are the most consciously unconscious: he simply lacked the flexibility and delicacy of mind to let his freely associating wrist really freely associate. We feel a cumbersome mental apparatus creakily governing the paronomasiac release, so that the metamorphoses of 'Phantasmagoria', 'Lozanne', and even 'Salvador Dali' are uninformative in their remorselessly arbitrary confutation of expectation. But as Gascoyne begins to emerge from Surrealist discipline, his mind begins to assert a subtler domination-from-below of the witty transitions. Poems like 'Antennae' and 'Educative Process' follow the phases of a recognizable relationship in a consecutive, though never overtly sequential, arc: 'Not wholly unprepared Nor entirely unafraid. . . . Forgotten mouths forget. . . . For us now we are suspended above life. . . . So evanescent that which binds us. . . . Our burning possession of each other Held in both Hands because it is all we have' ('Antennae') Unconsciously, as it were, Gascoyne's mind has learnt to move blindly, dictating movement and organizing surface from below. His own preconscious mind has begun to call the tune, to the detriment of Bretonesque arbitrariness. Occasionally the images show the process of their own formation—

> Foliage blown by the wind
> Streams into the memory of hair.
> ('Educative Process')

Sometimes they approach the ideal of Haiku—

> A river of perfumed silk
> A final glimpse of content
> The girls are alone on the highroad
> ('Educative Process')

In 'The Rites of Hysteria', this inner, pre-conscious logic is applied to political reality, with the result that an epigrammatic style explains the hysterical symptoms:

> And the owners of rubber pitchforks bake all their illusions
> In an oven of dirty globes and weedgrown stupors

Thus, the poem defies even its own inner irrelevances (reversions to Lautréamont such as 'the ashtray balanced a ribbon upon a syringe') to present to the world of reason and logic a reflection of its absurdities:

> A cluster of insane massacres turns green upon the highroad
> Green as the nadir of a mystery in the closet of a dream
> And a wild growth of lascivious pamphlets became a beehive
> The afternoon scrambles like an asylum out of its hovel
> The afternoon swallows a bucketful of chemical sorrows

There is in both Dada and Surrealism a degree of sheer
skittishness, of *épater le bourgeois*, which from the first attracted
the participation of jokers like Richard Huelsenbeck and light-
weights like Picabia. The wit essential to all Surrealist art
shades naturally into its profounder conceptions of the imaginative process. The metamorphoses of Surrealist poetry move
from one plane to another: 'Someone whose dress seemed to
have forgotten who was wearing it appeared to me at the end
of a pause in the conversation' (Gascoyne: 'Phenomena'). The
effect here is obtained by confuting the reader's grammatical
expectation by substituting a different *type* of termination for
the natural. These semi-humorous transitions of Surrealism are
linked, via the concept of wit, with the metaphysical conceit, as
understood in academic criticism. It is interesting that the
conceit came naturally to Gascoyne. Writing of Hart Crane, he
felicitously turns one of Crane's own favourite reverberations,
'antiphon':

> until
> the sea received you, azure antiphon
> whose octave answer is the sky
> where your wrecked smile drifts still.
>
> ('The Plummet Heart')

This is the fully-fledged metaphysical conceit, thoughtfully
elaborated yet briefly enough touched upon not to jeopardize
the haunting final image, which wisely conceals its visual
analogue—clouds. Like many images in Gascoyne, it has an
uncanny persistence in memory: I still find it impossible to see a
certain kind of slowly dissolving white summer cloud without
thinking of Gascoyne's lines.

The Crane elegy, 'The Plummet Heart' occurs among the
Metaphysical poems in the Collected Gascoyne. This section
stands uneasily halfway between the Surrealist poems and the
Personal Poems of the early 'forties. Uneasily, because with few
exceptions (the Crane poem among them) these poems fail to
break out of their elaborately metaphoric innerness. It is as
though the habit of the Surrealist phase—definitely and
consciously renounced by Gascoyne ('I no longer find the
navel-gazing activity at all satisfying')—died hard, and he had

to make a strenuous effort to bring his emotional experience
and obsessions into contact with the objective world. The process itself is described in 'The Wall', another of the Metaphysical Poems that keeps its inner and outer worlds clearly
distinct. The Surrealist period is symbolized by a wood—

> At first my territory was a Wood:
> Tanglewood, tattering tendrils, trees
> Whose Grimm's-tale shadow terrified but made
> A place to hide in: among traps and towers
> The path I kept to had free right-of-way.

A fair summing-up both of the Disney–Grimm imagination of
so much Expressionist-Surrealist art (for example, Henri
Rousseau's jungles, and Max Ernst's rain-forests), and also of
the element of escape, if not escapism, in the choice of Surrealism. The second stanza takes up the image of the Well—
'reputed bottomless', but in fact conducive more to narcissistic self-contemplation than to the search for truth, for 'the
secret source of nothingness'. Finally, the poet finds his way
through the Wood, beyond the Well, to a Wall, through which
he feels he must smash his way. Significantly, the poem ends:
'To persevere'. Gascoyne is henceforth to display in action that
native moral will which always underlay his Surrealist fantasy,
and consorted ill with it. For Surrealism demanded the abnegation of the self, and Gascoyne could never achieve this aspect of
the programme. His self-abnegation is very much that of the
man of strong will, and the best of the Surrealist poems give
expression to states of hysteria and tension rather than freely
associate in the manner prescribed by André Breton: the
Surrealist verse is born of disgust (which its formal procedures
were to 'purify'). Henceforward, Gascoyne produces a poetry
more and more marked by heavy almost monotonous rhythm,
and metaphoric procedures bordering on the metaphysical in
their often over-elaborate thoughtfulness. But the Surrealism
had sheltered him from the sclerosis of knowing self-denigration,
of irony and 'wit' in the Empsonian sense. So that the Self-
Knowledge that makes so much of his later verse painful to
read derives genuinely from the painful abutments of reality.

But Surrealism did more for Gascoyne than secure him im-
munity from irony. It gave him access to a world that lived out

its myths in streets and hotel bedrooms: Gascoyne's overtly
Surrealist poetry graduates inevitably, if at times awkwardly,
into the Personal Poems of the 'forties, with their milieu of
Nightwood bars and night-walkers, the Paris of Cocteau, Radi-
guet, Edith Piaf. Seen from one angle, in fact, Gascoyne's
poetry is more interesting than Auden's and Spender's simply
because made out of more complex and significant experience
than the literary tea-parties, country house weekends and
evasive relationships that went into their poetry. Gascoyne's
'Noctambules', one of the finest of the Paris poems, celebrates
the *demi-monde* of *poètes maudits*, absinthe-drinkers and *fin de
siècle* lovers familar to us from the novels of Djuna Barnes, Jean
Rhys and other expatriates. But it is compact of a haggard
complexity of involvement which will always, to some, seem
more rewarding in its rich despair than the 'responsible' life.
The fatigue of the poem *is* hellish, so is the gulf of emptiness it
opens up:

> more cries are heard
> Which, merging with the wind
> In wordless tumult, blend
> In an inconsolable dirge
> And desperately press
> Onwards in waves across
> Acres of wet roofs, on
> Across the unseen Seine,
> Away beyond the Madeleine
> And deep into the gulf that yawns
> Behind the Sacré Cœur. . . .

Yet this life of emotional despair and spiritual laceration is
preferable to a life of nothing, and the bourgeoisified existence
embraced by Gascoyne's English contemporaries does seem
nothing.

In other poems of the period, the relationship with the Surrealist period is even more pronounced. We see that only the
conceptual frame distinguishes these 'objective' poems, which
take place in the normal streets and hotel bedrooms of ordinary
life from the Surrealist fantasies sealed off in their own air-tight
jungle. The mirrors in 'The Fabulous Glass' frame a world as
disturbed as that of 'The Rites of Hysteria': the basis of the

verse-form is still the metamorphosis. The cone the poet planted at the beginning of the poem becomes a tree, which in turn falls,

> And where it lay
> A centipede disgustingly
> Swarmed its quick length across the ground.

It is perhaps the adverb 'disgustingly' that both places the image outside the territory of Surrealism and testifies most effectively to Gascoyne's technical skill. The placing of the word disproves at one stroke the fundamental notions of Flaubertian aesthetics, with its *Don't-state*, *render* normatives. No 'rendering' words could evoke half as economically and tellingly the emotion of disgust Gascoyne overtly states. In some cases, it is better to state. At the same time, we recall that in Surrealism there can be no loaded words. Words like 'disgusting' are emotive; that is, they do not denote or describe facts, they prescribe response. Such vocabulary is not consistent with Surrealist aesthetics, since Surrealism has burned its boats, and knows no way back to the world were emotively loaded words, prescribing moral response, are valid. It cannot confess to disgust or to horror, even when evoking them. All the time Gascoyne is a living reproach to himself: he cudgels his experience, and bruises life, as D. H. Lawrence once accused the thinker of doing:

> O you are tangled up in yourself
> Poor little man, poor little man!

This conflict of will against life provides the subject-matter or at least the impulsion behind some of the best of the Personal Poems. In 'Chambre d'Hotel', a perfect relationship poem that should be in every modern anthology, the poet and the woman lie

> entombed
> Deep in unspeaking spleen.

When he tries to take her hand and bridge the appalling gulf between them she springs up and goes to the window, staring out into the street, and silently putting

> A riddle without answer and
> As old as earth's disgrace.

It is difficult to think of any other contemporary poet capable of
rendering so well the tension of deadlock in sexual relationship.
One must go back to the earlier Lawrence for adequate comparison. Surrealism also seems to have preserved Gascoyne
from any of the stock ways of setting up his cameras and choosing his angles: the action of these poems is as original and
affecting as the imagery and tone. In 'Jardin du Palais Royal',
for example, the poet focusses attention on

> The central fountain's dance.

The lovers, again, are locked in strained silence:

> but you rocked
> Backwards and forwards
> And never spoke

Again the poet can make no effectual move. He stares at the
fountain

> trying to see
> Into the constantly disintegrating core
> Round which the fountain ever climbed again.

The poem ends with a return—having failed to break the 'pain
that kept us dumb'—to the arcade that runs around the square.
This time the arcade is made symbolic in a quite straightforward gesture:

> That cold moment made the garden seem
> Too like our loves, abandoned in a cave of time
> Boxed in by the frustrating and decayed
> Walls of the haunted memory's arcade.

The awkwardness with which the emotional experiences are
related to their actual 'setting' perhaps betrays the out-of-
practice stiffness of the poet who has spent too long inside the
hermetic jungles of the Surrealist nightmare. But the success of
the poem tells us that the poet knew the rain-forests of Ernst
and the moonlit cities of Chirico and Dali as spiritual realities:
'Jardin du Palais Royal' is, as it were, a Surrealist poem taking
place in broad daylight. Like 'Noctambules', and many other

poems of this period, it emphasizes the extent to which the world of the Surrealist imagination coincided with the actual life Gascoyne saw and experienced in Paris.

Perhaps as a result of his Surrealist apprenticeship, Gascoyne emerged, when he did emerge, as a far more archaic poet than many who had never been as significant exponents of the international *avant garde* style as he had. Rhythm and metre in the latter poetry are regular and almost bookish, the diction is sprinkled with 'e'en' and 'O'er'. Moreover, he never attained a facility which might have compromised the strange originality of conception which marks not only the Surrealist pieces, but the later poems of relationship. He remains a slightly stiff poet, which is remarkable in someone who wrote something as mature as *Roman Balcony* in his seventeenth year. His poetry is at once the most archaic and the least conventional of its time, and the antique ungainliness of much of his work really does seem essential to its effect. 'Spring MCMXL', for instance, celebrates the vernal goddess with an unabashed Botticellian paganism. Yet the goddess is seen, and the ancient celebration was never less stale:

And through the smoke men gaze with bloodshot eyes
At the translucent apparition clad in nascent trembling green
Of one they still can recognize, though scarcely understand.

The sober tread of the rhythm in these lines reminds one, again, of what has really all along been a dominant characteristic of Gascoyne's verse—an incapacity for inner release, abandon, the Dionysiac frenzy. Gascoyne is the man of will, dominated by the ego, who perhaps for this very reason chose Surrealism, the idiom of 'the unconscious', which only to the uninitiated appears to offer freedom and release, but in fact demands a total denial of the self. The sober, forthright rhythm of Gascoyne's later poetry never becomes academic, yet it never gets its feet off the ground. It moves forward with a uniform tread, earnest yet exploratory:

Beside the stolid opaque flow
Of a rain-gorged Thames; beneath a thin
Layer of early evening light
Which seems to drift, a ragged veil

> Upon the chilly March air's tide:
> Upwards in shallow shapeless tiers
> A stretch of scurfy pock-marked waste
> Sprawls laggardly its acres till
> They touch a raw brick-villaed rim.
>
> ('The Gravel-Pit Field')

Not only the rhythm here, but the painstaking realism of the observation, testify to the effort of will Gascoyne was called upon to make to complete the transition from outright Surrealism only partially effected in the often excessively interior Metaphysical Poems. In contrast to the Pylon poets, who all went into relatively early decline, Gascoyne persisted and persevered to produce his finest poetry late in life. It needs luck to be born a poet; courage and strength to stay one. For the time being, Gascoyne laboured: many of the poems he produced at this time are descriptive in the pejorative sense of the term. Poems like 'Walking at Whitsun', 'The Gravel-pit Field', and 'The Sacred Hearth' are called upon to carry an enormous burden of observation, the whole being held together only by a remorselessly earnest effort of the will. This will is not rhythmic like that of Yeats—Gascoyne's rhythms are fairly uniform—it is rather strength of moral determination. The strange thing perhaps is that so many of his apparently ungainly descriptive assemblages do in fact hold the attention. So that although there is not often the felicitousness of observation that stamps the poetry of Day Lewis, for example, the painstaking closeness repays our attention by so patently not being mere orchestration: heavily though these poems are scored, their observations hardly ever provide mere background or fodder for 'meaning' to breed upon. Thus, while it is hardly possible, without ingeniousness, to provide satisfactory explication in thematic or structural terms for the series of facts narrated in a poem like 'A Wartime Dawn', the significance of the poem is still curiously inseparable from the dense descriptive clutter:

> Nearest within the window's sight, ash-pale
> Against a cinder-coloured wall, the white
> Pear-blossom hovers like a stare; rain-wet
> The further housetops weakly shine; and there
> Beyond hangs flaccidly a lone barrage-balloon.

For succinctness and wit the poem as a whole cannot match Edwin Muir's excellent 'A Wayside Station'. Muir's poem ends, like Gascoyne's with the day waking to war; but it is achieved with greater deftness. A stream

> starts its winding journey
> Through the day and time and war and history.
>
> ('A Wayside Station')

Gascoyne's punch-line is significantly more ponderous:

> And one more day of War starts everywhere.

Yet the lines quoted earlier demonstrate the subtlety of feeling that informs the *un*subtle concentration of his poetry: the strange memorability testifies to the presence of something much more fundamental and valuable than the 'quality of the reporting' noted by Kenneth Allott.[2] One remembers the first poem printed in the *Collected Poems*—'Slate', from 1932, with its strange, deliberate association of the slate in a quarry with the clouds 'behind the hill, monotonously grey'. And one cannot quite say why the parallel remains so persistently in the mind. In 'A Wartime Dawn', the sky is compared to 'the inside of a deaf-mute's mouth'; a whole series of subtle gradations of whiteness, off-whiteness, greyness, takes the eye from the 'ash-pale' Pear-blossom to the 'lone barrage-balloon' hanging 'flaccidly' (we applaud the typically careful excellence of the adverb). More than fine reporting is in evidence here: the capacity for feeling in the presence of rare affinities displayed in the passage springs from the same sensibility as created the Surrealist poems, tutored by the Surrealist discipline.

But the Surrealist who emerges is likely to find himself lost, especially if he returns to England. The return to England and the coming of the War left Gascoyne stranded, high and dry on the mud-flats of a dubious reality. Much of the best poetry he wrote over the next ten years was about war. (It is remarkable how much of the good poetry in English written about the Second World War was written by civilians: Edith Sitwell,

---

[2] *Contemporary Verse* (Penguin Books, 1950), p. 246.

Dylan Thomas, T. S. Eliot, Stephen Spender and Gascoyne all wrote fine poetry during the Blitz.) Gascoyne is decidedly *un*decided about the events: the War is seen as an ignorant disaster, in which neither side can claim the moral right. Perhaps it was precisely his total estrangement—as Paris-oriented ex-Surrealist from culture, as pacifist from the War effort, as night-walking poet from social 'responsibility'—that gave Gascoyne in one way a more real appreciation of his position than partial integration in the corpus of society could have. For the poet is always alienated. Gascoyne's alienation was unusually complete. There could be no better symbol of the essential alienation of the poet than this Francophile ex-Surrealist pacifist wandering through a utility England.

Gascoyne's finest expression of his position comes, I think, in the poems of the 'forties. Few poems express better than 'Reported Missing' the pathos and the absurdity of the poet's vocation in the modern world: opening a door in a house (which he does not own), the poet finds himself in a bedroom left as it was when the man who had occupied it left it. The poem is an account of the poet's discovery of the unexpected room, of the 'subjugating charm' of the missing soldier's eyes in the bedside photograph; then comes the commemoration,

> a few unasked-for lines
> Which must leave the essential once more all but quite unsaid.
> ('Reported Missing')

It is difficult to imagine a finer balance of sympathy: one is moved equally by the kept-up room which is in the process of becoming a mausoleum, by the waste of the young man's life, and by the pathos of the poet's own intrusion. Somehow these 'few unasked-for lines' lie close to the nature of poetry itself, an activity which, for all its ancient prestige, remains, outside the universities, a curiously marginal thing.

If the poet's lines are always unasked-for—even if requested, those he supplies will never be quite what was wanted—so the poet himself is always a vagrant, whether married or single, jobless or in work. Gascoyne's poem 'A Vagrant' skirts and traverses some extremely treacherous terrain. The possible false stances are legion, from the self-justification of the poet 'in whom the means of livelihood swallowed up the primary vocation',[3] to the ranting of the bohemian parasite battening on to bourgeois fat, or the scrawny failure's whine of self-approbation. What Gascoyne's interior monologue discusses has been the poet's theme since Rimbaud. The approach is admirable, pugnaciously anti-bourgeois, yet un-shrill, and without a trace of hollow self-vindication. Indeed its final message is to admit a failure as total in its way as that of the bourgeois he despises. He admits that the 'job-barker's programme' (an invitation to join the crowd and get fitted up with a niche, a cell and a prison-number) cannot really appal him with its prospect of work-fatigue, since his own routine (that of the jobless poet) 'wears the will out just as well'. Indeed he says, the job-barker's line

> may in the end
> Provide me with a noose with which to hang myself should I
> Discover the strain of doing nothing is too great
> A price to pay for spiritual integrity.

His contempt for the 'sleepy-sickness-rotted sheep' (the wage-slaves) is desperately close to the worst kind of adolescent posing; yet something in the tone, the unusual fullness, perhaps, of the contempt (he writes as though no one had ever tackled the subject before), tells us that he is on the level, and that his decision to join the outsiders, 'the lowest tribe of patient prisoners and ex-convicts and all the victims of the guilt/Society dare not admit its own' really amounts to something. Perhaps it is the straightforward admission towards the close of the poem that his own life is filled with boredom and emptiness, for all his scorn of bourgeois 'sleepy-sickness':

> Awkward enough, awake, yet although anxious still just sane,
> I stand still in my quasi-dereliction, or but stray
> Slowly along the quais towards the ends of afternoons
> That lead to evenings empty of engagements.
>
> ('A Vagrant')

It is fascinating to observe the echo of the Surrealist wit made to yield so much: the unexpected transition from space to time

---

[3] Spender, *Engaged in Writing*, p. 20.

reminds us of the witty metamorphosis of the early poems, yet here it carries the weight of a lifetime's labour.

If we compare this poem with another interior monologue of similar purpose (Roy Fuller's 'The Ides of March'), we shall get a good idea of the relations between Gascoyne's tradition and that of the school of Auden. Where Fuller's poem closes on a wincing ambiguity, the conflict the whole piece is made of still unresolved, Gascoyne's ends with a question, half-rhetorical, half-real, which raises the possibility it apparently despairs of:

> What, oh what can
> A vagrant hope to find to take the place of what was once
> Our expectation of the Human City, which each man might
> Morning and evening, every day, lead his own life, and Man's?

Fuller's Brutus also in good faith wishes to build the Human City, and we are reminded that both Fuller and Gascoyne shared an early faith in Marx. The winces of embarrassment, self-doubt and irony of Fuller's poem are familiar properties in Auden's tradition. Brutus begins by laughing at himself—

> Fireballs and thunder . . .
> A vulgar score, but not inappropriate
> To my romantic, classic situation.
>
> ('The Ides of March')

And he goes on to give us a clear account of the anomalies of his own self-contradictory position. Too clear, we might feel. Turning to Gascoyne's more laboured, sober poem we cannot fail to be struck by the contrast between 'the self-ironical, self-distrustful attitudes' of the poet who hates his bourgeois position enough to ridicule it but not to change it, and the poet who has thought the bourgeois life incompatible with 'spiritual integrity' and has gone so far as to refuse it in consequence. Hence, there is nothing in Fuller's poem so simple or so moving as Gascoyne's recognition that the stupid carousers and himself are gnawed by the same knowledge,

> knowledge of its lack of *raison d'etre*
> The city's lack and mine are much the same.
>
> ('A Vagrant')

The difference between the ironies of Fuller and this plain, painful statement is like the difference between the wry dissonances of the wrong-note school of Stravinsky and *Les Six*, and the total harmonic testament of Schönberg and Webern. The basis of Stravinsky's harmony is the concord spiced with the wrong-note, just as the basis of the Auden school is the 'normal' attitude spiced with self-irony, self-mockery. Gascoyne, like Webern and Schönberg, saw the necessity of a fundamental break with the conventional. Whence, the greater importance of Gascoyne for young poets today. To achieve the self-knowledge that counts, something more profound, more far-reaching is required than a refurbishing of the old with irony; just as Schönberg saw the necessity of a fundamental re-thinking of the very matter of musical thought, so the great poets of the century have found it necessary to exorcise the clogging properties of what we might call diatonic poetry. Irony in poetry could only serve a purpose as limited as the wrong-note tricks and pastiche of the Diaghilev Stravinsky, or the earlier self-mockery of Laforgue. The man who mocks himself probably does so in order to avoid a more fundamental re-volution within himself. In parading his self-awareness he keeps himself from self-knowledge.

In much of the poetry he wrote after the war, then, Gascoyne seems lost—lost in a world of friends now married, lost in the demotic, egalitarian England of Attlee and Cripps, lost in the cultural turmoil in which the Surrealists in France were also confessing bankruptcy.[4] The poetry is correspondingly heavy-hearted, plated with observations that only occasionally raise themselves above a disenchanted accuracy. Yet the proof and reward of a lifetime's dedication to poetry and the life of a poet (in a more serious sense than that of the saloon-bar parasite, the part-time publisher or the don) was only to come much later, when Gascoyne wrote the work that seems likely to be his greatest achievement, the *Night Thoughts* of 1955.

What 'Noctambules' is to the world of sexual embroilment, *Night Thoughts* is to the wider-reaching world of meditation—a cry of and for sympathy. It begins in the world of the Sur-realist poems, of 'Noctambules' and *Nightwood*—the ocean of

[4] *Viz.* Tzara's *Le Surréalisme et l'Après-Guerre* (Paris, 1947).

night in which isolated souls founder. It is the world, in fact, of *avant garde* art since Baudelaire and Rimbaud. Yet what is perhaps most impressive about a poem whose seriousness any-way puts to shame the socialized decline of most of the poet's contemporaries, is that what begins in *avant garde* isolation ends in the generalized human condition. Through no conscious act of extension, Gascoyne's theme becomes genuinely universal: it is all men the poet addresses at the end when he writes:

> Greetings to the solitary. Friends, fellow beings, you are not strangers to us. We are closer to one another than we realise. Let us remember one another at night, even though we do not know each other's names.

The poem is, in a way, the triumph and the vindication of the symbolist *veillée*, the nocturnal vigil so familiar in poetry since Rimbaud. The vigil is of course much older than Rimbaud. In English we can return to Edward Young, whose title Gascoyne borrows, but farther, to Vaughan, whose poem 'The Night' really inaugurates the whole tradition. No modern English poet can be unaware of great moments in Wordsworth, such as the apocalyptic passage in Book X of *The Prelude*[5]; or of Coleridge's 'Frost at Midnight'. Yet still it is probably to the later generation of Hölderlin and Leopardi and in particular to the child of this generation, Rimbaud himself, that the modern poet turns most naturally;—Rimbaud raised the *veillée* to a way of life, and in doing so, provided his successors with the great image few of them have been able to resist for long. In *Les Illuminations* Rimbaud speaks of the poet's lone lighted room in the sleeping city as a ship:

> *Les lampes et les tapis de la veillée font le bruit des vagues, la nuit, le long de la coque et autour du steerage. . . . La mer de la veillée.*

In 'Enfance' the room is a subterranean cell; later, in *Une Saison en Enfer*, it is submarine, suffering beneath the keel of the morning—

[5] Wordsworth, *The Prelude*, Book X, 11, pp. 70–93. 'With unextinguished taper I kept watch.'

*Un grand vaisseau d'or au-dessus de moi, agite ses pavillons multicolores
dans les brises du matin.*

(Rimbaud, *Une Saison en Enfer*)

Gascoyne himself sails dangerously close to the wind:

> My message is sent out on the waves
> Of a black boundless sea to where you drift
> Each in a separate lit room, as though on rafts
> Survivors of the great lost ship, *The Day.*

(*Night Thoughts*)

It is probably Gascoyne's own need to extend outwards to reach
others (that need for comradeship so magnificently absent from
Rimbaud) that lifts *Night Thoughts* so high above the academic
veillée poem.[6] The poem, in fact, does not exist to demonstrate
the poet's own specialness; it does not even strive after those
spiritual rewards Rimbaud sought with such tenacity, though
this search is the essence of the vigil. While *Night Thoughts* is in
one sense the culminating poem in the European *avant garde*
movement, in another it annuls the *raison d'être* of the *avant
garde.* Its confessed aim is

> to break through the silence and the noise in the great night
> Of all that is unknown to us, that weighs down in between
> One lonely human being and another. . . .

The will of the whole poem is to break through to those other
islands of humanity, to reach the drifting rafts of those who,
being alone, are also ready to make contact. Gascoyne's *avant
gardisme* at this point joins him on to the rest of the human race in
the most surprising way: by cultivating in the extreme degree
the isolationist anti-conformism of the traditional *avant garde*
poet, he discovers in himself the need which can actually succeed in bringing people together, where all the injunctions and
exhortations of humanism and religion have failed.

Hence, although the 'Megalometropolitan Carnival' (Part 2
of the poem) mocks the hellish world of Everyman as consumer-
society addict, it is nevertheless Everyman he finds himself

---

[6] As an example of which see John Holloway, 'The High Tide'.

speaking to, not publically, as in Beethoven's Ninth Symphony, but privately, in isolation. The satirical central section of the poem recalls Buñuel rather than Dante, and reminds us that good satire is only to be written by one who knows himself to be part of what he satirizes. The satirist must know himself also to be a Yahoo. Gascoyne's attitude towards the neurosis-ridden, barbiturate-sodden inferno of Megalometropolis is too much the distant disdain of the untainted outsider, and the overriding impression is of enlightened priggishness.[7]

The final section, *Encounter with Silence*, breaks through to an encounter not just with silence but with what silence masks, the Universe, nothingness, oneself. The lifetime's intent listening yields first the harvest of (almost) imperceptible sounds:

Decrepid dust-blown tinkling of a crumbling pagoda's bells . . .
Intensely complex tight-screwedup tattoo of tiny drums
The velvet-padded hammering of life-blood's changing pulse
The pulse of changing life is the deep underlying constant.

Once again we must admire the sheer meticulousness of the detail; these are the *trouvailles* of the seer, the mystic, not of the Literary Man out for effects. Moreover, the great sense of the 'deep underlying constant' clearly does derive from the intent concentrated waiting of the three preceding lines. The great abstraction is one Gascoyne has won the right to use. These 'observations' could have been gained only from long concentration. Concentration on what, though? On nothing, it appears, for silence, as the poet discovers, is illusory, a mesh of tiny sounds 'to which it would be too tiring to pay conscious attention'. Similarly, what stretches out before the poet's eye in the country night is not Nothingness, either, but everything—the Universe. It *is* nothing and the nothing is everything. At last, the problem of Will that has dogged Gascoyne all along is solved into its component dilemmas. All the while, he had been waiting, listening, tiring himself 'with doing nothing'. Yet what had it been? What was it he was listening to? and for? This is the dilemma of symbolism—to listen, to wait, to attend, yet to nothing, or rather, 'an utterly unqualifiable something'.

---

[7] It is unfortunately this section which has been chosen to represent *Night Thoughts* in the *Penguin Modern Poets* selection.

All the while, that is, it was his will that was preventing him from hearing—actually hearing nothing—'the nothing that is All'. He had been deafened by the act of listening.

Hence, he discovers—in the act of writing—that 'it is I myself that am nothing'. This is not to be confused with a statement of modesty or humility ('Humility is the only virtue'); it is an epistemological not a moral discovery. Yet this epistemological discovery—made by hearing what he was hearing—entails humility, or rather makes humility possible. In this way, art moves from the Humean 'is' to the Humean 'ought'. With the humility comes companionship. Gascoyne comes out the other side of himself, and having done so, returns to his own ghosted body, and to his wife.

> All of us talk and talk of all and everything and shut ourselves up in ourselves and with the curtain of the words shut out the fact that we are blind and dumb.

The dread of nothingness has made it possible for him to realize that 'yet he was a man'. When he returns to himself, to his wife,

> The open air, the space about him had first stirred his heart, he lifted up his heart and it had opened, and the wind that blows when it will and comes from nowhere that we know and passes on as unaccountably, had inspired it with its more vital, lighter, unrestricted and revivifying breath.

There are no shortcuts to this wisdom. Nor can it be summarized as I have seemed to do here. In David Gascoyne's poetry we can trace a genuine progress from darkness to light.

As far as the argument of this book is concerned, David Gascoyne's poetry is especially interesting because its tone and seriousness are so English: paradoxically, Gascoyne's Surrealism, his choice of the European rather than the Anglo-Saxon tradition, helped him preserve that very quality for which the great poetry of the existential tradition is so precious. The almost morbid earnestness of Gascoyne's verse places it alongside that of Edward Thomas and Thomas Hardy, rather than that of Eluard and Char. Yet this paradox is really quite easy to unravel. The main purpose of the present book, indeed, is to show that the various strategies adopted by the poets I am treating as lying outside the ironist-intellectualist tradition were adopted precisely because they helped the poets who adopted them keep in touch with a more exalted, a more truly serious and committed conception of poetry than that which restricted the compass of poets like Auden and Empson and their American equivalents.

7 Dylan Thomas:
Merlin as sponger

Dylan Thomas, another poet of stature who escaped irony by embracing Surrealism, acquired a fatal kind of popularity—acceptance by the literate, non-specialist middle class. The intellectualist response is fairly represented by the review Robin Mayhead wrote for *Scrutiny*[1] when the *Collected Poems* appeared. Having derided in assured tones Thomas's admirers, he goes on to complain about Thomas's special mannerism, 'this habit of clutching at the apparently striking image that comes to hand, without a working out of its implications or a proper consideration of its appropriateness.' Far less radically oriented critics have made the point before, and one would suspect the Leavisite critic who did not make it. But although one can agree about the inchoate and unrewarding nature of some of Thomas's poems, it is difficult to agree that Thomas's images came to hand in quite the way that is implied in the above quotation. Mr Mayhead also observes that 'Mr. Thomas is characteristically borne on a kind of Shelleyan "aery surge" through a dazzling flood of image and sensation.' Although this idea is not worked out, and is indeed abandoned for other criticisms, there is implicit here an accusation that Thomas wrote in a coma during which images came to him like rays of light and for no better reason. One gathers that there is a parallel case to be found in Shelley; Thomas is the modern Shelley, and Shelley of no greater consequence than his modern self.

Now not only does this betray an extraordinary lack of interest in English Romantic verse—Mr Mayhead cannot have read more than a few Odes and the essay in *Revaluation*—but a fundamental misunderstanding of the function of imagery in

[1] *Scrutiny*, Vol. XIX, 1952–3.

symbolist and surrealist poetry. It is true that there are reservations to be made about aspects of Thomas's output. The man-in-the-street's protest against the wilful meaninglessness of many of the early and middle poems is not without foundation.[2] It is true that he frequently did not write to make 'sense' either to others or to himself. Much of his verse was written in accordance with the principles of Surrealism, in so far as Thomas wrote in accordance with anything. The output of Surrealism is exceedingly uneven, largely because of the hit-or-miss nature of its processes: a Surrealist image is either right or wrong, with no intermediate stages possible. In the end, pure Surrealism (Surrealism that adheres to the doctrine of arbitrariness propagated by André Breton, the Confucius of the movement) evens out all talent: the poems become arbitrary selections of images, and Picasso is as 'good' a poet as Eluard. Yet it served its purpose, in literature as in painting, and even, as Pierre Schaeffer demonstrated, in music. Certainly, the grip of poems such as Thomas's 'Poem in October', 'And Death Shall have no Dominion' and 'Do not go gentle into that good night' has passed the limits of phrase-forging, and the fluent incoherence of the overtly Surrealist pieces, for example,

> A stem cementing, wrestled up the tower,
> Rose maid and male,
> Or, masted venus, thro' the paddler's bowl
> Sailed up the sun
>
> ('A Grief Ago')

in which the sexual basis of the imagery does not maintain any hold upon the visual framework of the poem. It is, certainly, difficult to see the value of many of these poems, except in the hints they divulge of Thomas's psyche. There can, as well, be little value for the poet himself, who is denied the satisfaction of objective form, and the benefits of discipline. But the ultimate consequence of the Surrealist apprenticeship (which exacted its own kind of discipline) was to give Thomas's verse a total independence of the ruling literary cliques and conventions—of irony and the sclerosis attendant upon it:

---

[2] See for example Professor Joad's diagnosis of decadence in Thomas's verse, *Decadence* (London, 1948), p. 312. Joad's repugnance is echoed at a higher critical level by Dr Davie, *Articulate Energy*, pp. 125–6.

> Not for the proud man apart
> From the raging moon I write
> On these spindrift pages
> Nor for the towering dead
> With their nightingales and psalms. . . .
>
> ('In my Craft or Sullen Art')

The exalted tone, the powerful exploitation of a richly loaded vocabulary—these qualities, so important in Thomas's work, reflect a vision unhindered by the self-conscious cramp of most of his contemporaries. Surrealism had, moreover, given Thomas an automaticity of hand which selection was to alchemise into something Shakesperean: poems like 'Fern Hill' and 'Poem in October' have an amalgam of clarity and complexity difficult to match in English poetry after Keats.

There is on the face of it no reason whatever why the verbal complexity of Thomas's poetry should not impress the Empsonian critic as much as it impressed a practitioner as wily as Theodore Roethke[3]; or the strength of his language the Leavisite critic. No poet ever played more cleverly or resourcefully upon the ambiguities and overtones of the English language than Thomas, or showed a greater sensitivity to the sources of its strength. If poetry could really be defined in Pound's terms as language charged to the utmost with meaning, Thomas's poetry would approach as close to the ideal limit as any poetry of recent times, including Swinburne's. My hypotheses are disingenuous, of course: I am aware that Thomas's researches were often carried on within a kind of local vacuum, word breeding word, association association. But it is also unfair to concentrate exclusively, as Dr Davie has, on Thomas's most inchoate passages, to try to prove that Thomas's language for all its concreteness, is really inert through lack of syntax.[4] In point of fact, Thomas's best verse—and there is enough of it —exploits syntax in an intelligent and rather magnificently simple way. The point could be illustrated by a number of poems—'And Death shall have no Dominion', 'Caught in an octagon of unaccustomed light', 'I have longed to move away'. Let us take one of the superb Blitz elegies instead, the 'Refusal to

---

[3] See *The Glass House* by Allan Seager (New York, 1968), pp. 192–3.
[4] *Viz. Articulate Energy*, pp. 125–6.

mourn the death, by fire, of a child in London'. The first two of
the poem's four six-lined stanzas, and the first line of the third,
make up one powerful compound sentence, composed of two
conditional clauses and a main clause. These lines state the
intention of refusal, and the ample scope afforded by the conditional clauses allows Thomas to create a rich, clear and
complex image of 'life'. The third stanza itself explains the
refusal—although the orator's impassioned hauteur has already
sufficiently given us the reason—as a refusal to murder 'the
mankind of her going'. Finally, the last stanza—the first to use
the present tense—changes key, and darkens its tone-colour:

> Deep with the first dead lies London's daughter,
> Robed in the long friends,
> The grains beyond age, the dark veins of her mother,
> Secret by the unmourning water
> Of the riding Thames.
>
> ('A Refusal to Mourn')

The whole poem is braked by that rhythm of the 'riding' water;
it remains for the orator to close his words with a now famous
aphorism, 'After the first death, there is no other', which gives
the lie to the poem's title. But in fact the whole poem is sustained on its high note of compassionate indignation precisely by
the intention of refusal: the rush of the exciting but carefully
manipulated religious words—the 'round zion of the water
bead' that so puzzled Professor Joad, but seems to possess such a
simple mystical significance now—gives us all the veneration for
the life from which the child has been excluded. Like so many
of Thomas's best poems, it is a celebrating and a regretting at
the same time. The curiously beautiful timbre of Thomas's
voice, in fact, surely derives from this sure mélange of life and
mortality: he has such a powerful instinct for something un-
dying, yet such a fine nose for the decaying flesh. He is a
strangely pure poet, for all the clogging facticity of his beloved
Anglo-Saxon monosyllables—numb, dumb, wax, track, etc.

What galls the ironist critics, I fancy, is this doggedly incor-
ruptible tone in such a soiled, beer-swilling hearty. But a more
serious failure has been the blindness to the true role of the
rhetoric in the verse. Charles Tomlinson, who should know

better, lets this allow him to prefer an utterly unremarkable
poem by Austin Clarke to the most powerful of modern
sonorities:[5]

> Myself
> The grievers
> Grieve
> Among the street burned to tireless death
> A child of a few hours
> With its kneading mouth
> Charred on the black breast of the grave
> The mother dug, and its arms full of fires.
>
> ('Ceremony after a Fire Raid')

Thomas has found here a form which actually looks like a
knell, and soon we come to the inevitable clang, the booming
phrase, because sooner or later Thomas cannot resist the big
effect—

> Among the street burned to tireless death . . . .

In the Surrealist trick evocation, the death (ie., expiration) of
the street turns into Death personified among the mobile
flames ('tireless'). The idea runs slickly off the tongue, as
though Thomas were a declaiming actor, inserting knowing
asides. And this *is* Thomas—a strolling player, with more than a
little Vincent Crummles about him, a sonorous lay-preacher,
willing to speak a few lines for a small consideration. . . . His
skill and sincerity (sentimental, he easily warms to his work)
nearly always guarantee that the customer is satisfied. At this
stage, I need hardly say that I regard this as perfectly valid
behaviour in a poet, far more valid indeed than the really
unattached, unasked-for 'responsibility' of the academic poet,
whose confessions of inadequacy and intimations of unease are
worth little to anyone but the poet himself.

The continual playing upon and with words evident in the
example quoted above (the pun, syntactical and semantic, on
'the mother dug', the deliberate misuse of the preposition
'among') became obsessional as Thomas got older: far from

[5] Charles Tomlinson, 'Poetry Today', B. Ford (ed.), *The Modern Age*, *The
Pelican Guide to Modern Literature*, vol. VII, pp. 460–61.

being 'unthinking', indeed, as the Scrutineers suggested, his
poetry, like Hart Crane's, errs on the side of over-deliberateness.
The poetry of Empson is classically limpid by contrast with the
incessant punning and verbal harmonizing of Thomas's. Often
it is drowned out by the rhetoric, to which it is always however
lending subtle support. Robin Mayhead could hardly, in fact,
have mistaken his man more spectacularly. Consider for example the following extract from a less endearing side of
Thomas's mind:

> In fountains of origin gave up their love
> Along her innocence glided
> Juan aflame and savagely young King Lear
> Queen Catherine howling bare
> And Samson drowned in his hair
> ('Into her lying down head')

The associations of the images court banality: Juan aflame,
Lear savage, Catherine bare, and, crowning gesture, Samson
well in need of a haircut! In 'Fern Hill' we meet 'happy as the
grass was green' and 'Once below a time'. The boy in the
poem changes colour in six lines, from 'green and carefree' to
'golden in the mercy of his means', because, having fixed
firmly the image of apples, the poet sees green as the obvious
adjective for immaturity, then, proceeding to images of
happiness, it is not youth and growth that need to be symbolized,
but the birthday card memories of endless days of boyhood,
Talbot Baines Reed and the 'Ode to Autumn', why of course,
golden days, so down goes golden. The use of it here is characteristic of all Thomas's writing. One can feel throbbing the
heart of the poet, ready to squeeze every drop out of every
image. Nothing is too low. *Under Milk Wood* was the logical
conclusion—a vast, timeless battlefield in which Thomas could
shoot every cannon in his armoury, every banality, every old
music-hall joke—mother-in-laws, arsenic-brooding husbands,
frustrated old maids—in it goes, helter-skelter, and the good
images perish with the rest. Perish, or survive, for *Under Milk
Wood* remains, for all its vulgarity, very much alive.

The methods he employed are relentless: the old hackneyed
associations stand shoulder-to-shoulder with the new ain't-I-
awful bombshells: 'happy as the heart was long ... my sky-

blue trades ... the lamb-white days ... fire green as grass.'
It is not merely that Thomas did not spurn the age-old
associations, but that the whole conception of imagery in his
mature work is completely deliberate, and within this deliberate framework, he achieved bright effects. I do not think
much would be gained by quoting at greater length, or by
analysing one of his poems right through. It would be a simple
matter of repeating again and again that Dylan Thomas wrote
as consciously as anyone of his time, that the effects in his verse
are considered for their rhetorical effect, their power of surface
suggestion, and their ability to maintain the surface texture of
colour and noise. The reference to Shelley therefore is absurd.
Linking Thomas with Shelley is itself a fair enough measure of
the misunderstanding both poets have suffered in the ironist
era. The question of status does not enter into it, it is a question
of difference of kind.

Dylan Thomas's name is still associated with the New
Apocalypse: it is possibly of him that Mr Alvarez is thinking
when he refers to 'choking incoherence' as the defining weakness of 'forties poetry.[6] But really Thomas has little in common
with the Apocalypse, and nothing at all with the willed loose-
ness of George Barker and W. S. Graham. No poet was ever
more conscious of what he was doing. Surrealism gave him a
belief in the absoluteness of imagery, and imparted to his verse
the swinging fluency of contour it never lost; it certainly did not
offer what he never took—a brief for not thinking about what he
was doing.

It is natural to think of David Gascoyne when considering
Dylan Thomas, if only because they were the outstanding
British poets of their time who availed themselves of the Surrealist discipline. Further than this, the comparison does little
to help us. Thomas's Surrealist imagination was as fluent and
unanchored as the *Mabinogion*, Gascoyne's as concerned and
painstaking as *Beowulf*. They chose Surrealism for different if
related reasons. Gascoyne required a more interesting meta-
physic than English life afforded, Thomas protection from a
snide literary world.

Thomas's strategy was one of the classic modern gambits: a
country-boy scared of the metropolitans, he threw up the

[6] Introduction to *The New Poetry* (London, 1963), p. 20.

Surrealist word-wall to shield a basically shy and simple personality from hard-boiled scepticism. It was only when he had won
respect and reputation (largely by dazzling the London critics
with an incoherence they mistook for Sybilline—'blinding them
with science'), that he began to express more naturally the
exalted and truly naïve vision he had of the countryside of his
childhood home, South Wales. His *Eighteen Poems* bewildered
the literary world of 1936: they appeared to come from beyond a
frontier, like the delphic utterances of a Cocteau:

> I fellowed sleep who kissed me in the brain . . . .

'I fellowed sleep' is probably Thomas's most deftly ungraspable
Surrealist piece: it recalls the dream scenes of Chirico and
Chagall with a Celtic fluency of movement beyond David
Gascoyne:

> I fled the earth and, naked, climbed the weather
> Reaching a second ground far from the stars;
> And there we wept, I and a ghostly other,
> My mothers-eyed, upon the tops of trees;
> I fled that ground as lightly as a feather, . . .
>
> ('I fellowed sleep')

The determinedly 'concrete' verbiage, too ('each grave-
gabbing cloud') is purified of the Anglo-Saxon clogginess that
so often drags Thomas into thickets of obscurity:

> How light the sleeping in this soily star,
> How deep the waking in the worlded clouds, ...

To say that this poem is 'ungraspable' is not of course to say
that it is incomprehensible: on the contrary, it is not even
difficult. Its dream action is perfectly fluent, and the questions
one suspends are questions that can't really be framed. Essentially it inhabits a world one feels Thomas had access to simply
as a Celt: Surrealism connected up with a deep layer in
Thomas's being—the Celtic a-logicality. Thomas's Surrealist
poems are often merely catalogues of mystical yet fanciful
transmogrifications, in which his own being and body is
scattered through the physical world—

> My world is cypress, and an English valley . . .
> I piece my flesh that rattled on the yards
> Red in an Austrian volley.
> I hear, through dead men's drums, the riddled lads,
> Strewing their bowels from a hill of bones,
> Cry Eloi to the guns.
>
> ('My World is pyramid')

The almost carefree (yet somehow not joyous) mysticism of this verse is something one can find in the *Mabinogion* itself, and in the lyrics of the Irish *Danta Gradha*.

Dylan Thomas's sense of the poet's vocation is ancient, as old as Merlin. He will not express himself 'plainly' (whatever that might turn out to mean). He will not say, for example, 'I have written nothing for three months', but,

> On no work of words now for three lean months in the bloody
>   Belly of the rich year. . . .
>
> ('On no work of words')

Again we have to remind ourselves that the notion of poetry's necessarily being possessed of the virtues of good prose, and in general straightforwardly mirroring a consecutive line of reasoned sense, though not new, is at least isolably neo-classic. Dylan Thomas reminds us of an older conception of poetry, and one which in many ways, like Milton's, makes better sense: for after all, no moral or rational theory can really justify poetry except as mnemonic. Its original appearance historically is mysterious until we remember by how much it antedates linear thought and discursive prose.[7] Thomas's rhetoric, like his bardic stance, his unfailingly exalted tone and his inability to make the 'plain' statement, have a much longer and more impressive lineage than the reasonable tidiness of academic verse, with its Aristotelian roots. What, after all, *is* the function of verse? As argument, as reason, what are its clauses, its terms? None, that could persuade us to forfeit the serviceability of discursive prose. There must be other reasons for choosing to express oneself in verse. The very least we can say is that

---

[7] See Cassirer, *Language and Myth*, trs. S. K. Langer (New York, 1946); especially the final chapter, 'The Power of Metaphor'.

Thomas's—in so far as one can extrapolate them—are as good as any.

This is not to encourage a MacLuhan-ish retreat into primitivism. It is, though, to reject a certain parochialism in much modern criticism (I am thinking of New critics like Yvor Winters) which seeks to impose upon poetry a narrowly rationalistic and ethical function. The conception of poetry embodied in Dylan Thomas's verse is both older and more convincing than academic puritanism acknowledges. For there is always something savage and regressive in good poetry, no matter how urbane its appearance and tone. Alexander Pope is perhaps the best example in English: what basic (and base) antipathies and animosities his intricate formalism conceals! Dante, too, enacts in the *Inferno* primitive rituals of vengeance and aggression, consigning his personal enemies to everlasting torment. Behind these ceremonies lies the ancient belief in the power of vocables and incantation to inflict pain or bring relief. 'The original bond between the linguistic and the mythico-religious consciousness is primarily expressed in the fact that all verbal structures appear as *also* mythical entities, endowed with certain mythical powers, that the Word, in fact, becomes a sort of primary force, in which all being and doing originated' (Cassirer, *op. cit.* p. 45). This belief in the Word Magic connects up with the pre-civilized regressiveness of poetry like Dylan Thomas's, which restores to perception the oceanic stage of a society which genuinely believed in magical transformations:

> Flower, flower the people's fusion,
> O light in zenith, the coupled bud,
> And the flame in the flesh's vision.
> Out of the sea, the drive of oil,
> Socket and grave, the brassy blood,
> Flower, flower, all, all and all.

In such a process of dissolution and restoration, Dylan Thomas remakes the world.

It is the wholeness of his dedication to himself and to his role which most distinguishes Thomas from those other contemporaries or elder contemporaries who also chose to

answer the predicament of the mid-twentieth century intellectual through myth, or through some older conception of the poet
than the post-Romantic looker-into-the-heart. Wholeness of
dedication, and of course, the possession of the armoury that
counts—subtlety and power of rhythm, purity of sensibility,
sheer word-power. Do we have to return to the authority of
Pushkin to remind ourselves that learning, intellectual gravity
and earnestness cannot serve to outweigh talent? *Mozart i
Salieri* spells out a lesson many a cultural savant has found
difficult to swallow. Charles Lever no doubt thought himself
a more 'serious' and important novelist than Dickens. Robert
Graves, with more justification, clearly regards himself as
vastly more significant than Dylan Thomas. If Graves were not
in general so unreasonable about his contemporaries, one
would be more puzzled at his failure to see in Thomas a
descendant of the old Welsh bards studied in *The White
Goddess*. The continuity of tradition, the body of lore and
Knowledge, these of course have gone. But that goes with the
entire development of modern civilization: Graves writes as
though it were mere possession of arcane lore that made Taliesin
a poet and that repossessing himself of that lore he can put himself in touch with a current of 'truth' denied his contemporaries.
But this is from any point of view a fantastic belief, a cancella-
tion of the past thousand years. Sure enough when we turn to
Graves's poetry we find not a reincarnation of the old bards but
a highly accomplished inheritor of the sixteenth-century love
poets, filtered through the sensibility of the Georgians. His love
poems have their content prescribed by the Romance tradition,
and lack the true mystic force of the old poetry which he
admires so much, and of which we catch echoes in Dylan
Thomas. Characteristically, Graves fails to consummate his
imagery. In 'Love in Barrenness', for instance, the north wind
image is beautifully handled, but faced with what to do with it,
Graves produces a couplet so little relevant as to be able to
conclude *any* love poem:

> O wingless Victory, loved of men,
> Who could withstand your beauty then?

Every discrete part of a poem should have the air of being created for and of its own context, and for no other. In this poem,

the image is arresting, but the poem is unable to round it off—
to consummate his image. Having something to say is a common way of expressing this. Giving significance is another.

In Edwin Muir's poetry also a technical conservatism accompanies a regressiveness of attitude, only in his case the
concern is not with the mythology of Romantic love, but with
the most serious appraisal of twentieth-century man. Muir, one
recalls, was a co-translator of Kafka, and the Czech allegorist
did more for the poet than (obviously) inspire the title of one of
his volumes (*The Labyrinth*). Kafka's influence emerges in a
general tendency towards parable and allegory to the detriment of a more direct addressing of experience. Perhaps a
majority of the pieces in *Collected Poems 1921–1958* have a
literary or mythological basis; and where such a basis is absent
there is frequently a tendency to treat the subject with a
somewhat portentous detachment. Poems like 'The late wasp'
and 'The late Swallow' for instance parallel those later poems
of Stephen Spender's in which an impersonation of Rilke or
Seferis usurps the poet's own voice. Muir's wasp for instance
dives down 'through nothing and through despair'; his swallow
'shakes out ... pinions long untried'. We know what has
happened here: too long a sojourn among the great writers of
the past has gradually informed the poet with a sense of
importance which makes the natural treatment of the actual
seem simply beneath him. The fact is that that great literature
was itself created out of naturalness, even if it was often a
conventionalized, rhetorical naturalness. One need not em-
brace the modern cult of the wholly natural style to feel that
Muir has become detached from his own fundamental sensibleness here. I have already mentioned[8] an excellent example of
the actual subtlety of feeling which Muir displays when he
ignores the tone of the classics and looks at what is going on
around him: 'The Wayside Station' is superior to most of
Muir's poetry largely in virtue of its 'realism'. Occasionally,
however, Muir produced poems which appeared to justify or at
least redeem the eclecticism—too occasionally, in my view to
justify the high estimate some have of him. A familiar example
is the often-anthologized poem, 'The Combat', which provided
in the early 'fifties an allegory of war astoundingly illustrated in

[8] See p. 111 above.

Vietnam. The poem is wholly successful, and the allegorical presentation positively instrumental in producing its curious effect of pathos and alarm. How oddly familiar, for instance, is the imperialist antagonist, a dream image of bellicosity which conflates several war-mythologies without restricting itself to any:

> Body of leopard, eagle's head
> And whetted beak, and lion's mane,
> And frost-grey hedge of feathers spread
> Behind—he seemed of all things bred.

A satiric reference to the melting-pot theory, one would have thought; the opponent at any rate might have come from a G.I.'s nightmare of the Vietcong: 'A soft round beast as brown as clay'. At first, there seems to be no contest—'One would have said beyond a doubt / This was the very end of the bout'— except that 'the creature would not die'. And at the end of the poem, it is still going on, the eagle throwing in bigger and bigger forces:

> The killing beast that cannot kill
> Swells and swells in his fury till
> You'd almost think it was despair.

The whole poem has the tone and quality of prophecy, which is to say that it is possessed of a preternatural clarity of vision which sees the future in the seeds of the present. But it also has a disturbing matter-of-factness, which serves to create the backyard quality of the allegory. Such a matter-of-factness is fatally absent from the vast majority of Muir's ballads, sonnets and parables.

But occasionally, again, the rather bland clasical tone of Muir's georgic allegoricalizing hardens into a different sort of relevance. In poems like 'The Horses' Muir explores the possibilities of science-fiction with a brilliance difficult to match in contemporary poetry:

> The radios failed; we turned the knobs; no answer.
> On the third day a warship passed us, heading north,
> Dead bodies piled on the deck. On the sixth day
> A plane plunged over us into the sea. Thereafter

Nothing; the radios dumb;
And still they stand in corners of our kitchens,
And stand perhaps, turned on, in a million rooms
All over the world.

The allegory here, of course, has popular idioms behind it.
There is no questioning the poem's superiority over most of
Muir's exercises in Kafkaesque Angst (see 'The Interrogation'
—'And still the interrogation is going on': W. H. Auden had
travelled that border-land before Muir.) But in 'The Horses'
the subtle, simple narrative can count on all our dreads, and the
archetypal horses which come and offer themselves to the
survivors complete an honest and bold schema:

Since then they have pulled our ploughs and borne our loads.
But that free servitude still can pierce our hearts.
Our life is changed; their coming our beginning.

It is just this quality of fable, morality and yet straightforward common-sense and humanity which one misses, by and
large in the work of another outstanding poet of Muir's time
who like Muir sought a structural principle in myth and arche-
type, Kathleen Raine.

Here surely is an *œuvre* that is consistently well-achieved—
few of her contemporaries have so completely mastered their
means—never less than wholly serious, and concerned with
wholly serious themes. And yet one misses something, and it is
difficult to say what. It is not intensity ('Fiends tear me to
blood / And slivers of torment'); it is not personal involvement;
it is not lucidity; or depth; or any of the usual convenient
hypostatizations critics use to rationalize their judgements. It is,
perhaps, not necessary to place Miss Raine at all: it might seem
enough to state that her *Collected Poems* contains far fewer bad
lines than those of most poets. But her intelligent, human and
orderly poetry poses the critical dilemma in a particularly acute
form. What, after all, has Dylan Thomas got that she has not?
He is not more intelligent, and she knows more about the
symbolism of religion, for instance, than he does. I suppose it is
something to do with a kind of emotional reserve that comes
through Miss Raine's verse. At any rate it is difficult to
believe that Kathleen Raine or any one for that matter has

experienced less than Emily Dickinson; and certainly no-one would want to accuse *her* of emotional reserve. It is possibly something to do with Miss Raine's perhaps excessively fluent trafficking in the archetypes: it takes a great deal of energy and inner resistance to relate the self to the world of archetypal significances as Rilke does, for instance, or Dylan Thomas, in poems like 'And Death shall have no Dominion'. Honesty and a quiet intensity are rarely absent from Miss Raine's verse, yet one might venture to suggest that the following statement, though both sincere and interesting, amounts in significance to less than it should:

> I have heard too much silence,
> listened too long to the mute sky.
> ('At the Waterfall').

This is a form of distress women poets are professionally prone to (for example Marianne Moore's 'the strange experience of beauty / its existence is too much', and numerous ejaculations of Emily Dickinson). The 'mute sky' is peculiarly Miss Raine's own; but the entire statement made somehow falls short of the surprise which is so close to the heart of poetry. This absence of surprise is explicable, it seems to me, in terms of a fundamental failure in *engagement*: Miss Raine is not, so to speak, ruthless enough, and her solitary communings with sky and landscape do have something of the air of escape about them. And if it should be felt that I am relying upon a response to Miss Raine's non-masculinity, let me give as an instance of a poet possessed of the ruthlessness of a poet of stature, Edith Sitwell.

The example of Edith Sitwell is particularly instructive. For she won through after a great deal of tricky twentyism to write major poetry after the Second World War. In her earlier verse there is something disquietingly easy in the way she rings the changes on sight and sense impressions in her efforts to re-vitalize the language. In a sickness of synaesthesia, she produces a mixture of shocks, tricks, surprises and cute interchanges of sense-mode which was from the start unlikely to stabilize the language with the spark of energy it needed after the Georgians. Her intramodal jugglings, like the acrobatics of e.e. cummings, left the language in a state of utter debilitation. It is not possible to go on for long like this—

> The wind's bastinado
> Whipt on the calico
> Skin of the macaroon
> And the black Picaroon
> Beneath the galloon
> Of the midnight sky.
>
> ('The Wind's Bastinado')

Soon everything becomes elevated like a pink cloud, everything is unusual visual and aural effects. Yet the poems she wrote during the Blitz in London and after the Hiroshima bomb rank among the finest and most serious statements about war in our time. In contrast to the dancing-tricks and the typographical clowning of the early poems, these late pieces are counterpointed harmonized recurrences of a small number of images (gold, red, corn) which seem to take command of her. It is like the moaning of a powerful harp in pain:

> The last faint spark
> In the self-murdered heart, the wounds of the sad
>   uncomprehending dark,
> The wounds of the baited bear,
> The blind and weeping bear whom the keepers beat
> On his helpless flesh . . . the tears of the hunted hare.
>
> ('Still Falls the Rain')

That she has never really been accorded the honour such poetry deserves is largely due to the hostility of the ironist era to the bohemian aura that stuck to her throughout her life. The truth is that, absurd as her arty camp was, it probably helped her retain a sense of her destiny as a poet and enabled her to win through to the serious poetry of her last period, written at an age at which most of her contemporaries had given up trying.

8 The Legacy of Auden:
the poetry of Roy Fuller,
Philip Larkin and Peter Porter

I

No doubt, hindsight will reveal a fairly judicious amalgam of Auden and Empson at work on the impressionable young poets who followed them. Apart from Dylan Thomas and the New Apocalyptics, who took a nose dive into Celtic mysticism to rid themselves of the hard sensible vision of the 'thirties, most poets of the 'forties and 'fifties took their tone from Auden, both in technique and attitude. The attitudes involved a straight, class-guilty Marxism and a fairly pitiless judgement of the poet himself and the bogusness of his role in bourgeois society. Technique followed Auden's methods—the closely assembled montage, proceeding by the steady accretion of social detail, the rhythm either matter-of-fact or inert, the stanzas sensible and conformist. Roy Fuller instantiates the type to perfection, and at his best approaches Auden's accuracy:

> Children play on the by-pass, with the peaks
> Of gasometers haunting them, and factories
> Like lingering shapes of the past. Beyond, in fields,
> Are massive artificial animals
> And haystacks like Tibetan hats—the strange
> Art of the simple. Lanes lead to villages
> Selling beer and petrol as stores to mad explorers:
> Behind the walls are superstitious rites,
> Performed under pious mottoes worked in wool.
> ('Pleasure Drive')

Fuller lacks—it is clear even in so excellent a paragraph—the brisk assurance, the sheer speed, of Auden's mind, solving

problems of rhyme and meter several lines in advance, so that
the *aperçus* fall pat into place with neither overlap nor blur. Yet
Fuller's slowness, his stolid image-gathering and number-
counting (note the pedestrian walk of his rhythm, which never
alters, no matter what metre he adopts) allow a more thorough
investigation of what he feels to be the essential corruptness of
the bourgeois artist's position. There is perhaps nothing in
Fuller Auden did not know already, and throw out *en passant*
himself. But Fuller's interior monologue, 'The Ides of March',
provides the bourgeois Marxist poet with a more perfect
persona than anything in Auden: Brutus awaits the conspirators
in his orchard, vaguely horrified and offended by the vulgar
absurdity of the whole cloak-and-dagger farce, hovering, yet
intellectually convinced of the rightness of his course. He knows,
he says, that

> what we built had no foundation
> Other than luck and my false privileged role
> In a society that I despised.
>
> ('The Ides of March')

Fuller's unremitting hounding of the poetic consciousness—its
momentary absurdities, its self-importance, its narcissism, its
corrupt pity—makes him good medicine for any young poet.
His role in this respect is roughly parallel to that of Kenneth
Rexroth in the United States. Both are (or were) Marxist, both
are savage on the ridiculously winsome dishonesties attendant
on the awareness of poetic talent, especially in a society the
poet despises. But ultimately, this mercilessly serious watch on
integrity seems, if not itself corrupting, at least disabling. For
Fuller, it is impossible for the poet to be right in anything: his
action and his inaction are alike culpable and dishonest. Revolution—a possible answer—Fuller himself rejects, as his social
position (poet-solicitor) suggests, and his Oxford lectures
emphasized. The only course left open to the poet is a continuous unmasking of himself: he can neither endorse the
society in which he finds himself placed, nor commit himself to
the anarchy of revolution. What he can do is give constant
expression to his sense of his own dishonesty. Bad faith, in the
Sartrean sense of the expression, is really the theme and sub-

stance of Roy Fuller's poetry. Like Sartre and Auden, Fuller
naturally arrived at Marxism as the most powerful condemnation of his own and his own class's guilt. The Marxism of the
English poets of the 'thirties is, as I have said, a function of
bourgeois guilt rather than a genuine political manifestation.
Fuller emphasizes the real weakness of Auden's position: class-
guilt, the mill-stone of the bourgeois poet, is not only inadequate,
it can actually succeed in drowning the sensibility that makes a
man a poet rather than a solicitor, or rather that makes him
also a poet and not *just* a solicitor. Fuller would be quick to
reply that he was just a solicitor. Yet I do not think this can
really be accepted. And at this point, we approach again the
real crux of the matter: unless the poet can regain some of that
sense of the importance of the profession of poet that informed
the work of T. S. Eliot, for example, and Yeats, it will be impossible for him to undertake any fully serious poetry in the
modern world. The attitudes and preconceptions of the Auden
tradition militate strongly against any such sense.

It would not be difficult to conclude that Fuller was not
really a poet at all: his language 'does' little, his rhythm is
pedestrian and predictable. Like Auden's, Fuller's language is
a glass through which social phenomena are observed. The
conclusion would not be justified, in fact. The particular
assemblage of Fuller's concreta testifies to a poet's pleasure in
experience, and in the 'Mythological Sonnets', in which his
debt to Auden's Freudian allegoricalizing is most apparent, he
does achieve a plasticity of marshalled *aperçus* with genuine
symbolic resonance:

> The murdered father's head leans by those doors;
> The brothers' quarrel stands behind the doom
> Of one life's sickening and recurrent wars;
> And the smooth tongue that offers love is built
> On teeth ground flat in violent dreams of guilt.
>
> ('Mythological Sonnets, XIX')

It is supremely appropriate that the sequence should end thus,
on the word 'guilt'; Fuller's Audenesque explorations end in a
cul-de-sac, from which he cannot extricate himself without
going into a stultifying reverse. For the Marxist, this reverse
has always been utopian. Fuller's most beautiful poem is at

once his most utopian, and his most despairing: an Eclipse is indeed an adequate symbol for Fuller's conception of the human condition:

> So last night while we slept the moon
> Crawled through the shadow's long black spear. . . .
> ('Eclipse')

(In passing, we may observe that, after Fuller, no one need attempt the eclipse poetically: he has done it in that image for good and for all.) Immediately after these superb lines, Fuller proses in typical 'thirties 'disillusion'—

> Finding in all that sun-ruled void
> The darkness of the human sphere.

In these lines, the limitations of Fuller's technique, and the traditional rhetoric in which it is grounded, are almost embarrassingly apparent. They conform to conventional ideas about how a poem should be made: the rhymes and stanzas set up the 'morals' which are as predictable in content and tone as they are banal in rhythm and rhyme. The poem's conclusion is in a way the last peep of Marxist optimism left in Fuller:

> I pass into the house which wears,
> As architecture must, its age:
> Upon the rotting floor the moon
> Opens its pure utopian page.

The page is new and utopian, even though the floor (or the stage suggested by the 'age' rhyme) is rotting and 'wears' its age. So that the hopelessness of the English bourgeois does not quite sink the theoretical optimism of the committed Marxist, just as the formalistic conventionalism does not quite succeed in destroying the astonishing purity of the imagery.

The versification, the stanzaic procedures, the entire poetic methodology represented in this verse, belong to the past in a significant sense. Following Auden, Fuller retains the rhetorical preconceptions of a dead tradition shattered by T. S. Eliot and requiring the insane energy and purpose of a Yeats to yield anything new in the middle of the twentieth century, but one nevertheless patiently reassembled by Auden, as though *The Waste Land* had never been written. In a real sense, the methods of Auden merely update those of the Georgians. The imagery comes from towns instead of the countryside, and Freud replaces Lewis Carroll; otherwise the techniques are not really dissimilar.

Behind this clogging traditionalism there is the residual disillusion of the ironist school. The form-content dichotomy has in fact been reaffirmed. It is apparent that for Auden and for Fuller, 'form' is a specific, bottle-like thing, a hoop the poet must jump through to prove himself a poet, a kind of penalty ritual he has to go through in a forfeits game: what the poet has forfeited is the dignity of silence, just as in giving expression to his guilt he renews it. So that the form of the poetry has ceased to have any real significance. In his essay, 'Writing', Auden compares the free verse poet to Robinson Crusoe on his desert island. Most free verse poets are, he thinks, the victims of inevitable squalor—of 'sheets on the unmade bed, and empty bottles on the unswept floor'. Thus, for Auden, stanza, rhyme and symmetry guarantee tidiness, rather than the more portentous 'order'; no specific aims or intentions are involved, just an overall sense of good housewifery.

Such a conception of 'form' must produce a poetry padded with the appurtenances of tidiness. Hence, form, for Auden and Fuller, is both a genuflexion to the reading public, and a kind of interior decoration. It confesses their guilt at the same time as it apologizes for the insolence of breaking silence by at least making the reader some sort of offering for the pains he has taken in picking up the book. As I have tried to show, Fuller's formal conservatism connects up with his inability to sustain rhythm except of a cerebral kind. Moreover, as good Marxist, he is committed to scorn the supreme bourgeois impertinence of *vers libre*. Thus, in the final analysis, Fuller's formal timidity, like Auden's, bespeaks the inner uncertainty which undermines the entire ironist tradition.

II

This absence of inner compulsion is explained by, as it explains, the loose complex of attitudes that underlie the poetry of Auden and his followers. In the earlier poets, these attitudes are subtended by a basic Marxism, which, doomed as it is to absurdity in a bourgeois community from which the poet has no intention of breaking out, withdraws from the poet's observations their ultimate significance. In the later poets, the Marxism itself, which gave at least a semblance of meaning to the poetry, has withered away to be replaced by the often churlish dumb insolence of post-war anti-establishmentism. Technically, Philip Larkin belongs to the Auden stable. His poetry is easy and lissom in gait. Rarely hard-up for a rhyme, never for an accurate observation, he accomplishes with more music, though less brilliance, than Auden, the next stage of the English intellectual's self-immolation. The Marxism has gone, leaving a residual self-distrust, leavened by wit. An early airy-fairy Romanticism was cured by the significant discovery of Thomas Hardy. 'One book I had at my bedside,' Larkin observes in his introduction to the later re-print of *The North Ship*, 'was the little blue chosen poems of Thomas Hardy.' The influence is a significant one: as so often, the English poetry influenced by intellectualist precepts is saved from the self-conscious and often pretentious cleverness of so much American verse of the same period precisely by the awareness of the hard integrity of Hardy and Thomas and Lawrence.[1]

For all the importance of the Hardy influence, Larkin can really only be said to have found himself when he had mastered the precise social annotation and self-deprecating tone of W. H. Auden. Hardy successfully pricked the Yeatsian afflatus of *The North Ship*. But it was Auden who gave Larkin his instrument, and made it easier for him to find his social orientation, though he also imparted to him a jaunty mockery of tone that has kept him permanently out of favour at Cambridge.[2]

In *The Less Deceived*, there are still vestiges of the Yeatsian poesy that served the shy-boy-who-didn't-dare to express his longings. The gracefully evasive love lyric 'If my Darling' is an excellent example. There is, moreover, evidence of a deeper

---

[1] Mr Larkin's *Oxford Book*, with its thirty-nine pages of Hardy, confirms the general point. Dr Davie's *Thomas Hardy and British Poetry* (London, 1973), also emphasizes the growing awareness in English poets of the importance of Hardy's contribution.

[2] See J. R. Newton's review of *Whitsun Weddings* in *The Cambridge Quarterly*, Vol. No. 1.

duplicity; explaining his own refusal to join in the social round,
Larkin comments

> Why be out here?
> But then, why be in there? Sex, yes, but what is sex?

Oh, come now: 'what is sex?'! The alienation of the mode
allows the shy boy to get away with it, here; but the last lines
exact savage retribution:

> both are satisfied,
> If no-one has misjudged himself. Or lied.
> ('Reasons For Attendance')

This is a bull's eye. The poet's own musicality has enabled him
to reach a truth he had perhaps been hiding from full consciousness. 'Poetry of Departures', however, lets the future
librarian of Hull get away with it completely. Explaining this
time why he does not 'do a Rimbaud', a Gauguin, or a W. H.
Davies, Larkin tells us he would 'go today', if

> it weren't so artificial,
> Such a deliberate step backwards
> To create an object. . . .
> ('Poetry of Departures')

No: that has a bogusness Larkin would not have let pass later.
Both Larkin and Auden, like so many other poets, foundered
on Rimbaud: Auden mistakes a mawkish hero-worship for
genuine respect, Larkin merely rationalizes his own timorous-
ness. It is the lesser of the two deceptions, so perhaps his title
justifies itself.

The point is of some importance because Larkin's great concern in the volume is with being less deceived. So he goes
through the possible postures, the modes of deception, one by
one, unmasking their seductiveness: the Wordsworth–Richard
Jefferies childhood ('The Place's Fault'), the various heroisms
open to the book-worm, religion, hearty *Gemütlichkeit*. . . .
Eliminating the bogus is in fact Larkin's chosen profession. His
representativeness for his time is still unlimited. He is *the*

modern poet, the proletarian boy of talent and sensibility, horrified by the hearties, scared of sex, anti-gregarious, in love with the life of the poet, yet half-afraid he will not have it forever, and quite certain he will not have the courage to make the break, and refuse the organized horror-camp of the working world as Rimbaud and Gauguin did. For such a man, the idleness of the sixth form, and later of university, retains an irresistible attraction, and quite rightly: these are the only years given to the poet merely to *be* a poet. (Later, in *The Whitsun Weddings*, Larkin haunts his Oxford years—returning in horrified fascination to the well-carpeted world of dons and May Balls.)

The sensibility displayed is superior to that of Roy Fuller. The tone and musicality of the verse lift the perceptual sequences higher than anything in *Brutus' Orchard*. *The Less Deceived* still seems superior to *The Whitsun Weddings*, though it contains more mistakes. The quality of the sensibility, bathing in a numinous aura the sensitive observations, can best be observed in 'Coming', his most perfect and beautiful poem; and one which demands either no quotation, or quotation in full:

> On longer evenings,
> Light, chill and yellow,
> Bathes the serene
> Foreheads of houses.
> A thrush sings
> Laurel-surrounded
> In the deep bare garden,
> Its fresh-peeled voice
> Astonishing the brickwork.
> It will be spring soon,
> It will be spring soon—
> And I, whose childhood
> Is a forgotten boredom,
> Feel like a child
> Who comes on a scene
> Of adult reconciling,
> And can understand nothing
> But the unusual laughter,
> And starts to be happy.

The poem happened to Larkin here; it came upon him, as he came upon it. It seems one of the finest lyrics of the time.

If *The Less Deceived* funks 'joining in', as well as the Rimbaud myth, it shows more fight than the later volume (*The Whitsun Weddings*) towards those Toads, the Toads of work Rimbaud himself had funked:

> Why should I let the toad *work*
> Squat on my life?
> Can't I use my wit as a pitchfork
> And drive the brute off?
>
> ('Toads')

Larkin's acknowledgement of the question, and then his tackling of it, give his two major volumes a broad representativeness. The world of *The Less Deceived* is gentle, made up of sunsets and dusks, country churches (not, in fact, debunked, though the reverence is awkward, the outsider-ness rather flaunted); it is the world of any and every young English poet. The sensibility displayed is, correspondingly, silky and delicate. On one side is the fear and the shyness of the virgin; on the other, the virgin's fear of 'fulfillment's desolate attic'—the real theme of Western poetry since Wordsworth, Coleridge and Goethe. The attitude towards love and sex on the one hand, and towards work and success on the other (two complementary kinds of failure), meet up in the poet's central dread of satisfaction. Suppose he acted upon those private nocturnal cravings of the erotic imagination? Suppose, on the other hand, he 'made it' in society, in life, at one at last with the hearties and the success men every poet secretly yearns to impress and be accepted by? (Larkin's novel *Jill* enacts both these perennial fantasies with extraordinary frankness.) It is dread of some such fulfillment that informs and heightens the poet's exquisite experiences in the natural world. The poet always wants to hold onto his unfulfilment, to keep intact the narcissistic purity of his own world. Yet steadily he moves towards the demolition of this world; he cannot accept the perpetual postponement of satisfaction; he feels it to be unreal, and he cannot rest until he has wrecked it, breached it for good, put himself up on the sad shelf of achievement alongside Wordsworth and Coleridge.

It is appropriately ironical that the desolation that came to
Larkin was not that of fulfillment but of frustration. The plunge
he took, to wake up disabused, was not into sex and licence, but
into work, industry, the treadmill life of grown-up men. The
Toad work whose authority he had challenged and flouted in
The Less Deceived, is now accepted as a comforting companion
for the dreary trip towards the grave:

> No, give me my in-tray,
> My loaf-haired secretary,
> My shall-I-keep-the-call-in-Sir:
> What else can I answer,
>
> When the light comes on at four
> At the end of another year?
> Give me your arm, old toad;
> Help me down Cemetery Road.
>
> ('Toads Revisited')

The Whitsun Weddings is a harsh book. The Romantic grace that
heightened and lifted so many passages in *The Less Deceived* has
evaporated for good, revealing the crabbed, ugly world of
suburban work he had all along known was awaiting him. The
adolescent poet's dread of nine-to-five routine, that informed
the original 'Toads' poem in the earlier book, pales before the
horror of dropping out of decent, regular security, like the
lonely old grubbers Larkin observes in the park,

> Waxed-fleshed out-patients
> Still vague from accidents,
> And characters in long coats
> Deep in the litter-baskets
>
> All dodging the toad work
> By being stupid or weak.
>
> ('Toads Revisited')

Thus, the horror of routine is transmuted slowly into a comfort:
the womb after all is a kind of cell, a kind of coffin: womb,
office and cell all advertise our 'desire for oblivion'.

Even now, the poet still cannot accept marriage. The failure
through shyness confessed in 'Wild Oats' convinces us more

than the rather ugly sneer of 'Self's the man', in which he derides the domestic life and equates the married man's dread of loneliness with his own inability to make sufficient contact with another human being as similar forms of selfishness. The insight has its point, but it is difficult not to hear in the tone the shrillness of shyness turned sour. Larkin of course is not unaware of this danger. Again and again in *The Whitsun Weddings* he returns to the past to compare his own life, that has developed into lonely bachelorhood, with the shaggy abject domesticity of those contemptible yes-men who got married as soon as they could. He wonders how Dockery, the old College contemporary whose son is now up, can be so convinced that he 'should be added to'. 'Why did he think adding meant increase?/To me it was dilution.' The suspicion that Dockery has got something from life that Larkin himself has missed is quieted by the poet's rationalization:

> Life is first boredom, then fear.
> Whether or not we use it, it goes,
> And leaves what something hidden from us chose,
> And age, and then the only end of age.
>
> ('Dockery and Son')

The suspicion one has here that Larkin is in fact co-opting Dockery into failure by generalizing his own fear is to some extent confirmed by the dread expressed in 'Mr. Bleaney' that ultimately nothing is worse than actual loneliness in ugly surroundings. 'Mr. Bleaney'—a perfect piece—really adumbrates the great theme of all Larkin's work: failure. The hired box Larkin decides to take in this poem from one point of view provides the perfect symbol for human failure as Larkin sees it:

> But if he stood and watched the frigid wind
> Tousling the clouds, lay on the fusty bed
> Telling himself that this was home, and grinned
> And shivered, without shaking off the dread
>
> That how we live measures our own nature
> And at his age having no more to show
> That one hired box should make him pretty sure
> He warranted no better, I don't know.

'at his age': it is the future and its ghastly possibilities that haunt Larkin now: after 'Mr. Bleaney', acceptance in some sort of the prison of responsibility and punctual attendance was inevitable.

But by the same token, even our successes are failures— in fact especially so, as the ending of 'Toads Revisited' emphasizes. Philip Larkin has achieved as much success as most men expect from life: he is a respected poet and a chief librarian. Yet he registers this, like the goods-laden stores of the new working-class affluence, as a sadder failure than the poverty of the depressed years it has replaced. The social poetry of *The Whitsun Weddings* has a harshness, which corresponds to the almost brutal contempt with which he tries to infuse his naturally mild, studious voice. ('Get stewed: Books are a load of crap'.) 'Here', 'Sunny Prestatyn' and 'The Large Cool Store' offer savagely poignant montages of working-class earning-power and the tawdry dreams it fosters and all but buys. So that it is no real surprise to find a poem like 'MCMXIV' catching with exquisite melancholy and nostalgia the days of Larkin's own cloth-capped father: the underprivileged queuing up to get slaughtered in the trenches

> As if they stretched outside
> The Oval or Villa Park,

Although the Great War and the brutal hierarchicalism it represented are seen as having shattered a world and a way of life, it is the beauty of that life (in contrast to the brashness of the new affluence) which Larkin is moved to celebrate, not its ugliness—

> Never such innocence again.

There is much bitterness and harshness in *The Whitsun Weddings*; frustration distorts Larkin's native refinement in poems like 'Self's the man', and 'A Study of Reading Habits'. Yet the most remarkable thing about the volume is that in spite of the fact that it celebrates the success of failure, and the failure of success, overriding everything else is a poetry of return and nostalgia, conferring upon every piece in the collection a dimension of clarification often not evident when individual poems are considered separately. Everything in the volume takes place within the decision about life that has been discussed above in particular poems: hence, the whole book shares a tone of bitterness, redeemed by the regret that accompanies it. Regret is never entirely unpleasant: it is a sweet, not an acrid, emotion. The dominant mood of the book receives its finest expression in the title poem, 'The Whitsun Weddings', which at once consummates the Larkin idiom and puts it in its grave. The montages are achieved more perfectly than anywhere else, and they are bound, shaped and directed with sure tact by the journey framework of the poem: the journey in itself represents something of a valediction. To what exactly, it is difficult to say. We are simply aware of one of those moments in the career of a poet ('Coming' celebrated another) when a juncture, a point of understanding, is reached and left at the same time. Hence, over the perfect parabola of the poem, we feel that Larkin is entitled to his orgy of exact *aperçus*—'An Odeon went past, a cooling tower,/And someone running up to bowl'. Upon it all his welcoming, valedictory gaze confers a mantle both of newness and of interest, the interest of something long known but only just now recognized, and in being recognized, left. Just as the poet only gradually realizes what is happening—'At first I didn't notice what a noise/The weddings made'—so only slowly does the deeper understanding emerge that the journey itself is more than through space, and time. It is through a whole phase of experience, and knowledge, so that in the end the awareness of having made an arrival coincides with the equal awareness of the life he has just wished goodbye:

> We slowed again,
> And as the tightened brakes took hold, there swelled
> A sense of falling like an arrow-shower
> Sent out of sight, somewhere becoming rain.

III

A generation younger than Larkin the London-based Australian poet, Peter Porter, demonstrates the tenacity and the continuing serviceability of the Auden idiom. In theme and technique,

Porter strikingly recalls Fuller and Larkin; Audenesque too is
the characteristic preoccupation with the lie:

> Dear lie, between the trusting chair
> And bashful fire, a world enough
> (Though schizophrenic air
>   Divides its real to worn and rare)
> Purports to watch. . . .
>
> ('Too Worn to Wear')

The verbal skill is all Porter's own—a sneeze becomes

>   a rage of stuff
>   Wasted upon a shift of air
>
> ('Too Worn to Wear')

Yet Auden is there in the versification, the stance *vis-à-vis* one's
own integrity, his 'responsibilities' *vis-à-vis* a society to which
he feels he owes nothing, yet which feeds him in return for
the work which joins him indissolubly to it. Most of all, Auden
has monitored the brilliant incisiveness of the observational
montage which provides the structure in Porter's best poetry:

> One girl undressed because she thought it right;
> Another, trained in truth, watched what she did
> Loving her mirrored love, her second sight.
> A judge of conduct gasped to see the fun,
> A valued impotence safe in his head—
> A private creature staring out the sun
> Not warmed by it is seeing by its light.
>
> ('Party Line')

The generality of the images approaches here closely the
argument by instance of the Auden poem; yet the framework of
the poem, as always in Porter, is provided by the particular
scene. He does not, like Auden, manipulate the 'typical'
instances in a forensic argument. His wit in general is more
considered than Auden's, and comes closer to the example of
Empson and the Metaphysicals:

> The labour-saving kitchen to match the labour-saving thing
> She'd fitted before marriage (O love, with this ring
> I thee wed)
>
> ('Made in Heaven')

The Australian freshness brought to bear on stale English scenes enables Porter to 'do' aspects of the London experience as no-one, perhaps, ever has. Perhaps only a colonial could 'see' Kings Road as Porter does. Certainly, no Chelsea Bird novel has anything like the fresh clarity of Porter's bitter disillusion. There is an autobiographical novel embedded in Porter's volume *Once Bitten, Twice Bitten*. The title suggests Philip Larkin, of course. Much more daring and earthy than Larkin, Porter has his nose rubbed in the mud, gets his fingers burned. *Once Bitten* should have made a dozen ephemeral novels superfluous. 'Beast and the Beauty', for example, brilliantly exposes one of the representative myths of our time— the colonial arriving in London and receiving there his initiation into sex, class and English society; and the myth also connects up with some of the great basic myths of literature, those of *Illusions Perdues* and *Great Expectations*. Having committed himself to the debutante he has attracted, the proletarian poet has to take the inevitable brush-off:

> Her family of drunks
> Were shrewd, wine-wise young barristers and gentleman-
> Farmers fought for her hand. In the loft there waited trunks
> Of heirlooms to be taken seriously.
>
> ('Beast and the Beauty').

In spite of 'the depth that lived in her soul', the capacity for 'the wonder in Kings College Chapel' which she had shared with the young outsider poet, it is the social verities that have to 'be taken seriously'. The poet's chagrin is horribly convincing—

> So he sits alone in Libraries, hideous and hairy of soul,
> A beast again, waiting for a lustful kiss to bring
> Back his human smell, the taste of woman on his tongue.

The mythic structuring, as well as the generally freer handling, lends Porter's Audenesque social montages a vitality often absent from Philip Larkin's more chaste disillusion. Fundamentally, his is an equipoise of virility and the disabusement of the tradition within which he works. Unlike Larkin, he really

likes sex, and has enjoyed it: when he speaks about girls it is with
a zestful sexiness:

> their sister,
> In love with a school teacher,
> Pushes back the sex in her measuring blouse.
>
> ('Once Bitten, Twice Bitten')

The disabusement, the yearning, has a sweet bitterness quite
different in tone from the soured virgin tone of the later Larkin.
This fresh bitterness, both sexual and social, perhaps lends its
weight to the poem in which the colonial myth is most overtly
expressed, 'Metamorphosis'. The metamorphosis is, of course,
the transformation of raw young Australian to passable London
advertising man:

> This new Daks suit, greeny-brown,
> Oyster coloured buttons, single vent, tapered
> Trousers, no waistcoat, hairy tweed—my own:
> A suit to show responsibility . . . .
>
> ('Metamorphosis')

The act succeeds—'The town will have me' socially and sex-
ually. But the poem parallels, roughly speaking, the courses of
'Beast and the Beauty': the beautiful girl he has arranged to
meet has ditched him for someone richer, more *au fait*:

> We talk of how we miss each other—I tell
> Some truth—you, cruel stories built of men:
> 'It wasn't good at first but he's improving.'
> More talk about his car, his drinks, his friends.
>
> ('Metamorphosis')

The beast of 'Beast and the Beauty' reappears at the end of this
poem, to add a dimension to the metamorphosis:

> As in a werewolf film I'm horrible, far
> Below the collar—my fingers crack, my tyrant suit
> Chokes me as if it hugs me in its fire.
>
> ('Metamorphosis')

And we remember the Daks suit, the 'hairy tweed' of the

original transformation, the 'tyrant suit' that, having helped
him get her, now punishes him for his presumption.

The technique and the feel of the versification, the general
approach towards the problem of building a poem, do not go
beyond Auden: though young, Porter is (in these poems) a
square. Many poems in *Once Bitten, Twice Bitten* are still
'observed' in a dangerously academic fashion—a party not
quite participated in, Somerset Maugham Tea Rooms—there
is perhaps a trifle too much 'wit': 'She showed his hands the
presentiment of clothes.' Both rhythm and the pay-out of the
lines (not quite the same thing) in general remain content with
the Auden gait, though his verse often rocks on its heels with
the resilience of a welter-weight. Yet Porter has digested and
confronted his London experience in a most impressive way:
almost all the Australian poems in *Once Bitten, Twice Bitten* are
routine and well-made academic pieces,[3] where the London
poems are mature, filled with a new sense of identity. Significantly, in 'Metamorphosis' he observes, looking at his reflection,

> I am myself at last.

This sense of finding himself occurs at that stage of a writer's
career when he becomes conscious of the myth he has both
created and been created by. Porter's myth strikingly parallels
Larkin's at certain points. Porter's 'What a lying lot the
writers are' echoes Larkin's coarser 'Get stewed. Books are a
load of crap.' 'Reading a Novel', which should be compulsory
reading for all those London publishers' readers and editors
feverishly seeking a myth of their own through other people's
confessions, suggests a tentative identification with the novelist's
own 'true Role—the man who looks and sees and is not
touched'—in other words, with the Larkin hero himself.
Poems like 'Reading a Novel' could hardly have come into
existence without the mediation of Larkin and Fuller. Yet the
Porter myth is at once more virile and more multiplex. 'The
man who looks and sees and is not touched' in the Porter myth
is touched.

[3] The brilliant exception to this generalization is the title-poem. 'Once Bitten,
Twice Bitten'.

IV

Mention has already been made (p. 48) of William Empson's influence upon the Movement poets of the nineteen-fifties. I am not concerned here with the influence Empson exerted upon a number of superficial poets, with the facile vogue of villanelle, for instance (Auden's 'If I could tell you I would let you know' in fact seems to have made a stronger impression than anything by Empson). What seems more important is his impact upon a far more impressive talent, Geoffrey Hill, and his pervasive influence at Cambridge.

Working on a smaller and smaller canvas, Geoffrey Hill has striven more rigorously and with more success than any of his contemporaries to realize the Empsonian ideal of a poetry of maximal, directed ambiguity. No poet of his time, on either side of the Atlantic, shows a more profound grasp of the working principles of the English language.[4] Moreover, the technical know-how is always mated with a stern seriousness, an impatience with any but the most ultimate and fundamental themes. Once more we note in English poetry of the middle twentieth century the same complex confusion of traditions: the emphasis upon irony here receives its strongest support, but informing it are the characteristically English modesty and so-briety. In some ways, in fact, Hill's poetry consummates the in-tellectualist tradition. Consummates, unfortunately, is quite the wrong word, with its associations of achieved release and fulfilment, not to say abandon. What Hill proves in the end is that the Empsonian obsession with consciously exploited am-biguity is ultimately stultifying: he succeeds in making room for the ambiguities at the expense of expression, so that for all the grandeur of his themes, he is like an expert with nothing to say. The verbal harmonies seem tendentiously 'accurate': 'foun-tains / Salt the sparse Haze' and the same poem has

idyllic death
Where fish at dawn ignite the powdery lake.

'Ignite', like 'salt' in the earlier example, is a typical piece of visual accuracy; but equally, both verbs are intended to hold

---

[4] Theodore Roethke comes, perhaps, closest to Hill.

resonance corresponding to and derived from the poem's theme announced in the title—'To the (supposed) Patron', and initiated in the first word, ('Prodigal'). The diction tells us throughout that the patron is the Man from Christ's parables and the puns and ambiguities re-enact the Rich Man's mortality. Thus, the Great Common-place enacted within the poem—the Rich Patron has to die no matter how suavely his wealth beguiles the fact into unconsciousness—invests the visually accurate verb, 'salt'—with its preservative significance, and at the end, the fish 'ignite', not only as their evanescent flashing suggests fire, to the eye, but as their fire suggests Life (though spuriously—this is the poem's irony) to the mind. The *mot juste* receives the support of the theme and works on two layers. This remorseless application of the Empsonian pun runs riot through Hill's otherwise sedate pages: the dead 'maintain their ground'; some are 'not past conceiving but past care'. The Shakespearean flavour of the latter example gives us the clue to Hill's derivation: Hill elaborates the weakness for a pun Johnson observed in Shakespeare into a poetic methodology. His should be—from the Empsonian point of view—the ideal poetry: it is all significance, every verb conceals its double meaning, and inserts its knife as the reader passes. If there is no absolute ambiguity of this kind, the verbs and adjectives are at least carefully precise: the 'dulled wood' of Christ's cross 'spat' blood on the stones. The salmon in 'Genesis' 'muscle', and the air contains 'wads' of sound. The expertise is considerable. So is that of the versification. Hill has studied carefully for example the art of exploiting the line-end to throw ironic or ambiguous emphasis onto particular words. Verb or adjective placed at the end of the line receives the weight and shadow of rhyme, yet always stands in danger of having its meaning or even its grammatical status altered by the following line:

> each deed
> Resurrecting those best dead
> Priests, soldiers and kings;

'dead' is first noun, then adjective qualifying 'priests, soldiers and kings'. We are forced to change our view of these dead: first they are the 'best' (of the dead), then quite the contrary, those who are best *when* dead. Fifty years ago Ezra Pound castigated the Georgians for concentrating on 'loveliness', on 'poetry', instead of keeping their eyes on the facts, and letting the poetry come in the back way, as it should: '... attempts to be poetic in some manner or other defeat their own end; whereas an intentness on the quality of the emotion to be conveyed makes for poetry.'[5]

Geoffrey Hill loads his poems with 'significance' rather as the Georgians loaded theirs with the 'poetic', with the result that poetry, and with it significance, often escapes him. A majority of his poems are about death. He writes epitaphs, some of them very fine. The lines for Osip Mandelstam, for example move and are moved:

> And again I am too late. There go
> The salutes, dust-clouds and brazen cries.
> Images rear from desolation
> like ruins across a plain ....
> A few men glare at their hands, others
> Grovel for food in the roadside field.

This is subtle and fine, with no distracting pun under the stone.[6] The poem holds onto that grief Hill so often allows to slip between his too clenched fingers. In poetry, significance should accrue from the feeling; in Hill, the poetry exists for the 'significances'. These significances plate and coat the surface of verse concerned mostly with the great commonplace of Death. A stiff morbidity is conveyed, and no one knows more about the English language's stock of double meanings. Yet the final impression is of a man who chose his themes, or allowed them to be chosen for him, in the absence of any very compelling response to life of his own. 'Life' is precisely what Hill's poetry lacks. For life he substitutes gesture:

> But we are commanded
> To rise, when, in silence,
> I would compose my voice.

Literary attitudes of this kind are not to be struck after the fact: they should arise out of natural grief and what seems to the

[5] Ezra Pound, *Make it New* (London, 1934), p. 162.
[6] There is one, of course, on 'brazen'.

poet an invisible and obvious mode of expression, which for
some quality of emotion, crystallizes into the 'classic'.

   The title of one of Hill's volumes, *For the Unfallen*, parallels
that of one of Larkin's: *The Less Deceived*. For Hill, the living
are merely those not yet dead, the Unfallen, for whom even now
we ought to be composing epitaphs. For Larkin one can hope
for nothing more than to be less deceived, less of a fool, than the
others—the hearties, the bullies, the rulers, and the ruled. Both
attitudes cohere within the ironist academy. Neither of the
poets appears to have been shaped by Leavis, yet their acceptance of either defeat of the pyrrhic victory of self-awareness,
does, I think, reflect his indirect influence.

V

Positively, Dr Leavis's reverence for the modest, the self-
aware, the quietly unpretentious, is admirable; no-one has
done better justice than he to those aspects of Bunyan and
Wordsworth, for instance. Yet in sum and influence, the
consequence has been to place an unnecessarily high valuation
on steadiness: poetry in the decades most exposed to Leavis's
influence—the 'forties, 'fifties and early 'sixties—has been too
concerned to be unpretentious, not-absurd, self-aware, (the
latter normally taken to mean awareness of one's own possible
delusions of grandeur). I have already observed the corrupting
effects of self-awareness when taken as an end, not as a means.
Quiet self-congratulation is the end-product, a stuffy complacency, a knowing sense of being in the right. Looked at from a
distance, there is little real difference between the poetry of the
Oxford Movement (for all its 'smart' *Angst*) and that of
'positive values' (the Cambridge equivalent). In both there is
the same pedestrian rhythm, the same carefulness, the same
absence of drive and transcendence, the same grayness of
academicism. Only in place of the often slick irony and self-
ridicule of the Movement, Cambridge poetry offers domesticity: for Lawrentian reasons, marriage and responsibility are
preferred to the Larkinesque single-man's disillusion. The result
is a connubial poetry, with the same 'preference for limits' of
Davie and Elizabeth Jennings, clogged with a dour pugnacity,
an at times intolerable heaviness of manner born of the poet's

awareness of having successfully avoided the snares of pride and self-importance, aestheticism and arty pretentiousness. As in the Movement poets, integrity is guaranteed by sufficient reservation and pious confession. Having parcelled himself out among the animals, for example, David Holbrook asserts his human differences:

> I walk upright, alone, ungoverned, free. . . .

The possibility of arrogance however is immediately quashed—

> Yet their occasional lust, fear, unease, walk with me always.
> All ways.

'unease': that is the clue. Together with the inevitable 'Yet' of qualification, *uneasiness* places the poem securely in the academic 'fifties. Unease, in fact, is really the key 'fifties concept. To confess to unease proves intelligent awareness, and the 'Yet' that never misses a trick safeguards the virgin integrity. Beneath the broad appearance of metropolitan affluence lies the 'unease' only the poet knows about: Cambridge poetry is resolutely anti-metropolitan. Dankwerts (a Holbrook character comparable to Larkin's Dockery) finds out all about the hollowness of the London affluence his Cambridge degree secures; he falls, 'albeit on a fat bank-balance of amoral earnings'.

David Holbrook's verse almost parodistically represents the Cambridge aethos. He has taken the paths Larkin refused, and could not but refuse—marriage, children, responsibility. 'Poor old horse' shows the ageing poet-supervisor contemplating the undergraduates going through their paces, but refusing to accept that he has had his day—

> I do not want to have had my day. I do not accept my jade.

Reading this poetry it is impossible not to think Larkin made the right decision. Holbrook's verse parallels or travesties Larkin's, almost as if to prove to Larkin that he had in fact been right all along. The impression that emerges from such domestic mishaps as 'Fingers in the door' is of sentimentality, rather like that of the Rückert songs Mahler set so lugubriously in *Kindertotenlieder*. The attempt to give the 'petty' incident some kind of cosmic significance through the use of literary appeals to 'dead bright stars' achieves the opposite effect of bathos: one suspects the seriousness of the poet, if not the sincerity of the father. Cambridge earnestness, in avoiding so sedulously the glib Angst of the Oxford novelists (Wain and Amis), mistakes sentimentality for humanity, humdrumness for seriousness, and patronage for humility.

If the self-deprecations of Larkin eventually wither away the capacity for further experience, at least his final acceptance of the bourgeois burden is compact of bitterness and fear. He is under no illusions, either, about the 'loaf-haired' secretary, or about that fact that he needs her. He is scared to death of the lonely old grubbers in the park, of Mr Bleaney's hired box, of the prospect of isolation and nothingness. He does not, like Holbrook, in 'As for living our supervisors will do that for us', try to nudge us into accepting that he is making some great sacrifice on behalf of the Dankwerts of the future. The 'integrity' of Cambridge poetry thickens into solid complacency. These 'positive values', this 'humanity', underline more stringently than any metaphysics could, the need in the human mind for a principle of opposition. The human spirit grows fudgy and smug unless it is at war with itself in a more fundamental way than is occasioned by academic irony and automatic self-deprecation. These are, *au fond*, ways of merely buttressing the ego: paradoxically, the ultimate consequence of watching one's own integrity is a more and more massive egotism, an egotism which exactly inverts and complements the self-doubt of irony. Oxford and Cambridge poetry in the 'fifties and early 'sixties is but the two sides of one coin. The Cambridge equivalent of Oxford irony is the corruption of the cult of self-knowledge—a care taken not to exceed known bounds ('a preference for limits'), and a culling of the rewards in a 'fat bank-balance of *moral* earnings' (to paraphrase Mr Holbrook). In a way, the temptations of the academic life are greater than those of honest Mammon. The stale smugness of academic poetry suggests as much; Auden's diagnosis of 'ingrown virginity' could be applied to the ultimate complacency of academic 'integrity'. The businessman or the publisher is unlikely to fancy himself a moral virgin; such a delusion is all too common among academics, as witness Mr Holbrook's 'As for living, our

supervisors will do that for us.' It is unfair, perhaps, to choose
Mr Holbrook's poetry to stand for this category: he has made—
so it seems to the outsider—a real contribution to education,
and probably does not regard himself as a poet at all. Nevertheless, the very clumsiness of his verse seems sufficiently
indicative of the sheerly inadequate aesthetic lying behind so
much academic criticism to justify the injustice.

VI

The impasse in which poetry found itself in the middle of the
twentieth century does not only appear in the form of academic
ironies and positive values. It is no less evident in the decora-
tive 'postcards-from-Corfu' poetry so common in the small
magazines and anthologies of the immediate post-war years (a
result, presumably of military service passed in exotic surroundings). In America also, writing became wholly consumed
by its percepts: Theodore Roethke, for instance, and Saul
Bellow (in *Herzog* especially) invest themselves too completely
in facticity upon which they are unable to confer significance.
In England, irony and picturalism are related: it is no accident
that so many of the 'forties postcard-poets became stalwart
ironists in the 'fifties. Robert Conquest, for instance, having
established himself as a minor scene-painter in the post-war
years became more famous as the editor of *New Lines*; and G. S.
Fraser, who had proclaimed the virtues of Nicholas Moore and
Ruthven Todd, went on to crystallize the 'academicism' of
the 'fifties in his anthology *Poetry Now*, with its remorseless
trend-hunting preface. No-one as concerned with eddies and
swirls as Mr Fraser can be aware of the real drift of the tide:
it is hardly surprising that he failed to detect the common
qualities of the forms of poetry he found so bewilderingly
various in 1952. From this distance in time, *Poetry Now*, like
New Lines before it and Mr Alvarez's *The New Poetry* after,
seems homogeneously composed of rather timid and unadven-
turous poetry: the poetry in these anthologies is unmotivated by
sufficiently powerful instigation, and the perceptions of which
it is made up—whether snapshots from Corsica or ironic asides
from Oxford—remain unwelded by any presiding consciousness,
any sense of the importance of the act of writing poetry.

The poets have shown themselves aware of this. Roy Fuller—
inevitably—has made the frankest confession of inadequacy:

> The poem should end here, its trouvailles all
> Exhausted, but there remains the moral
> ('Winter World')

The frankness is engaging, and like many similar avowals in
mid-twentieth century verse, is in a way offered as itself
answering the need. But it does not: frankness, confession,
admission of defeat are not themselves sufficient, either morally
or poetically, to justify the poetic stance. For Fuller, as for most
poets of his time, the imagery of poetry lies inertly out in the
world. There is no spiritual or mental synthesis; thus, there
is no real *raison d'être* for the poetry—as Fuller too well knows.
This inner weakness derives naturally from the intellectualist
programme. Like the 'partial fires' of Empson, the self-dis-
paragement of Fuller and Larkin produces a poetry of strictly
absurd observation-particles, unwelded by the sense of significance which is the essence of poetry. The weaknesses of academic
or ironist poetry, therefore, do not stem from a faulty methodology. On the contrary, the technical inadequacies (the poem as
bundle of trouvailles tied up with moral ribbon and powdered
with irony) derive from the fundamental lack of vision. The
technical forms of ironist verse—its pedestrian rhythms, inertly
presented observations and superimposed morals—are inevitable consequences of a fractured sensibility and of a dissociation
which was not to be repaired by salting conventional attitudes
with irony or sprinkling metaphors with dissonance. The cause
lay deeper. So long as the motives of excitation are the strict
identification with the sensuously perceived object, then the
basis for synthesis is assured; that is, so long as the object
demands identification, so long as it creates a relationship
where one had not previously existed. But when the object
becomes merely correlative, that is, the instrument of a ready-
made desire, so that desire loses its character in attaching
itself to something not strictly desired but merely presented,
then there is no ground for intellectual synthesis.

Such an intellectual synthesis demanded a more fundamental spiritual revolution than was attempted by the ironist

school—or than has been achieved merely by absorbing a certain amount of the technical sophistication of the Imagist traditions. Many of the remarks offered above about the various academicisms of the 'fifties and 'sixties have been made otiose by the gradual obsolescence of the older technical appurtenances, and the supersession of a freer series of verse-forms. But it is just as possible to remain trapped within intellectual and emotional inhibitions in free verse as in rhyme and stanza. A great deal of the poetry published in England in the 'fifties was relatively free in form, negatively speaking. But much less of it was deeply alive and spiritually awake.

9 Beyond Positive Values:
Ted Hughes

What I have all along been referring to as the English existential tradition remained unbroken through the Eliot revolution. Up to the present day, it has continued to produce much of the best and least fragile poetry written in England. It appears in the nineteen-fifties, for instance, in the poetry of R. S. Thomas and Jack Clemo, and, significantly modified by the agency of D. H. Lawrence, of Ted Hughes. Once again, we observe that the tradition manifests itself in *non plus ultra* situations. Each of these poets confronts a denuded reality. R. S. Thomas's world is that of the Welsh farmer, debased almost to animality by the struggle to wrest an existence from the stark countryside; Jack Clemo suffers from physical handicap of the most extreme order, and translates an anguish of spirit and tissue into the terms of the bare clay landscape of Cornwall; Ted Hughes meets nature and animality in a consciously head-on collision.

R. S. Thomas and Jack Clemo are poets who have been universally praised and are everywhere respected for a power of 'honesty' in their poetry. Every Sunday reviewer, every academic, every merely successful poet, must have felt shamed by their integrity: 'refusal to compromise' seems barely relevant praise—neither man seems ever to have been remotely approached by the possibility of compromise. The corrupt response, the easy lie, the facile acceptance, would seem as sheerly difficult for these poets as the life of ascetic renunciation would be to the literary butterfly, whose horizons are formed by the publisher's offer and the reviewer's sting. *Song at the Year's Turning* and *Map of Clay* represent the persistence of the English existential tradition in its purest form. Here, as in the poetry of Hopkins, or Edward Thomas, is the eschewal of metaphysical transcendence, the concomitant absence of display and conceit, the shrewd sense of mortality, and the close uncomfortable alliance with earth, with what I have repeatedly referred to as bedrock existence. Their poetry, like John Clare's at its finest, exists in intimate, lonely communion with the soil that runs under city and freeway, finally to surface either in Cornwall or Wales.

R. S. Thomas—a priest—seems to have sought out a terrain to suit his mind, where the human animal grubs along with the rest, just able gracelessly to survive:

> Poor hill farmer astray in the grass:
> There came a movement and he looked up, but
> All that he saw was the wind pass.
>
> ('The Lonely Farmer')

The characters in Thomas's poems are, like the lonely farmer, 'betrayed by the heart's need'. Their enclosed yet draughty lives are not fulfilled in the turning of the seasons, in communion with the earth, as Wordsworth had suggested they might be. On the contrary, they are frustrated by the earth's recalcitrance, barren, empty; Iago Prytherch, Davies the peasant, Cyndyllan, are as absurd as Beckett's tramps. The cold winds blast them out of feeling, so that the man hacking mangel-wurzels seems hardly to notice when

> the knife errs,
> Burying itself in his shocked flesh.
>
> ('Soil')

Cynddylan's new tractor makes him even more ridiculous than he was before; there is little sense, in Thomas's excellently bitter satire, of a superseded Wordworthian charm, compact of a natural organic communion which the machine has destroyed. Before the tractor, Cynddylan was 'yoked to the soil', and ludicrous as he now is—a knight errant

> breaking the fields
> Mirror of silence—
>
> ('Cynddylan on a Tractor')

he has acquired at least a swashbuckling cocksureness. Thomas's Wales is bare, barren, savage, the people ignorant, marooned.

In Wales, Thomas observes,

> You cannot live in the present. . . .

For

> There is no present in Wales,
> And no future;
> There is only the past. . . .
>
> ('Welsh Landscape')

The people are feudal superstitious peasants, whose belief in God has died:

> His wisdom dwindled to a small gift
> For handling stock, planting a few seeds
> To ripen slowly in the warm breath
> Of an old God to whom he never prays.
>
> ('The Last of the Peasantry').

The atmosphere evoked, like the people, reminds one strongly of Bernanos's *Journal d'un Curé de Campagne*, though without the French novelist's presiding theological values. The Christianity in Thomas's poetry is without metaphysics, without a code of right and wrong, to which we can refer for guidance. And it is precisely this naked, value-free confrontation with basic matter that lies at the heart of the English existential tradition.

Yet Thomas's poetry derives its real force from the awareness and love of human warmth and possibility; underlying these bitter observations is the deep faith in human potential that leads Thomas to invoke Shelley in what is perhaps his finest poem. The dream Shelley dreamed and which Thomas now thinks has decayed lies around Thomas's field of vision like a fading after-glow.

> Is there blessing? Light's peculiar grace
> In cold splendour robes this tortured place
> For strange marriage.
>
> ('Song at the Year's Turning')

It is almost possible to measure, in the distance separating Thomas's 'Song' from Shelley's *Hellas*, the extent of industrial man's pilgrimage. The belief in the man-angel has gone, and the returning of the seasons brings no real comfort in its adumbration of eternity.

> Winter rots you; who is there to blame?
> The new grass shall purge you in its flame.
>
> ('Song at the Year's Turning')

But this poetry exists in order to warn us against taking our relative, conditioned half-truths for the whole truth. Having presented Iago Prytherch to us—with shattering directness—

> His clothes, sour with years of sweat
> And animal contact, shock the refined
> But affected, sense with their stark naturalness
>
> ('A Peasant')

Thomas instantly warns us against the automatic civilized response he knows we have already made:

> Yet this is your prototype, who, season by season
> Against siege of rain and the wind's attrition,
> Preserves his stock, an impregnable fortress
> Not to be stormed even in death's confusion
>
> ('A Peasant')

For this primitive Beckett clown, with neither grace nor dignity,

> also is human, and the same small star,
> That lights you homeward, has inflamed his mind
> With the old hunger, born of his kind.
>
> ('Affinity')

Thus, R. S. Thomas reports back to us from the front-line of reality; and like the guilt-ridden civilians we are, we respond with a suspect warmth. Thomas's poetry possesses a dangerous power to move, and this power derives, I think, from the identity he can make us feel with his peasants. Ultimately, they become merely heightened metaphors for ourselves.

The nature of the relationship between Thomas's reality and our own is best suggested perhaps in 'The Evacuee', a poem, one fancies, which has left few readers quite dry-eyed:

And so she grew, a small bird in the nest
Of welcome that was built about her,
Home now after so long away
In the flowerless streets of the drab town.
The men watched her busy with the hens,
The soft flesh ripening warm as corn
On the sticks of limbs, the grey eyes clear,
Rinsed with dew of their long dread.
The men watched her, and, nodding, smiled
With earth's charity, patient and strong.

('The Evacuee')

So that although R. S. Thomas's poetry comes to us from the frontier of civilization, its paradoxical effect is to recall us to ourselves. It reminds us that it is we who are the sojourners, we who are absent from home. This great primal truth, the poetry of the existential tradition, with its insistence upon an elemental contact with the earth, exists to remind us of.

Jack Clemo provides perhaps the most literal embodiment of the tradition's ideals. His landscape is the metaphoric land-scape of Hopkins and Clare, made actual; his suffering takes place not only in the spirit but in the body. Clemo's Cornwall, with its tin-mines and its lunar weirdness of white clay, rain and iron, is the bare spiritual world of existential consciousness; Clemo lives, from day to day, a drama which, if it force its way into art at all, does so usually in a figurative form. Hence, his vocabulary relies heavily upon terms which themselves could have been extrapolated from the works of his spiritual pre-decessors, but which are as natural to him as breathing. In their contexts, these key terms—*bedrock*, *pit*, *solitude*, *stark*, for in-stance—assume absolute authenticity, yet seem, as Clemo uses them, but barely capable of conveying the heavy tragic sense behind the poetry. The poetry of Jack Clemo, existentialist in the only sense of the word that matters, is the summation of the whole tradition: after Clemo, English poetry had to find a new way. That sense of denuded reality, of life when little but existence itself remains, received in *The Map of Clay* (1962) its ultimate statement. Chance gave Clemo the means of fusing the spiritual and the physical, the symbolic and the literal—clay. The clay of the Cornish mine district—tacky, damp, white, luminous, heavy, dogging, inescapable, hateful, pure—becomes, in Clemo's hands, naturally symbolic of the flesh of Christ and of man himself. 'Why should I find Him here / And not in a church?' he asks in 'Christ in the Clay-Pit':

> I am one
> Who feels the doggerel of Heaven
> Purge earth of poetry . . . .
>
> ('The Excavator')

These lines explain the entire spiritual orientation of *Map of Clay*, with its odd Calvinism and its strange joy. For it would be facile to assume that Clemo's puritanism precludes pleasure or indicates a mean or partial response to life. On the contrary, the poet's privations yield him an intense ecstasy, a pristine sensuality that stands in astonishing contrast to the cramped normality of Philip Larkin, say, or Roy Fuller. Clemo's entire will has been bent towards making totally meaningful a world which to most of us would seem cruel and heartlessly denuded of comfort and hope. To Clemo, the nakedness of the mines-landscape is a source of joy, a genuinely sensuous pleasure:

> I feel exultantly
> The drip of clayey water from the poised
> Still bar above me; thrilling with the rite
> Of baptism all my own, . . .
>
> ('The Excavator')

Every true poet knows what kind of sheer well-being lies behind these words:

> I stand here musing in the rain
> This Sabbath evening where the pit-head stain
> Of bushes is uprooted, strewn
> In waggon-tracks and puddles,
> While the fleering downpour fuddles
> The few raw flowers along the mouldering dump—
>
> ('The Excavator')

It is in moods like this that poetry germinates, not in the glamour of kodachrome sunsets. To this extent, Clemo's aesthetic is centrally relevant to the modern scene. Since Rimbaud, the modern poet has striven, like Clemo, to outrun beauty, 'beauty and its old idolatries' in Clemo's phrase. Clemo's 'Sufficiency' might stand as prolegomenon to Symbolist and post-Symbolist poetics:

> Yes, I might well grow tired
> Of slighting flowers all day long,
> Of making my song
> Of the mud in the kiln, of the wired
> Poles on the clay-dump; but where
> Should I find my personal pulse of prayer
> If I turned from the broken, scarred
> And unkempt land, the hard
> Contours of dogma, colourless hills?
> Is there a flower that thrills
> Like frayed rope?
>
> ('Sufficiency')

But it would, in turn, be no less facile to accept Clemo's *Weltanschauung* blithely, with no acknowledgement of the suffering that underlies it, that justifies and explains it. If he sees in the white clay of Cornwall the flesh of Christ, he also sees in the process of mining—excavating, disembowelling, dredging, digging, tearing—a symbol of his own predicament. Just as Hopkins saw Christ as a torturer, a combatant, whose purposes must, in the end, be benevolent although they seem malign, so Clemo sees in the savage violence done to the earth in mining a parallel to God's onslaught on himself:

> There squats amid these pyramids
> The Sphinx-mood of a Deity,
>   Unfelt until he bids
> Sandstorms awaken and the choking dust
> Drive me across the moors of barren trust.
> Then I perceive the aloof grey shape, the scorn,
> Quiet veiled cruelty of the watching eyes:
> The grim mysterious Will all help denies.
>
> ('Clay-Land Moods')

The pyramids are the clay tips, of course, and the thunder proceeds from the machinery: the mine has become a persecuting being, as in Zola's novel *Germinal*. Both George Herbert and Hopkins had dramatized the wrestle with the Creator in more or less intimate terms. But there is no real parallel for the truly dreadful experience expressed in the next stanza of 'Clay-Land Moods', in which God's 'terror-mood' drives the poet, creeping

> down rain-grooves, cravenly slink to hide
> In caves of the pit, and bruised with panic prayer
> Unknown to Mammon's sober workmen there,
> I wait till lightnings, thunder-rasps have died
> And God allows His terror-mood to lift
> From off the senseless rift.
>
> ('Clay-Land Moods')

The final stanza of the poem only obscurely explains the phenomenon. At the 'mystic hour', when the godhead-mine assumes its most terrifying guise, ('Alive with darker power'), the poet confesses to guilt, a 'pale Ghost-self of primal guilt that drives the nail'. When he becomes aware of his guilt—however pale, however primal—then the Clay-Land Moods seem comprehensible:

> Then I begin to know
> Why I am tested so.
>
> ('Clay-Land Moods')

This may be, to some extent, the inevitable paranoia of one who 'had feared the cold glance more than the bomb'. At any rate, the sense of guilt and persecution drives Clemo not into morbidity and withdrawal but into exultation: in Clemo's verse, the verb *thrill* is almost as common as the noun-epithet *bedrock*. At important points the two notions come together, as when, in 'Clay Phoenix' he speaks of the 'bedrock of nuptial sense', and then, a few lines later of the soul's 'destined thrill'. The clay phoenix of the poem's title rises only when the bedrock (literally here, as often in Clemo) is pierced:

> when the vein is touched, the signal granted,
> Comes the sharp snap of blast
> As the agnostic rock is splintered and the barrier passed.
>
> ('Clay Phoenix')

The phoenix inevitably suggests D. H. Lawrence, and in another poem, 'The Two Beds', Clemo elaborates the Cal-

vinism implicit in this poem to arrive at a condemnation of
Lawrence's philosophy. Lawrence is seen, in terms at once
naively literal and daringly metaphoric, as a fellow mine-
denizen ('You were a child of the black pit'). But where Clemo's
clay brings him to light and self-transcendence, Lawrence's
coal-blackness entraps him in a limiting sensuality:

> You did not find the true flesh,
> Which needs no fire, though it is tempered
> By fires of spirit, and does not lapse or swoon
> In quest or consummation, nor taste oblivion
> In love or death; it knows only
> Life more abundant, which means consciousness
> Ascending to the All-conscious, finding otherness
> In vigour of the new Day, not slipping, gliding,
> Fading down the shaft of drugged sense to the dead
> Coal-forests where the dark gods reign, silently breeding
> The sensual theosophy, the second death.
>
> ('The Two Beds')

It hardly matters that Clemo has misrepresented Lawrence's
ideas here: a literary debate is justified not in its truthfulness to
its object but in the self-consistency of its own expression. Even
if it is not the actual D. H. Lawrence that is on view here, what
is on view is recognizable and intelligible. Boldly, Clemo
resurrects the Christian dualism: there is, he urges, spiritual
truth and energy which transcends the merely physical. Indeed,
he argues, the 'spiritual' is itself misrepresented and distorted
by traffic with the sensuous. His poem 'A Calvinist in Love'
eschews country kisses, 'the lift of the sap' in Spring, because
they would

> but entrap
> Our souls and lead to treason.

The Calvinist's love, denying Fallen Nature, draws upon 'older,
sterner oceans':

> Our love is full-grown Dogma's offspring,
> Election's child,
> Making the wild
> Heats of our blood an offering.

The poem is in itself an extraordinary revival of the Caroline
love-lyric, an amazingly realistic handling of what had, in the
seventeenth century, been mere convention, courtesy, hyperbole:

> This truculent gale, this pang of winter
>   Awake our joy,
>   For they employ
> Moods that made Calvary splinter.

This is not neo-Platonism, but unadorned statement of fact. In
much the same way, Clemo revives the superseded Cartesian
dualism, making of outworn conventions a virile spiritual
reality. The great paradox of his work, indeed, is that his
Calvinism, his denial of the physical, proceeds from the greatest
concentration on the physical—a concentration enforced by
nature. Clemo's is an almost autistic poetry, whose boundaries
and limits are immediate, formed by touch, smell, and dim
sight. In no other poetry I know is there so powerful a sense of
the immediate surrounding environment. By this I mean something quite different from the powerful blazing actuality of
Birds, Beasts and Flowers, or the rich density of Keats' Odes. That
is poetry of exuberance and enjoyment: Keats and Lawrence
enjoy the play and interplay of sense and recollection. In Clemo,
such 'projection' is at a minimum, and the really devastating
effect of his work derives from this final cruel actualization of
the existential universe. Clemo's position in English poetry is
crucial: in him, in all respects, we see the final form of the
existential tradition. It does not seem an exaggeration to say
that in no other language but English could Clemo have
written poetry at all.

That he has done so, of course, is a matter not of regret but of
celebration: his poetry represents an outstanding triumph,
triumph of the human mind and of the great poetic and linguistic tradition that breathes through every line. But plainly,
such a triumph is related to the difficulties it overcame. By and
large, the very virtues of Clemo's work condemn a tradition
whose strengths they also attest. In the poetry of Ted Hughes,
we find a new power, a new arrogance, a new life.

Ted Hughes was an immediate embarrassment to the critical
establishment. Edwin Muir praised *The Hawk in the Rain* for its

'admirable violence', for 'sensuous, verbal and imaginative' power and there was a general sense of something, at last, having happened. Yet the reception accorded to the volume was by no means unequivocal. Critics whose sights were still on Intelligence were unimpressed. The later acknowledgement of the turning of the tide was itself significant: *Lupercal*, which Mr Alvarez welcomed, (though in terms so vague as to stand application to any approved-of volume: 'What Ted Hughes has done is to take a limited, personal theme, and by an act of immensely assured poetic skill, has broadened it until it seems to touch upon nearly everything that concerns us') represents a development in Hughes not altogether to be welcomed. Precisely what was most original and refreshing in *The Hawk* has disappeared in *Lupercal*, or as least gone underground, and Mr Alvarez's adjustment to the general view of Hughes as an important figure wasn't something that gave Hughes cause for unqualified satisfaction. For Hughes had moved beyond the existential tradition, from which he so clearly derived, by means of and in virtue of a certain swagger, an arrogant consciousness of role, as disturbing to Mr Alvarez as to Hughes's Cambridge contemporaries. For Cambridge this 'showing-off' was easy to place, as easy, in fact as the fairly clear derivation of the style or styles on display: here was the Dylan Thomas bohemianism, along with a clear verbal debt to Hopkins and Donne. Yet Hughes' language really did have that body, that 'strength of the English language', Dr Leavis had always been so concerned to preserve:

> . . . he hangs as in clear flames
> Like a torturer's iron instrument preparing
> With dense slow shudderings of greens, yellows, blues,
> Crimsoning into the barbs. . . .

The theme of the poem from which these lines come ('Macaw and Little Miss') comes straight out of the later Dylan Thomas —the Thomas of *Under Milk Wood* and 'Into her lying down head'. The technique brilliantly recalls the flamboyant metaphysical exuberance of English Marinism, of Crashaw, and Gongora himself. Like Thomas, Hughes showed an early concern for the enlightenment of virgins; and the natural synaesthesia that interprets colour into heat, heat into colour, was something easily enough learned from the seventeenth century if not from the early Edith Sitwell.

But the influences release, they do not imprison. Moreover, the principles according to which the language is organized are already Hughes's own. The packed vocabulary is shouldered easily, and the slow sequential thoroughness of the metaphor— 'Dense slow shudderings'—gathers energy within itself; the life is gathered and diffused through the lines; it does not explode in verbal squibs. 'Wrecked', he writes of a Famous Poet,

> And monstrous, so,
> As a Stegosaurus, a lumbering obsolete
> Arsenal of gigantic horn and plate
> From a time when half the world still burned, set
> To blink behind bars at the zoo.
>
> ('Famous Poet')

'Density'? 'Concreteness'? 'Body'? 'The strength of the English language'? Surely, these lines have them, or the terms have no meaning. If Hughes, like Dylan Thomas before him, does not 'keep up' the English language, it is impossible to conceive what or who *could*. The failure of the academic world to acknowledge Hughes demonstrated that behind the concern for the 'body' of the language, lay the effectively dictatorial policy of 'positive values'; systematic self-denigration, and the ultimately corrupting concern for integrity. Against all these laws, Hughes offended grievously: neither interested in irony nor distrustful of himself, he did not seem aware of 'integrity' at all. He thereby raised in an uncomfortable form the doubts that must always have existed within the academic establishment: how much of significance can continue to be created by poets so obsessed with *showing* their awareness of their own intellectual transgressions, of the 'unease' they alone saw beneath the facade? The effect of power in Hughes's verse originated, clearly, in the poet's confrontation with experience of a far deeper and more intense order than was generally evident in contemporary poetry.

The strength of Hughes's verse made the ironist academics around him look the little poets they were. But what was most galling about Hughes was that he really justified swagger with achievement:

> The wind flung a magpie away and a black-
> back gull bent like an iron bar slowly.
>
> ('Wind')

There are no massive words in these lines from 'Wind', no display of power. But the bending of the iron bar in the flight of the gull is felt physically, 'laced with instress': no poet since Hopkins had shown himself so capable of reinforcing the inert vocables of everyday words with such tension.

It cannot be too strongly emphasized that to speak of Hughes's strength and power is in no way to suggest any deficiency in fineness. Quite the contrary. 'Wind' itself demonstrates clearly enough that Hughes is possessed of an at times alarming combination of tremulousness and force. This is manifest often in the strange delicacy of the imagery. The house in 'Wind'

> Rang like some fine green goblet in the note
> That any second would shatter it.

The fine note is linked significantly with the idea of the destruction of the house. Similarly, in 'October Dawn', the onset of winter's fierceness is felt first in the 'premonition' of ice that forms on a glass of wine left out all night. The film of ice on the wine suggests that 'The ice-age had begun its heave'—and it *does* heave! The language sweats and strains under the load:

> Soon plate and rivet on pond and brook;
> Then tons of chain and massive lock
> To hold rivers.
>
> ('October Dawn')

Yet the massive armoury of *The Hawk in the Rain*—the Stegosaurus, the Mammoth and sabre-tooth, the whole ark-load of pre-historic monsters that inspire Hughes with such awe and admiration—all this would be nothing without the inner energy, an energy of control and containment, which enables him to

hold the experience until it has been forced to yield up its
latent significances. This energy governs and is governed by
the dangerous responsiveness of sensibility that finds its most
powerful symbols in the delicate and fragile as often as in the
immensely strong:

> Now is the globe shrunk tight
> Round the mouse's dulled wintering heart.
> Weasel and crow, as if moulded in brass,
> Move through an outer darkness
> Not in their right minds,
> With the other deaths. She, too, pursues her ends,
> Brutal as the stars of this month,
> Her pale head heavy as metal.
>
> ('Snowdrop')

(The line, 'She, too, pursues her ends', by the way, demonstrates how much can be packed into the conscious play upon
words: I find nothing in Geoffrey Hill with the same impact.)
'To paint a Waterlily' quite deliberately contrasts the
exquisitely refined with the savagely unformed in which it has
its ground. 'Still as a painting' the flower hardly trembles,

> Though the dragonfly alight,
> Whatever horror nudge her root.

Hughes's feeling for the subtly poised as well as the brutally predatory emerges too in the superbly sustained rhythm of the
following lines:

> . . . so the eyes praise
> To see the colours of these flies
>
> Rainbow their arcs, spark, or settle
> Cooling like beads of molten metal
>
> Through the spectrum.

The sinuous drawing-through of the image (we follow while
the beads cool) demonstrates the penetrativeness of Hughes's
mind. The effect derives here partly from the nouns used as

verbs—'raise', 'rainbow', 'spark'—but it is due above all to the steady pressure of intelligence Hughes always brings to bear upon his imagery.

At this distance in time, the amazing power and the close control that enabled Hughes to harness the huge energy of the verbiage seem less extraordinary than this penetrativeness— this ability to force through the motif of the poem to some further revelation of its inner nature. To effect what was effected in poems like 'The Horses' and 'The Hawk in the Rain' meant continuing the most serious struggle in the poem at the point where most poets, exhausted, leave off, a handful of verbal victories in their inert hands. It is this courage rather than the enormous energy and epic scale of his poetry that most signifi- cantly marks him off from his contemporaries, from Thom Gunn, for example, or Geoffrey Hill. For the penetration through to the final mangled stanza of 'The Hawk in the Rain' represents sustained spiritual strain, such strain as can only be endured when the poet is possessed of a seriousness bordering on the morbid, a seriousness that goes much deeper than the ironist concern for keeping an eye on the integrity-quotient. Indeed, it is a seriousness that cannot function unless the 'integrity' of the agent can be taken for granted.

Hughes is far too aware of the nature of force, and of destruc- tive force, to be too worried about his integrity: reading 'The Hawk in the Rain' one has the impression that a mild exercise in irony would be welcome. The seriousness of Hugh's appre- hension creates an uncomfortable sense of nervous strain, com- municated through the powerfully clogging verbiage:

> I drown in the drumming ploughland, I drag up
> Heel after heel from the swallowing of the earth's mouth,
> From clay that clutches my each step to the ankle
> With the habit of the dogged grave,
>
> ('The Hawk in the Rain')

The hanging hawk, of course, is by now a literary property, and had been for a hundred years before Hughes's poem appeared. There are birds of prey 'hanging at height', admired in their predatory precision and punch, in Hölderlin and Tennyson, to say nothing of the Hopkins sonnet with which Hughes's poem most clearly challenges comparison. It is perhaps enough at the moment to observe that Hughes's poem surpasses 'The Wind-hover' in the more consistently intense, sustainedly watchful momentum of its language. Like Hopkins, Hughes is stuck on one end of the energic axis of which the bird is the other pole. But where Hopkins merely celebrates the 'achieve of, the mastery of the thing', Hughes moves from an always precarious wariness of observation to an abrupt crash, observed with a confused, close force that dislocates syntax and disrupts rhythm:

> ... suffers the air, hurled upside down,
> Fall from his eye, the ponderous shires crash on him,
> The horizon trap him; the round angelic eye
> Smashed, mix his heart's blood with the mire of the land.

The curious awareness of animal mentality is basic to Hughes, of course. The animal poem had crystallized into a genre long before Hughes appeared: Hughes's 'Jaguar' bears much the relation to Rilke's 'Jardin des Plantes' as 'The Hawk' does to 'The Windhover'. The genre originates in Blake. Apart from certain moments in *Paradise Lost*, where there exists a com-parable awareness of the superior striking-power and efficiency of beasts of prey, the animal had always figured demeaningly in bestiary or fabliau to illustrate ethical ideas. Since Blake, animals have become more and more wholly admired for their power and energy. Blake's Tyger is not *used* as a symbol: it is *seen* as a symbol, and the connection with the mysterious spiritual nature of Christ is made in virtue of the animal's perceived power. The descent *via* Tennyson to Rilke and D. H. Lawrence parallels a complex of Nietzschean ideas about the disabling effect of thinking upon action: the striking-power and direct efficiency of animals derive from the absence of the mentation that in man so often blurs act and decision.

It is important to bear in mind that Hughes achieved his breakthrough not by reaction against the native English tradition but by a still deeper immersion in it. Behind him stand not only Lawrence and Hopkins, but also lesser poets like Edmund Blunden and James Stephens. This is more than a matter of a common fascination with natural processes and animal vitality, though this in itself amounts to considerably more than a fortuitous coincidence of interest. A poem like Blunden's 'The Pike', for instance, seems to have influenced

Hughes immediately and directly, not only in verbal texture, but also in the weird rustic awe with which it celebrates, aghast, the power of the killer-fish:

> still as the dead
> The great pike lies, the murderous patriarch
> Watching the waterpit sheer-shelving dark,
> Where through the plash his lithe bright vassals thread.

Hughesian, too, is the savagery and panache with which the 'glutted tyrant', slaughters its next victim, leaving the miller 'amazed at the whirl in the water'.

In general, this poem of Blunden's seems closer to Hughes than anything by Lawrence: like Hughes, Blunden is appalled and fascinated at once by the ruthlessness of the fish. Where Hughes surpasses Blunden is in extracting from the emotion a generalizable meaning. Hughes's 'Pike' not only improves on Blunden's poem in shearing off the anecdotalism; it makes the fascination with the fish part of a broader vision. In the same sort of way, Hughes's 'Meeting' goes far beyond James Stephens' 'The Goat-paths', not just spiritually but methodologically. Stephens' poem evokes with some skill the tricky, subtly mystical silence of the goats, but the sentimental tradition within which he works leads him to a faint formalism which is the reverse of precise. Initially, the goats might be horses or donkeys which

> day after day
> Stray in sunny quietness,
> Cropping here and cropping there,
> As they pause and turn and pass,
> Now a bit of heather spray,
> Now a mouthful of grass.

It isn't just the sing-song that irritates here: it is more the way an unintelligent reliance upon an inadequate conception of verse-form is allowed to obscure the data that are the poem's *raison d'être*. Later on, these edge their way through the poetics, and even gain a delicate equilibrium with them:

> If you approach they run away,
>   They leap and stare, away they bound,
>   With a sudden angry sound,
> To the sunny quietude;
> Crouching down where nothing stirs
>   In the silence of the furze,
> Crouching down again to brood
> In the sunny solitude.

What of course Stephens really has to communicate here is just this pernickety unpredictability of the animals. What his Edwardian sub-Romanticism beguiles him into thinking he has to communicate is a 'thought' about the depths of his mind, so that the interesting nerviness of the goats, skilfully conveyed by the nicely poised rhymes, is dissipated—or rather smothered— by fay rumination. The goats, in other words, become mere fodder for Peter Pan's narcissism:

> I would think until I found
> Something I can never find,
>   Something lying on the ground,
> In the bottom of my mind.

Today, the animal poem is worn out. We accept the super- iority of the instinctual life of animals over our rationalizing grayness as a matter of course—another element in the liberal blanket that covers our white, bourgeois European shame. In its specifically modern form, the great formative influence has of course been D. H. Lawrence. Spiritually, Hughes owes more to Lawrence, I think, than to any other English poet, except perhaps Hopkins. The two men could scarcely seem more different: Hughes so powerful, so much the forger of well-made poems, the wielder of a verbal pneumatic drill, Lawrence so finely intuitive, telepathically attentive to the movements of natural life, the diviner of unique free-verse organisms. Yet the nexus is there. But we must recall that the power and muscu- larity of Hughes are always complemented by the tremulous awareness that enables him to find the wave-length of the otter and the cat. Furthermore, just as Lawrence's perception that men were so much less men than lizards were lizards formed an integral part of an entire philosophico-religious conception and evaluation of civilized man, so Hughes's insight into the animal-ness of animals connects up with a profound vision of the nature of man, and a critique of man as he is now within the cage of civilization he has provided himself with. The cages of Hughes' jaguars and macaws are doubly ironical: man is so much more caged and imprisoned than the animals, and it is in virtue of his 'single vision' that he confines instinctive vitality behind bars.

Thus, the admiration for and kinship with a primitive and barbaric strain in the animal world has led Hughes to a con-tempt for 'mere' civilization and, even more, for the particular configuration of values and attitudes that has strangled man's native energy and perverted his force. He spoke with contempt of the 'rabble starlings of Trafalgar' at a time when it seemed obligatory for poets to chant and march in chorus; he can even 'see' the guts and character in the kind of Brigadier derided by John Osborne as 'pig-faced'. Hence, Hughes' radical dis-alignment with the attitudes of the current poetry goes deeper than a contempt for its namby-pamby techniques and auto-matic ironies: it reflects a profound philosophical negation of the complex of attitudes underlying it. It is a negation of the entire quiescent pattern of contemporary society, and a re-jection of facile political orthodoxy in favour of a re-discovery of more fundamental layers of passion and experience.

This is why he is fascinated by the primitively strong, by the cohesive energy of undifferentiated consciouness. In 'The Horses' he moves directly from the consideration of the horses themselves, megalithic creatures with a primitive statuesque-ness, 'draped manes and tilted hind hooves / Making no sound', to the eruption of a sunrise of a Beethovenian magnificence:

> Silently, and splitting to its core tore and flung cloud
> Shook the gulf open, showed blue,
> And the big planets hanging. . . .

There is nothing in English poetry of a comparable depth and power until we go back to the best of Dylan Thomas, or, further, to the Spender of 'Beethoven's Death Mask', and thence to

Lawrence himself. Hughes is fascinated too by war, by the
poetry of Wilfred Owen and Keith Douglas. His own poetry
takes place as on a dead planet, on a planet whose animation
has been suspended—or one whose time-scale has been dis-
located, so that a split-second takes an age to pass, as if

> the approaching planet, a half-day off,
> Hangs huge above the thin skulls of the silenced birds.
>
> ('Griefs for Dead Soldiers')

This sense of being the last man on earth reminds one strongly
of the only other contemporary English writer who has displayed gifts of the same order, Alan Sillitoe.

Like Sillitoe (and, I think, Colin Wilson), Ted Hughes has
both achieved success and remained isolated in an alien
society. All three have seen the necessity for a new and more
vital life-principle. In Hughes's case, it is in this way that we are
to answer the superficial cant of those critics and readers who
ask: 'When is Ted Hughes going to write about *People*?'. He
writes about people all the time. Incidentally, however, it is
worth remarking that there is more of what is misleadingly
called 'humanity' nowadays in *The Hawk in the Rain* than in any
other contemporary poetry except that of R. S. Thomas and
David Gascoyne. 'Griefs for Dead Soldiers', for example, after
showing us the public hypocrisy of the Cenotaph ceremony,
shows us the widow carrying on the daily life that has to be
carried on:

> Still she will carry cups from table to sink.

Like Lawrence, Hughes is impatient of the liberal mob-
spirit which, substituting a collective Dutch courage for its fear,
disguises the fear from itself. Hence, his respect for the pig-
faced Brigadier; for the last English wolf; the jaguar; for the
hawk roosting, that attacks out of the sun, and therefore has the
sun and all evolution 'behind' him. The stripping of humanity
down to the bare-forked animal is likely to run foul of *Lear* and
Hughes doesn't always avoid the trap: 'Horses' ('We were
born horses') substitutes a sententious literariness for archetypal relevance. But in 'Gog', Hughes strikes through to a

primal violence existing within the civilized man that is at the same time an intimation of a new awareness, a mutation almost, ready for the future. On the purely verbal level, it is one of Hughes' most carefully lithe achievements, its words vibrant with ambiguity, yet coming as though at the behest of a dream-consciousness:

> The dog's god is a scrap dropped from the table,
> The mouse's saviour is a ripe wheat grain.
> Hearing the Messiah cry
> My mouth widens in adoration.
>
> ('Gog')

The definitional finesse of the stanza quoted matches the semantic thoughtfulness of Geoffrey Hill, but shot through with the weird insight of Christopher Smart. As an act of spiritual archaeology, 'Gog' can be compared only with the finest moments of *The Waste Land*. Like Eliot, Hughes succeeds in returning to an ancient past which is at the same time a future barbarianism:

> My feetbones beat on the earth,
> Over the sound of motherly weeping. . . .

Like Lawrence, on the other hand, Hughes suggests the need for a new kind of man, a kind of mentality superior to the self-doubt of the liberal tradition, one which will extricate man before he is boxed up and herded by totalitarianism. These two processes—the archaeological analysis and the overreaching synthesis—provide the dynamism to Hughes's poetry. Indeed, the one is essential to the other: it is as the first English poet successfully to absorb the fact of D. H. Lawrence's thought that Hughes is so significant. Until the poet does something bigger than himself; that is, in some sense renounces the world of the schemes of emotion as Rimbaud did; he will be unable to achieve any significant composition. Hughes has expressed the need for this renunciation with chilling precision: 'Flowerlike' he wrote of his childhood,

> I loved nothing.
>
> ('May Day in Holderness')

Ignoring the distractions of self-awareness and positive
values, and also the disabused modesty the English had resigned
themselves to in their decline, D. H. Lawrence pierced to the
region at which new values, new consciousness, could exist.
This meant having the strength to ignore the self in order to
find it. Hughes too had this strength. Yet his own immediate
influence has not been healthy. Far from releasing English
poets from their self-consciousness, Hughes has reinforced a
tweedy anglo-Saxonism, a 'tough' menagerie-poetry, over-
conscious of its effect-mechanisms. Poets like Ted Walker and
Seamus Heaney are different poets from what they would have
been had Hughes never published; but they do not represent
significant advance in technique or consciousness. On the
contrary, their verse remains stuck in the back-lanes of Loam-
shire. I suggested above that the development from *The Hawk in
the Rain* to *Lupercal* was something of a disappointment. It was
no wonder that Mr Alvarez felt more at home with the second
volume: the technique was more under control than in the
Hawk, the debt to Hopkins no longer evident, and above all the
sheer arrogance of the title poem, of 'The Horses' and of the
love-lyrics (the finest modern examples, in my opinion, of poetry
consciously conceived along the lines of Donne's *Songs and
Sonnets*), had closed up into a dour reticence reminiscent more of
Edward than Dylan Thomas:

> But his stillness separated from the death
> Of the rotting grass and the ground. A wind chilled,
> And a fresh comfort tightened through him,
> Each hand stuffed deeper into the other sleeve.
>
> ('November')

'A fresh comfort'—as cold as this tramp's—tightens through
the whole of *Lupercal*. The general direction of development is
continued through *Wodwo* and *Crow*: the arrogant brio of *The
Hawk*—an inevitable victim of maturation, of course—seems to
burrow back into its own consciousness. The poetry becomes
harder and grimmer. Hughes now enters a subterranean world
within a world we normally inhabit. 'Wodwo' represents a new,
more paranoid use of the imagined consciousness more conventionally handled in 'Hawk Roosting'. Here there is no act of
projection, no pretended assumption of another consciousness,

but a sullen dissimulation. Hughes uses the Wodwo persona to set himself at bay, but not in the playfully serious way of 'Hawk Roosting'. Now, there is an almost morbid sense of profound alienation. Hughes seems deliberately to have set himself apart from us. This trend is pushed still further in *Crow*, a more consciously fundamental utterance, perhaps, than anything else in the language. Hughes has by this stage abandoned normal perspectives, normal landscapes: he has bracketted out the world of custom and tradition for a sub-atomic universe of intensely seen fragments and flashes. It is not possible yet to evaluate this poetry. What perhaps we can say is that Hughes has consciously ceased to be a model for younger English poets. He had always tried to shrug off the hero-role foisted onto him after *The Hawk in the Rain*, yet claimed by him in the volume. It seems fair to say that another turn had to be taken before English poetry could utilize the spiritual energy released by Hughes.

Hughes's poetry is, I have emphasized already, essentially a continuation of the native English tradition. He informed the existential sobriety of the English rural idiom with a new intensity, and a new sense of role and purpose. *Crow* makes it clear how far he was prepared to push this idiom: it is an often frenzied affirmation of the sense of existence that informs the greatest works of the tradition to which it is something of an end-game: what, we may imagine Hughes asking himself, must I do now? Where can I go—in what direction? The answer was downwards, downwards and inwards. Unable to change, but aware of the new climate in which he was working, Hughes simply thrust down into the earth at his feet. He pursued himself from an awareness of existence—the sense in 'Gog' of man having just that very second alighted on this earth—to an exploration of the foundations of this existence. *The Hawk in the Rain* has lost none of its force and freshness, but what appeared in the Cambridge of 1956 an alarming display of violence now seems a rustic idyll. By his late 'sixties Hughes was fighting for his creative survival, as his own 'Famous Poet' had refused to fight. *Crow* is a logical continuance of the direction insisted by the earlier books, but it is also a fairly desperate manoeuvre by a poet feeling himself out-flanked.

Yet the general direction of the book seems to have escaped notice, and along with it the imaginative mechanism of the

individual lyrics themselves. They represent a final concentration of Hughes's masculine energy: they smash through the
fibres of personal psychology (though nobody but Hughes could
have written them, these poems are completely de-personalized),
and of language itself. Their characteristic effort is to shatter
the appurtenances of consciousness, their characteristic movement from obscurity through density to clarity. Each lyric is a
drill trying to burst through to the other side. The other side
of what? The terms do not really matter—the other side of
consciousness, of matter, of pain, of ecstasy—the other side!
To emerge is the aim of the Crow poems. The whole book wants
to say with Lawrence, look, we have come through. The poet
tries to reach a peace in annihilation, and occasionally succeeds.
'Robin Song' ends with the world rolling 'to crush and silence
knowledge'. 'Conjuring in heaven' ends with Crow 'cataleptic'.
'Crow goes hunting' sees him finally 'speechless' with admiration. He hears 'the wingbeat of rock, and his own singing'.
Another conclusion finds him 'lonelier than ever'. The catalogue could be extended to include practically every poem in the
volume. Starting in horror and mess, the lyrics seek to force
their way through to silence, to peace, to non-being, to isolation
—to horror, perhaps, but a horror clean and without distraction
from itself. It is in this way that *Crow* finally destroys the existential tradition. Like Beckett—a writer who has interested Hughes
much over the past decade—Hughes too wants to be left just
with the consciousness of existence, even if this is Absurd.

In the *London Magazine* interview with Egbert Fass (obligatory reading for anyone interested in contemporary writing)
Hughes refers to Eliot and Beckett more than to any other
writers. The importance of *Crow* in relation to Western
literature in the mid-twentieth century cannot be over-estimated: it annihilates—and transcends in annihilating, a whole
phase of European consciousness. It does so by the exercise of
that enormous masculine energy I have already referred to. To
refer to it again, is to do more than to praise once more the poet's
endless metaphoric dynamism (the images zip off the page in
Crow with more demonic intensity than ever); it is rather to try
and focus the peculiar significance he has for poetry now. There
is nothing left to chance in Hughes's verse, nothing uncon-
trolled, nothing random. To a fault, his language is tightly

reined, and let out very much at the poet's discretion. The force of his writing in fact derives precisely from this. An effusion, a release of violence, such as we see in most of Dali's painting, and in the novels of Ian Fleming and the later films of Hitchcock, does not create anything like the sort of impression made by Hughes's poetry. The power of Ted Hughes's verse derives substantially from the containment of force, not from the release or indulgence of it. Hughes's masculinity is Faustian, Orphic—a refusal to allow the feminine its due. It is an asseveration of the Will, like Beethoven's music and Dürer's painting, or Milton's poetry. In the *London Magazine* interview, Hughes offers a historical hypothesis—owing much to Lawrence and Robert Graves—which goes far to explain his own mechanisms. He suggests that modern England has rejected the presence of the great goddess of the ancient world which Catholic countries have managed to retain in the figure of Mary. He uses Shakespeare's *Venus and Adonis* to stand for a basic conflict between reason and libido: 'Venus in Shakespeare's poem if one reads between the lines eventually murdered Adonis . . . she murdered him because he rejected her.'

He might have gone instead to Euripides, for the *Bacchae* dramatizes just this quarrel. What is interesting, however, is less the theory itself (Graves' *White Goddess* has put the case already) than Hughes's relations to its fundamental premise. Hughes equates Adonis with 'logical rationalism', and as it were sides with Venus in rejecting *his* rejection of her passionate unreason. Throughout the *London Magazine* interview, in fact, the poet puts all the weight of his massive personality behind the veneric principle, behind Dionysus, behind fertile and wise anti-rationalism. He sees his own role as bringing to light some of the otherwise fouling force of the id, and justifies his own 'poetry of violence' in terms of the much more evil violence wrought in the name of conscious restraint and 'logical rationalism'. So far so good: Hughes is a Dionysiac agent. But does he not himself reject Venus? On his reading, no, he doesn't. He sees his task, as I have noted, as releasing through his verse the violence pent up inside himself and ourselves by the kind of reason represented by Adonis (or Pentheus). Yet, on the other hand, he does: because he, more than anyone else, represents the dominance of the masculine will. He rejects the Bacchante because they insist upon the human spirit's being possessed, i.e. *dis*possessed, made female, passive, yielding. Hughes like Lawrence (see the scene in *Kangaroo* in which Kangaroo actually embraces Somers, and Somers all but dissolves, just holding on himself by the sheerest thread of masculine will which resists being melted into another) can never bring himself to submit to the law of the feminine. He is dangerously responsive to the tremors of the ether: he is an agent of the occult. Or is he not a double-agent, one who receives information and uses it for other purposes than the transmitter intended for it, one who cannot be trusted, *enfin*, one who will therefore be torn apart by the enraged Maenads?

Inevitably, talking about Ted Hughes means, sooner or later, getting back to mythology, for he is a great mythologist himself. Ironically, Jonathan Raban senses this: 'The interview itself is a marvellous piece of myth-making.'[1] The adjective is of course deflationary; 'marvellous' here means not to be taken seriously, much as one talks of a marvellous piece of camp in the theatre. The implication is that there is a lot of self-deception, self-delusion going on. Yet this activity—derisively styled myth-making by Mr Raban—is precisely the mode in which poets habitually work. Hughes is myth-making all the time, as we all are in fact, but with enormous intelligence and mental energy. And the key to the understanding of his very important role in modern writing lies in the interpretation of his personal myth. Hughes's relations to his own cultural past and to his fellow-poets in America and latterly in England can only be judged correctly if we learn to read his own explosive yet strangely subtle mode, and to set it against the quite opposite mode practised by Allen Ginsberg and his successors. Both Ginesberg and Hughes refused the 'logical rationalism' of their immediate cultural environment, but in different ways. It is not Hughes who is the Dionysiac agent, but Ginsberg. But the continuation of the argument belongs to the final chapter.

I have said that it is too soon to evaluate *Crow* yet. It seems necessary, nevertheless, to sound a warning at least about its reception. Perhaps because of the American Indian origination of some of its material, *Crow* was the first of Hughes's books to alert the American reading-public to the existence of an English

[1] J. Raban, *The Society of the Poem* (London, 1971), p. 165.

poet of greater weight and consequence than Charles Tomlinson or Thom Gunn. English readers should not let what is in fact a typical insularity in American responsiveness deter them from making a judgement about *Crow* which they are in a vastly superior position to make. *Crow* is a logical continuance of *Wodwo*, the predictable outcome of the development that began with *The Hawk in the Rain*. It is, still, a somewhat inhuman, even brutal book, with none of the broad strength of the best of Hughes's earlier poems. It remains to be seen whether Hughes's abandonment of a human perspective is ultimately justifiable.

10 The New Poetry in England

Out of the complex of techniques, attitudes and preoccupations that we have for convenience called the ironist or intellectualist position—the position defined by the criticism of Richards, Empson and Leavis—there grew a concept of intelligence so pervasive as to be invisible. This notion of intelligence seems totally inadequate to the appreciation and creation of serious poetry today. In the 'fifties this complex of ideals and idioms had congealed into the academic poetry usually referred to as the Movement: the Movement was based upon Oxford, and vaguely associated with Anger, but in fact it was the basic poetry published in England between the death of Dylan Thomas and the publication of *The Hawk in the Rain*. The rebellions against the Movement in the 'fifties can be taken with a granule of salt. *New Lines*, *Poetry Now*, and the P.E.N. anthologies mainly derive from the same source as the Movement and display the same academicism.

It is on the face of it the joylessness that so appals one about Movement poetry. Linguistically, poetry had never been more dead; it maintains a dualistic relationship with its subject-matter, which is observed through a window—reported on, in fact. This tendency is already apparent in the poetry of the Auden school. Poets like Roy Fuller are quite disabused of any magic in their symbols, which are not symbols, therefore, but merely images—'the image noted' in Fuller's wry phrase. This joyless, unvibrant quality in academic verse derives not from any given technical methods, nor from a mistaken ideology. It is a much more fundamental question, a question of attitude, of belief, of a way of life. The poets in Robert Conquest's anthologies[1] give the impression not only of leading dull lives, but of knowing too well that they do. Philip Larkin has treated this fundamental subject intelligently and profoundly: he made it the subject matter of his poetry, which is in itself a limited but valid strategy. Most Movement poets merely yawned and pottered along noting down the images, with, it goes without saying, appropriately ironic comment. A *T.L.S.* reviewer of a recent volume of Mr Conquest's noted this quality of disbelief in the validity of his imagery, without commenting on the implication of the fact:

> 'An image has its points, you may agree:
> I hardly find them adequate myself.'

It is hard to know whether the poet is now dissatisfied with the triteness of the moral pointers or simply issuing a warning that Movement poets never meant their readers to take all this wit-writing literally.[2]

But this is spiritual malaise, anaemia—the sclerosis of irony. And this is something much more disturbing than any mistaken theory of language. Poetry cannot be written without intense inner conviction, making for intellectual synthesis. Such a synthesis was attempted by ironist criticism, but its attempt was external, and irony is at most a purgative. Any more fundamental restoration must come from improved vision.

What is true of metaphor and image holds true for rhythm. Eliot's dictum that poetry should have at least the virtues of good prose is heretical, and led ultimately to the rhythmic paralysis of the Movement. It suggested parity of prose and poetic rhythm. The state of rhythm of a poem is the level at which it calls for sympathy and understanding. The rhythms of prose are by nature less wound-up, less involved with themselves than those of poetry. Only, we may say that the more prose tends towards the stasis of poetry, the more are prose values likely to elude genuine plastic statement. Similarly, the closer verse-patterns tend towards the elasticity of rhythmic

---

[1] Robert Conquest edited two anthologies entitled *New Lines,* published in London by Macmillan in 1962 and 1963. G. S. Fraser's *Poetry Now* (London, 1956) and Alvarez's *The New Poetry* make similar revolutionary claims in introductions prefacing basically the same kind of academicism.

[2] *Times Literary Supplement,* 7 August 1969, p. 872.

prose, in fact, the more genial becomes the poet's attitude, the less does the poet's peculiar grasp of values hold together. At a certain level we may fairly demand from the poet the argumentative coherence of good prose, and from the prose-writer the articulate fusion of poetry. The vision of Joyce's prose is inseparable from the words used to express it, and Eliot's *Four Quartets* show him using imagery in an immaculately referential manner, yet gaining, as he puts it, 'by the form'. But these extremes underline the main point: that prose and poetry values are severely different. Movement poetry paid the penalty of its underlying scepticism by becoming indistinguishable from rhymed prose: any revolution had to involve attitudes.

A new group of poets, for the moment identified as the Liverpool poets, rather as the early *City Lights* editions exposed the San Francisco poets, has taken over the position of the English *avant garde* from a slightly older London group, of whom the best known are Michael Horovitz and Pete Brown. (These statements are already dated as I write but I am concerned with diagnosis, not with documentation.) The Beatles played a notorious and over-advertised part in the emergence of the Liverpool poets. They guaranteed Patten, McGough and Henri a degree of publicity and a certain identity. Moreover, the sophistication of English pop music has cancelled the heavy American debt that has always burdened Horovitz. The whole scene, in fact, in which the first and the second English *avant garde* wavelets were set going, has altered decisively enough to account for the greater confidence and elegance of the best of the Liverpool writing. Horovitz and Brown were self-consciously isolated 'Beat' poets, American in orientation. Brian Patten, by contrast, owes as little to American poetry (and as much) as the Beatles themselves owe to Elvis Presley. Patten would never have written anything so crudely derivative from *Howl* as Horovitz's 'For Modern Man.'[3]

The whimsical anti-intellectualism in Horovitz (an Oxford product) derives directly from the Columbia students who wrote *Howl* and *On the Road*. The Liverpool poets draw their bias partly from the anti-metropolitan working-class animus that makes Everton supporters hate Arsenal supporters, partly

[3] Michael Horovitz, 'For Modern Man', *Wholly Communion* (London, 1965), pp. 54–7.

from the new status of Pop music in a world from which
intellectuals have abjectly abdicated. In both cases a fatally
naïve whimsy augments the McLuhan-ized bias against
serious thinking and deep feeling. Horovitz's whimsy is the
educated man's refusal of the values of reason, control and
analysis, in favour of Blakean Poetic Genius and Whitmanesque
Love. Patten's naïveté takes the form of a tremendously
simplistic anti-establishmentism: 'I'm dreaming of a white
Smethwick.' The attitudes in his poetry are naïvely taken over
wholesale and without question from the brutally simple-
minded world of protest songs, and hence lack any kind of real
conviction. The pie slackness of the attitudes expresses itself in
cummings-ish whimsy—'She's eating roses on toast with tulip
butter.'

But Patten is (or was at the time these poems were written) a
very young man. So the naïveté and dishonesty of his protest
poems is perhaps less surprising than the exceptional sophistication of the best poetry he had written by the same time. There is
in his best poetry a mature ease of movement, both in the
handling of the experience and in the verse itself, which can
perhaps only be achieved by a poet of promise young enough
to be able to act instinctively, yet old enough in experience to
compel our interest. In passing from Michael Horovitz to
Brian Patten, one is making the transition from an underground polemicist to a real poet; one is also moving from a
middle-class graduate to an uneducated man forced into early
maturity in the backstreets of a big city. Nothing in Horovitz,
for all the casualness of its Love, matches the curiously magic
realism of the best of the lyrics in which Patten describes the
semi-vagabond life of casually poignant sex he had so early
embraced.

The sophistication of 'On a Horse called Autumn', for instance, with its sexual ambiguities—the poet dreams of 'nude
horsemen breeched in leather', and his girl 'journeys among
lies' the poet made real—seems disproportionate to the
poet's youth. The air of opportunist slyness about these poems
is what marks Patten off from Roger McGough, and lends his
narcissism an almost Rimbaudian grace. 'A Talk with a
Wood' informs the subtle accuracy of Philip Larkin ('quiet
things soaked in rain, I saw through your thinning branches

The beginnings of suburbs') with a poignant release:

> quite alone there
> I thought of nothing but my footprints
>
> being filled, and love, distilled
> of people, drifted free, then
> the woods spoke with me.[4]

The remarkably deft purity of 'love distilled of people' ensures that the final de la Mare-ish fayness gets by. The companion piece, 'Travelling Between Places' (Rimbaud on the poetry-reading circuit), seems to me to have caught more delicately than anything else Patten has written to date the strange lost pathos that is his most intimate quality—a sense of having moved, too young, beyond purpose and point, and of having experienced in weariness and disillusion the beauty of nothingness that in one sense *is* the poetic insight.

This delicate awareness—arrived at through a blindly sensitive evasion of the ideational modes of language—can easily fall foul of whimsy precisely in avoiding the 'responsible':

> She attempts to understand why a sentence made of kisses
> is followed by the image
> of somebody wandering alone through semi-colons
>
> but cannot fathom out
>
> whose dawn she belongs in,
> so among them is silent[5]

So far so good; too good for the psychedelic pop-song ending:

> She will make love in technicolour
> She will be the fruitful lady of dawn.

It remains to be seen whether the subtly graceful tact of his language and feeling will give in to the 'little boy lost' charm—

> none to lead me
> away from here, none
> to lead me there.[6]

The love poems which are his best achievement to date are all

[4] Brian Patten, 'A Talk with a Wood', *Penguin Modern Poets 10* (Harmondsworth, 1967), p. 121.
[5] Patten, 'The Fruitful Lady of Dawn', *Penguin Modern Poets 10*, p. 123.
[6] Patten, 'On the Dawn Boat', *Penguin Modern Poets 10*, p. 124.

curiously written in the margin, epitaphs to evanescent oppor-
tunities better for not having been seized doggedly, but merely
touched in passing. They are therefore Romantic, and this is their
beauty, but also their lightness. In such a young poet this should
hardly matter: already 'Room' and 'Song for Last Year's Wife'
have achieved in their bleakness a sufficiently moving plainness:

> I imagine you,
> waking in another city, touched
> by this same hour. So ordinary
> a thing as loss comes now and touches me.[7]

It is strange that a man so young, and dedicated to the Beat-
Pop religion of maximum pleasure, should so soon have achieved
so soiled a sadness, and have found himself most authentically in
fatigue. The Romantics, it is plain, have much to teach us.

Patten's books, *Little Johnny's Confession* and *Notes to the
Hurrying Man*, hold out little promise of a mature poetry outside the confines of the lyricism of love and disillusion he had
mastered by the time he was twenty. Where he attempts to
'confront' the political and religious realities of the modern
world, he is jejune, childish even, glibly purveying the stock
attitudes of the Beat-Pop world. The other poets of the Liverpool triumvirate confirm the general impression of lightness,
though with interesting variations. Adrian Henri is, like
Ferlinghetti, the Lepidus of the outfit and need not detain us.
Roger McGough has none of Patten's grace: he is very much
less 'a poet', substituting a skittish fantasy for Patten's lyricism.
Where Patten is Romantic, McGough is domestic. Yet when it
comes to 'the human condition' (that old music-hall joke),
McGough reveals an incomparably greater capacity for common
sympathy. Patten admits the workers and the underprivileged
into his narcissism only by a selfconscious act of Protest, as when,
for example, he patronizes 'Delicate John'. Thus, while situation poems like McGough's 'The Fish' have little or nothing of
Patten's romantic aplomb, there is nothing in Patten with a
tithe of the 'compassion' of McGough's semi-humorous,
quasi-fantastic 'My Bus Conductor', or 'What you are':

> you are the distance
> between Hiroshima and Calvary
> measured in mother's kisses

[7] Patten, 'Song for Last Year's Wife', *Penguin Modern Poets 10*, p. 106.

> you are the distance
> between the accident and the telephone box
> measured in heartbeats
>
> you are the distance
> between power and politicians
> measured in half-masts[8]

McGough's habit of taking a straight look at things he finds both funny and heart-breaking redeems the frequent rhythmic slovenliness of his shapeless verse, and imparts to his sometimes merely zany gabbling a convincing continuity of voice-tone:

> increasingly oftennow
> you reach into your handbag
> (the one I bought you some xmasses ago)
> and bringing forth
> a pair of dead cats
> skinned and glistening
> like the undersides of tongues
> or old elastoplasts
> sticky with earwigs
> you hurl them at my eyes
> and laugh cruellongly
> why?
> even though we have grown older together
> and my kisses are little more than functional
> i still love you
> you and your strange ways[9]

It needs considerable genuineness to be able to write a line like 'i still love you'; it needs far more, by way of skill and verbal know-how, to make it mean as much as McGough makes it mean here. The things she finds in her handbag, too, are at once grubbily real (how exactly he has caught the 'handbag' feeling) and weirdly surrealist. McGough's best gift in fact is his clever sense of everyday surrealism; though more 'fantastic' than Patten's, his inventions have a more real applicability. The straightness of a gaze that has no social or intellectual illusions about itself, yet can see the pathetic and the contemptible for what they are, condenses the collapsed perspectives of

---

[8] Roger McGough, 'What You Are', *Penguin Modern Poets 10*, p. 78.
[9] McGough, 'You and Your Strange Ways', *Penguin Modern Poets 10*, p. 68.

pathos and absurdity that make up the tangled complexity of modern urban life. The man in the wheel-chair run over by a bus reminds McGough of something in his cultural background:

> But something else obsessed my brain,
> The canvas, twistedsteel and cane
> His chair speadeagled in the rain
> Like a fallen birdman.[10]

It is the relevant irreverence, the not-being-coerced into the stock response of respectable pity, that has so far produced or sponsored McGough's most successful writing. Rarely very interesting technically, never possessed of grace, his verse nevertheless expresses an odd off-beat objectivity that serves his genuine sympathy for the non-U better than the self-important would-be toughness of Patten. But for the accidental incidents that led him to write poetry in the first place (ten years ago he would hardly have), McGough might be just one among the fifty thousand pairs of eyes at Anfield or Goodison Park.

II

The Liverpool poets have been largely a *succès de publicité*, a success of no less significance than the English Pop breakthrough which helped them into existence. The sophistication of English Pop music in the early and middle 'sixties was never harnessed to verbal intelligence of the type displayed by Bob Dylan and Paul Simon in the United States. The Beatles' lyrics, in spite of the cooked-up Colour Supplement vogue of Lennon's Stanley Unwin-ish *In His Own Write*, have never risen to literary respectability. Although less banal than those of the Rolling Stones, the Lennon-McCartney lyrics merely gesture towards meaning. Sometimes this has been enough, enough, that is, to help the music itself to its often very high level. In songs like *Eleanor Rigby*, *A Day in the Life*, *Penny Lane*, *Norwegian Wood*, the distinguished melodic invention receives just enough support from the idea-content of the words to compensate for the lack of real verbal wit, and lift the entire article above the Gershwin–Cole Porter level some critics seen to want to peg it

---

[10] McGough, 'The Fallen Birdman', *Penguin Modern Poets 10*, p. 66.

at. It often happens in song-writing that the composer finds in the words he sets just enough unarticulated emotion to afford him a valid terrain for invention.[11] Schubert found in Müller, George Butterworth and Vaughan Williams in Housman, something better for their expressive purposes than great poetry: powerful but incoherent emotion which they in turn proceeded to refine and fill out into expression. Ten years ago, McCartney and Lennon would have been a good Tin Pan Alley team in a world which had no interest in content and demanded a more professional if more vulgar style of performance. As it was, accidents of time enabled them to exploit the Beat breakthrough in poetry and the psychedelic world's hunger for spiritual food, and to create something more significant.

Experience and recent history suggest that significant literary advances tend to proceed out of the universities. Certainly, the limitations of the Liverpool group stem from their cultural illiteracy. The American Beat breakthrough was engineered and masterminded by Columbia graduates working upon the groundwork of extremely cultured older men such as Rexroth and Olson. The Simon and Garfunkel lyrics, for instance, reflect an intellectual level greatly superior to that of McCartney and Lennon. The anti-intellectual bias of so much of Kerouac and Ginsberg should not blind us to the fact that considerable cultivation of mind is needed to focus the aims and ambitions of an artistic *avant garde*. Hitherto, the English *avant garde* has lacked this kind of cultivation. It has taken its lead from semi-literate Pop music. When it has been possessed of literacy, as in the case of Michael Horovitz and the amateur Pop composer Jonathan King, it has been under the worst aspect of Ginsberg's influence—the stupid disavowal of intelligence.

Michael Horovitz's *Afterwords* to his anthology of English Underground poetry[12] is admirable: it hits the right targets and has the right spirit. But its intelligence (shown for example, in the awareness of the necessity of a Milton-oriented revolution in poetic theory and practice) allows itself to be swamped by the true-yet-useless 'All you need is love' chant—*Amor vincit omnia*

---

[11] See Susanne K. Langer, *Feeling and Form* (London, 1953), for discussion of this subject.

[12] Michael Horovitz, Afterwords to *Children of Albion: Poetry of the 'Underground' in Britain* (Harmondsworth, 1969), pp. 317–77.

(ironically quoted in The *Canterbury Tales* Prologue, putting Horovitz roughly in the Prioress's shoes). Poetry has, I feel, to be more hard-edged than this euphoric gush. Mr Horovitz intimates as much himself by falling back regularly on the 'right' intellectual influences—Marcuse is there ('the exclusively mechanic directions of a technological millennium'), and Marshall McLuhan, backing up William Burroughs as hollowly as ever. There is something tired and mechanical in Mr Horovitz's rosary-telling of the Establishment's evils, and the virtues of not washing and of making love. This is especially so since Michael Horovitz's idol, Blake, based his life upon hard work and precision. The greatest poets—Milton, Shakespeare, Eliot, Wordsworth—have always been concerned to be fully alive and aware in the mind. Having gained a victory over the totally inadequate academic conception of 'intelligence' (something Empsonian and self-denigrating), it seems a pity to throw it all away by appearing to have stopped thinking altogether. What we need is a super-awareness, not a mental sleep.

To some extent the social backgrounds are responsible. It is difficult for an educated Englishman not to take sides in the clearly articulated class set-up of English society. Moreover, the idea of a poet who is at once academic and abreast of the most advanced current feeling (where indeed he is not creating it) is inconceivable in England. Yet this is precisely the position of, say, Robert Duncan in the States. And the explanation lies in the possibility of the existence of an institution like Black Mountain College: Dartington Hall is the nearest approach to Black Mountain in England, and Dartington, for all its elegant *sang-froid*, sadly lacks the cultural sophistication and forwardness that marked Black Mountain in its best days.

No serious literary idiom is possible without the co-operation and participation of the greatest intellectual sophistication available in the society in which it occurs. The time when intelligence in poetry meant something of an Empsonian order has passed. Major poetry can only be written when a great deal more of the mind and the emotional being of the poet is engaged than appears active in the poetry I have described as academic. It cannot do without indefinite flexibity and suggestibility in 'form' and movement—the kind of flexibility, say, afforded by the researches of Eliot, Crane, the Imagists and the Surrealists. No genuine poetic revolution can be carried through without a fracturing of the currently practised poetic idiom—for poetry is a way of knowing and doing, as well as a way of expresssing, and what is known alters with the creation of new techniques. Or, to put the same thing in another way, new techniques are demanded for new intuitions. 'The medium is the message' is meaningless, but it seems to indicate that fragile relationship between 'form' and 'content' which reactionary minds of every era have been blind to. A conception of 'form' such as W. H. Auden has expressed [13] is incompatible with the creation of the highest poetry.

But equally, no revolution can be carried through in the absence of a compact body of spiritual aims and beliefs at variance with the received orthodoxy of the time, and its associated modes of knowing. As Wordsworth was sustained in his great purpose by a new theory of mind and by a profounder insight into the deeper spiritual drives of humanity, and as T. S. Eliot adapted the spiritual ideals of symbolism, so the new poetry today has broken through the fog of academic withdrawal into a climate of keen observation, flexible, attentive and adventurous: in this breakthrough it has been informed by a loose and wide-ranging complex of spiritual ideals.

Although the revolution has had to be through a disruption of forms, a by-product of the process has been a revitalization of traditional rhyme and stanza: even the relatively whimsical use of limerick by Roger McGough shows a more functional approach to the question of rhyme than the quite mechanical, unthinking adherence of academic poets like Laurence Lerner or Geoffrey Hill, whose technique has little relation to the specific occasion. In England there has been only a partial and fragmentary free verse tradition. D. H. Lawrence has had to wait until now for any real appreciation and anyway is a notoriously dangerous model, since his verse depends entirely upon the intensity of voice by which it is always governed. For

[13] W. H. Auden, 'Writing', *The Dyer's Hand and other essays* (London, 1963). Auden writes at one point: 'Rhymes, metres, stanza forms, etc., are like servants. If the master is fair enough to win their affection and firm enough to command their respect, the result is an orderly happy household. If he is too tyrannical, they give notice; if he lacks authority, they become slovenly, impertinent, drunk and dishonest', p. 22.

the most part, English free verse has been the province of amateurs like Herbert Read and Richard Aldington, and American-oriented imagists like Charles Tomlinson and Basil Bunting. Almost alone among English *avant garde* poets, Edith Sitwell developed her initially irresponsible free verse fantasy into a powerful and flexible instrument able to take on themes as profoundly important as the Blitz and Hiroshima.

The great obstacle of free verse—the dream of absolute spontaneity that amounts in practice to a steady diffusion of intensity—is a legacy of Surrealism still active in the writing of Jack Kerouac and the poetry of Gerard Malanga. Because of this, Anselm Hollo, the best known of the English free verse poets who achieved any sort of publication before the days of Penguin New Poets, only occasionally allows the delicate rhythm of cool, modern jazz to find in his scattered phrases the subtly rocking momentum that embodies not only the spirit of jazz but the feeling for a way of life:

> Walk by,
> Walk on by.[14]

The values of the world of modern jazz fuse, via the relaxed influence of the American Negro, into the field of Indian and Chinese mysticism and psycho-religion later popularized and debased in the publicity-conscious flirtation the Beatles carried on with the Maharishi. The Zen cult has in fact played a profound part in the Beat revolution:

> A man
> standing
> in the road, in the way
> of himself
> standing, being
> himself
> too exactly, to tell you
> the road or
> the ways of
> the town:
> >   see him
> >   —waving his arms![15]

[14] I have been unable to check the source of these lines. The poem appeared, however, in the London periodical *Residu*, no. 2 (1967).

[15] Hollo, 'The Struggle', *And it is a Song* (London, 1965), p. 25.

The debt to a whole way of thinking in these lines of Hollo's does not diminish the performance; on the contrary, it goes far to explain their confidence. The insight connects up with much of the ideational content of the poetry of Levertov and Creeley, and rests upon the foundation of the Beat absorption of the Tao and Zen. We note, too, the fully-functional ease of Hollo's play upon the key-word of his poem—'way'. The man stands in 'the way' of himself in the sense that he is an obstruction to himself, and also is too much himself to traffic in 'life' and communication (he cannot tell us 'the road or / the ways of / the town'). His chosen personality, or rather the personality that happened to him through absence of wise choice, stands in his way, yet the 'way' (= Tao) is the man, is himself. Hence he blocks himself in being himself. This compression and elusive certainty of touch is made available to Hollo by the sophistica-ted technical means at his disposal.

A ragged a-rhythmic annotationism often gets in the way of this kind of semantic and rhythmic limpidity. (The extent to which the rhythm makes the 'meaning' accessible both to Hollo and to us in itself clarifies and justifies the technical revolution we have witnessed). His poetry frequently ambles and dawdles through rhythm after rhythm without really finding a pulse, nor yet throwing up in definition any remarkable observation.

For free verse demands a quiet inner discipline, the discipline, for example, of D. H. Lawrence, closely organizing, waiting for the moment of its inner fulfilment. Hollo's carelessness derives perhaps from the negative side of the Beat programme: since academic techniques are mostly irrelevant to expression, let us open our mouths and speak whenever we feel like it. The true poet must know when to resist opening his mouth, must resist gratifying his petty impulses to impress or merely to appear in front of himself in words. If we compare Hollo's 'Our Lady without nipples' with John Wieners's 'A Poem for Museum Goers', we cannot help observing the greater definition of Wieners's images, even though, like Hollo's, these images are 'inner', inspired by the expressionist fantasies of Edvard Munch:

                    The nets are down.
                    Hugh seasnakes
                    squirm on shore

taking away even
the beach from us.[16]

Hollo's poem gropes after the rhythmic counterpoint of his own best verse, but fails anywhere to consummate its own imagery. The resultant symbolism lacks wit:

imagine a rifle
charged with a bullet
growing larger and longer
it remains in the rifle—
if you let the bullet get big
it will break the rifle when it comes[17]

Yet at its best, Hollo's poetry again demonstrates how superior Beat poetry is to the academicism it displaced, even in fields that would seem cut for the sober-sided 'responsible' poets of the academies and the literary journals. Sex, and the celebration of it, certainly belong more naturally to the Beat movement: the new Lawrentian–Reichian attitudes towards sex and inhibition have always been an important part of Beat ideology. But sex within marriage, and a more or less straight domesticity, would appear more naturally suited to academic poetry. Actually, this is the reverse of the truth: we find that Beat poets like LeRoi Jones and Anselm Hollo treat their wives with greater tenderness and poetic feeling than academic poets like David Holbrook, Edwin Brock or even Stephen Spender. Confronted with the family and the long-suffering wife (those enemies of promise), Spender and Holbrook, for example, immediately lose interest: the poems they dedicate to their wives and children become heavy labours of conjugal duty, devoid of love and pleasure. The family is not just resented: it is to be reminded of father's genial considerateness by having a poem devoted to it. The poems in question, needless to say, become exhibitions of father's extreme sensitivity. Thus, after his child's departure from the house, Spender tells us how he put the toys away,

Each plaything that he'd touched, an exposed nerve.[18]

[16] John Wieners, 'A Poem for Museum Goers', Donald M. Allen (ed.), *The New American Poetry* (New York, 1960), p. 372.

[17] Hollo, 'Our Lady without nipples', *And it is a Song*, p. 4.

[18] Stephen Spender, 'Empty House', *Collected Poems* (London, 1955), p. 191.

Edwin Brock is better at confessing—confessing his inadequacies, his loud-mouthedness, his selfishness. The trouble is
that we believe him, and do not see any especial beauty in the
act of confession:

> My own two kids could tell them: the slapped
> face and the breakfast roar of the bore who sat
> cuddling himself in the flat's best corner.[19]

A comparison of Spender and Brock as domestic poets would
tell us quite a lot about the development of the poetry of confession, of failure, of inadequacy, over the past thirty years.
Much more realism and reality is now demanded of the poet:
Spender's evasiveness would no longer pass muster. But essentially the comparison would demonstrate yet again the
definiteness, the actuality, of the tradition I have been referring
to variously as academic and ironist, and would in fact best be
described simply as square. The task of the poet is still basically
the same in Brock as in the 'thirties poets: to unmask his own
inadequacies and his sense of 'unease', thereby intimating his
'self-awareness' and ensuring his own integrity.

This kind of domestic verse is ugly: a painstaking reminder to
the wives of the poet's 'consideration'. Love, being largely
identified with de Rougemont romance, plays little part in it.
Hence, this extraordinary fact that the poetry of the 'irresponsible' hippies and beatniks is more 'responsible' towards
wives and children, for instance, than that of the wage-earning
insider poets. The Beat ideals, often stridently and childishly
trumpeted, must in fact be taken seriously: it is a matter of the
way life is lived, not of the techniques with which poetry is
written. In his 'domestic poem', '& with your hearts', Anselm
Hollo reproduces some of the mannerisms of jazz erotica a
shade too carefully, but still convinces at the point of orgasm:

> Dawn. Dusk. Dawn. Dusk
> We could stand here forever
>   blind
> with what is jetting through[20]

[19] Edwin Brock, 'On Being Chosen for a Schools Anthology', *Penguin Modern
Poets 8* (Harmondsworth, 1966), p. 20.
[20] Hollo, '& with your hearts', *And it is a Song*, p. 31.

The Hemingway-ish passage earlier in the same sequence would serve admirably too, to illustrate the free intercourse of Beat symbolism which can be noted also in Robert Creeley:

> When the lines are cast
> the nets are set and waiting
> the tunnies come slipping through the moonlit sea
>
> soft and low
> they go
>
> even their speed a slowness, as it is
> with us at night

The blues rhythm—'soft and low / they go'—achieved by syncopatedly timed repetition of sound is still more effective in these lines because of the 'domestic' subject-matter, and the wholeness it implies. Anselm Hollo is perhaps too consciously an English Beat poet to have reached any very marked stage of individuation. More often than not the very distinctive subtlety of rhythm I have tried to describe above is lost within a loose jacket of all-permissive Beat mannerisms. He seems to have been impersonating an American poet for so long that it seems to have escaped his notice that he has acquired a voice of his own.

Anselm Hollo's poetry is still a slight achievement, slight in movement and in content. But its sophistication of technique is symptomatic of the new assurance in English poetry. The revolution has, so to speak, taken place. Michael Horovitz's Penguin anthology, *Children of Albion*, contains much that is ephemeral, slack and modish—the usual fay in-jokes and slovenly Beat narratives, and, of course, much less palatably, the obligatory stock of Protest, which remind us for the millionth time that nothing is so distasteful as righteous indignation, particularly when the rumble of the bandwaggon wheels accompanies its shrillness. The Love-hallucinogen euphoria too strikes one even now as datedly feminine: there is a tough, revolutionary discipline in the best American Beat poetry. But there was always in Beat polemics the fatal vulnerability to sensation, to Huxley-esque swooning. It is difficult to see how the regeneration of Albion is to be effected in this way. Probably, this is because Mr Horovitz himself is a 'dated' figure (but

aren't we all?), a persevering acolyte of Allen Ginsberg—a
Beat poet, in fact, in a world from which they have already
passed away. The new poetry is no longer Beat poetry: it is
something much suaver, more accomplished, already aware
that Love is a far more complex and dubious thing than
Horovitz suggests, that it is not only *not* the panacea but a
psychologically dangerous quantity, made up of ambivalence,
narcissism, jungle warfare and the *Wille zur Macht*. This new
awareness suggests the filtering through of the influence of D. H.
Lawrence, and the craftier, slyer side of William Blake, that
subtle knower of what perhaps no one should know. Certainly,
reading the poetry of Mark Hyatt—the strangest and most
talented poet in *Children of Albion*—one can almost accept the
fact of a new Elizabethan age in which language again is
natural to the tongue and the mind.

Hyatt writes like a newcomer to language, to the worlds it
opens up. Like the prose of Elizabethan mariners, merchants
and explorers, his poetry strikes metaphor at every turn. His
words have had no traffic with idea and concept, they are like
stones:

<blockquote>

am I
the damned tormentor? Out for the infernal
banquet, a feared king of darkness, fat on
fragments of huge committed mankind, violent with
my shadow, a countryside poverty, the desperately
fallen marriage of laughing-shock, with unmasked
documents about the rendezvous, freely lavishing
on a lady's honour, meanwhile the years go on, the
triumph of the spectators, flogs on sight.
The jugglers work below on small talent, in the
human legions, out to kill, me with my adventurous
deeds, there's no intermission on any vice, the
idleness of wealthy knowledge flies, teeming with
sad shepherds, beginning to end, chilled relaxation
with an emperor's heart, the victim of a curse. . . .[21]
</blockquote>

And so it goes on, medievally in the centre of its own universe,
soliloquizing in a Jacobean psycho-drama, asking no questions
of its metaphor, taking for granted the public relevance of its

[21] Mark Hyatt, 'Eleemosynary', *Children of Albion*, p. 157.

language. One does not have to know the facts (if any) behind this paranoid scene to appreciate its structures and therefore its meaning. Here comes the villain:

> Now I am flying towards the experienced champion,
> and I am stuck in the middle of a cob'web, soon the
> beast will come down and suck my body, a sunbeam
> will bring confusion, it must be the adversary, the
> task of conquering must be choice, wrinkled and bent
> she comes, this queen engages the gigantic circus
> crowds to recognize the enemy, with promise and pledge
> she comes forth, dragging her injections of new tortures. . . .

This magic carnival of words is rounded with a confession of the ambivalence that nerves up the whole performance:

> my killer is
> a friend, unable to make any answers, it's the onlookers
> that slash the mind, for death.

A far cry from Michael Horovitz's idyllic republic of letters.

III

At the time of writing, the best proof of the effectual existence of an English poetic renascence is probably to be found in the two volumes of Lee Harwood, *The White Room* and *Landscape*. Or rather, in the volume of slight but technically sophisticated verse Harwood's eclectic love-poetry makes it possible to ignore. The accomplishment of poets like Spike Hawkins, Dave Cunliffe, Libby Houston and Hugo Williams for instance testifies to the power of the undertow much as the skill and finesse of Campell, Moore, Hunt, Rogers, etc. gave evidence of the overall breadth and strength of Romanticism. It isn't easy to gauge Harwood's stature at this stage. His is an agile, fluent, assured, flexible idiom, free of strain, unconcerned with making effects. The very existence of such an instrument is in itself impressive: there is behind it a subtle, absorbed tradition.

Harwood owes nothing whatsoever to Allen Ginsberg. This in itself is not unusual or surprising: there is practically no trace of the heavy Rock idiom in contemporary poetry in either England or America. On the contrary, the earnest *Howl* chant

has disappeared, to be replaced by a cool, refined, often wil-
fully 'degenerate' idiom. Harwood owes much, as any poet
working in London must, to the post-*Howl* tradition of American poetry—to individual poets like Michael McClure, for
instance, and LeRoi Jones. And it would be a mistake to ignore
the huge fact of American poetry after Ginsberg and Corso in
favour of the French Surrealist debt. Harwood edited (or edits?
I do not know for certain) a periodical called *Tzarad*, in homage
to Tristan Tzara. There is an element of immaturity in the
choice of *maître*: why Tzara? Whoever read anything by Tzara,
or André Breton, for that matter, apart from the manifestoes?
Or de Sade, or Lautréamont? These cult-figures are really just
names. Harwood's Paris derivation is if not spurious at least
ambiguous. In the 'fifties (when Harwood was maturing) Paris
still meant experiment to the London-based writer, release from
tweedy irony and academic conservatism. It was for America to
provide the positive spiritual blast-off, in poetry as in painting;
and the real force behind Harwood is not Tristan Tzara or
French Surrealism but the whole complex phenomenon of
recent trans-atlantic culture with its amalgam of raw optimism
and sophisticated disabusement.

Harwood takes from Surrealism what David Gascoyne and
Kenneth Patchen had taken earlier—a freedom of reference,
the melting metamorphosis of image into image, the subtle
juxtaposition of context and tone, the whole battery of mind-
imagery—jungles, forests, deserts, mountains, moonlight. At
some points, Harwood definitely recalls Patchen. Compare this
by Harwood—

> In a mountain sun
> pursued by my own phantoms
> monsters lurking in the forest
> > in my head
> an innocent forest out there
> mountain flowers and meadows
> the swirl of grass and pines hissing[22]

with this by Patchen—

> The columns of death glow faintly white
> Within the forests of this destroying planet

[22] Lee Harwood, 'For John in the Mountains', *The White Room* (London, 1968),
p. 35.

> Here gleeful beasts track each other
> Through lanes of winter and rotting heroes.[23]

The jungle, mountain, forest and bestial images so common in Surrealist poetry are abundant in Harwood, and with much of their traditional metaphoric force. But they come interspersed with an almost Auden-esque apparatus of military and social imagery. 'When I see you again', one of the best love-lyrics of *The White Room*, begins on the traditional Surrealist frequency—

> without you
> my star roams hungry
> a confusion of galaxies
> my charts don't work anymore.[24]

The last line has already introduced the quasi-military metaphor-structure of journeys and explorations which continues in the next group—

> hunch over my navigation table
> bears running free in the restroom
> my hand bleeds.

Hereafter it becomes impossible to plot the poem's course, so free are its transitions, so assured is its interchanging metaphor pattern.

> I float in your eyes
> lake half seen through the tall marsh
> grass
> sun swallowed
> and now inside your head
> dazzling me.

The first metaphor there is obviously blue eyes seen through lashes—but that does next to nothing to explain the sensuous impact of the writing. The whole poem is unanchored, free *yet* (and this is what counts) it is a statement, in a tone of voice recognizably Harwood's own. The Surrealist hermeticism has

[23] Kenneth Patchen, 'These Unreturning Destinies', *Selected Poems* (New York, 1957), p. 4.
[24] Harwood, 'When I see you again', *The White Room*, p. 15.

gone completely. Where in Dylan Thomas and the early Gascoyne the imagery exists in a vacuum, Harwood is always speaking to someone, or at least writing in a tonal idiom which the poet knows has common acceptance: this is a poetry of vocal context, which is to say of common values and shared experience. This is the crucial difference between Harwood's poetry and that of the Surrealists. It is the difference, largely, between the essentially alienated, negative culture of France, which looks backward to Rimbaud, Mallarmé and Lautréamont, and the energetic forward-looking culture of America.

Alienation in fact appears as a fact in the landscape rather than a matter for concern. Gone for good are the tortured am-I-being-honest-with-myself? wrangles that preoccupied Roy Fuller and Philip Larkin. Nothing seems more ironically significant of the general change in intellectual climate than the fact that Roy Fuller (in his role of Oxford professor) could spend so much time castigating the irresponsibility of the 'younger' generation. Fuller's own poetry is so hung-over with a crisis which has become comfortable with usage that it is incapable any longer of expressing experience. Turning from *Brutus' Orchard* to *The White Room* is turning from death to life. The fact that Harwood's political poetry is no more successful than Brian Patten's may mean nothing more than that this kind of right-thinking radicalism can no longer generate spiritual interest. Harwood's 'Cable Street' is even more callow than Patten's 'I'm dreaming of a white Smethwick', a shallow melange of tired attitudes occasionally springing into narcissistic life—

> the river slides smoothly
> under many bridges[25]

only to relapse into a feeble pastiche of the worst Ginsberg—

> testes, balls. cock of great
> space galaxies.
>   Do the presidents know what they're doing?

Do the *poets* know what *they're* doing? Certainly, no English poet, with the exception of Roger McGough, has produced any

[25] Harwood, 'Cable Street', *The White Room*, p. 27.

political poetry with a fraction of the power of 'Death to Van Gogh's Ear' or 'Mutation of the Spirit'. Ginsberg and Corso are older men, with their roots in the old radicalism. The new poets have a *feel* for affluence, even though economics may deny them a taste for it. There are vodkas and martinis and jets and cadillacs and white denim suits in Harwood. One thinks of Kerouac's *Desolation Angels*, with its Corso character Raphael, tired of Beat squalor, and it may be that the materialist stigma that dogged Auden and his contemporaries has lost its hold.

The best poems Harwood has so far produced are those which express love, pain and separation. 'Plato was Right Though' loosely and casually discusses the poet's role, yielding the free-falling parachutist chosen by Stuart Montgomery to illustrate the title-page of the volume as ultimate analogy for the poet's role—

> A lone parachutist drifting down through the blue . . . .
> And even if he *is* shot dead in his harness
> by the border guards, who really cares?
> He has the same chances as anyone else.
> 'When you're facing death or junk, you're always on your own
> and that's exactly how it is,' he said. It became daily
> more obvious that such clichéd truisms were only too true.[26]

This poem with all its Auden furniture—border-guards, expeditionary forces, house-parties, the élite waiting for the end —can for the time being stand for Harwood's quality—a stateless refusal to take too seriously the social charade that has within it a knife-edge of ruthlessness. The tone is interestingly fay (things are 'pretty' with ribbons on them), America stands (frankly) for the advertisers' good things. Meanwhile there is the complex ease of perfect pieces such as 'No—All the Temple Bells', which perhaps encapsulates more succinctly than any other poem of his the sophistication of the Surrealist realism that is his best gift—

> an elaborate stringball
> rolling across a green desert
> whose orange and humid night

[26] Harwood, 'Plato was Right Though', *The White Room*, p. 103.

I now eat and offer you
'Let us reconsider . . . I mean these
mountain problems'
a car starting in quiet side street.

Index of Authors and Critics

Bold references are to chapters or sections of chapters.